Monitoring poverty and social exclusion 2007

Guy Palmer, Tom MacInnes and Peter Kenway

JOSEPH ROWNTREE FOUNDATION

New Policy Institute
poverty.org.uk

The **Joseph Rowntree Foundation** has supported this project as part of its programme of research and innovative development projects, which it hopes will be of value to policy makers, practitioners and service users. The facts presented and views expressed in this report are, however, those of the author[s] and not necessarily those of the Foundation.

Joseph Rowntree Foundation
The Homestead
40 Water End
York YO30 6WP
Website: www.jrf.org.uk

First published 2007 by the Joseph Rowntree Foundation

ISBN: 9781859356203 (paperback)
ISBN: 9781859356241 (pdf)

A pdf version of this publication is available from the JRF website www.jrf.org.uk or from the poverty statistics website (www.poverty.org.uk). Further copies of this report, or any other JRF publication, can be obtained either from the JRF website (www.jrf.org.uk/bookshop/) or from our distributor, York Publishing Services (Tel: 01904 430033).

A CIP catalogue record for this report is available from the British Library.

Designed and produced by Pinnacle Graphic Design Ltd
Printed by Alden Press

Monitoring poverty and social exclusion 2007

Available in alternative formats

This publication can be provided in alternative formats, such as large print, Braille, audiotape and on disk.

Please contact:
Communications Department
Joseph Rowntree Foundation
The Homestead
40 Water End
York YO30 6WP
Tel: 01904 615905
Email: info@jrf.org.uk

Contents

Acknowledgements

This report has benefited enormously from the support we have received from many different people and organisations.

We would, in particular, like thank to the members of the Advisory Group, convened by the Joseph Rowntree Foundation, who have taken considerable time and trouble to help us at every stage of the project. They are: Ruth Lister of the University of Loughborough, David Darton of the Equal Opportunities Commission, Gabrielle Preston and Francis McGlone of the Child Poverty Action Group, Lisa Harker, Stephen McKay of the University of Birmingham, Katherine Rake of the Fawcett Society, Anna Pearson of Help the Aged, Jane Barrett and Laura Adelman of the Department for Work and Pensions and Sarah Morgan from the Department of Communities and Local Government.

The data used in this report comes from a wide range of official government surveys and sources. In particular, we would like to thank George Johnson and Valerie Christian of the Incomes Monitoring Team and Robert Chung of the Family Resources Survey Team at the Department for Work and Pensions for supplying us with datasets ahead of schedule. We are also very grateful to staff from the many government departments who have supplied us with data, either directly or via the internet. These include, but are not limited to, the Department of Communities and Local Government, the Department for Children, Schools and Families, the Office of National Statistics, the Scottish Executive, Welsh Assembly and Northern Ireland Statistics and Research Agency.

Finally, we must again thank the many staff at the Foundation responsible for putting this challenging document together in such a short timescale. Of particular note here has been the advice and guidance of the ever-helpful Chris Goulden.

As ever, responsibility for the accuracy of this report, including any errors or misunderstandings, belongs to the authors alone.

Introduction

The *Monitoring poverty and social exclusion* series

This is the tenth in a series of annual reports which began in 1998. Its aim is to provide an independent assessment of the progress being made in eliminating poverty and reducing social exclusion in the UK.[1] Over the years, many of the reports have had a special theme. This year, that theme is the differences between men and women.

In line with past practice, the report contains 50 indicators each comprising two graphs. The first graph typically shows progress over time while the second shows how the problem varies between different groups within the population, divided variously according to either income level, social class, economic or family status, gender, ethnicity etc. Given this year's theme, gender differences are shown wherever possible (including sometimes in the first graph of the indicator pair as well).

In keeping with past practice too, the indicators are grouped into themes and the themes into chapters. The organisation of the chapters themselves is, however, quite different from usual. Instead of the core of the report being arranged around age groups (children, young adults, working-age adults 25 and over, and pensioners), this report is arranged around subjects. They are:

- low income
- lacking work
- disadvantage in work
- childhood and educational disadvantage
- ill-health
- housing and exclusion

The reason for this changed structure arises from the choice of gender as a special theme. In exploring differences by gender, differences by age – but within the usual four age groups – emerged as an interesting sub-theme in its own right. But these do not always naturally fit within the age groups structure; for example, poverty rates differ markedly between those young adults under age 22 and those over. Differences by gender are also not always conveniently presented in an age-based chapter structure and so this subject-based structure was therefore chosen instead. Since it is actually what has been adopted for our special reports on Scotland (2002, 2004 and 2006), Wales (2005) and Northern Ireland (2006), it is not alien to the series as a whole.

These reports are only one part of the output of *Monitoring poverty and social exclusion* and there are also separate reports for ethnicity (2007), Scotland (2006), Wales (2005) and Northern Ireland (2006).

www.poverty.org.uk

In their turn, all of these reports are themselves only a small subset of the complete set of indicators which have been created as part of this project, all of which are available on the project website www.poverty.org.uk. Anybody wishing to reproduce material from the report is also encouraged to visit the website to check for a more up-to-date version of the graph. Via the webpage www.poverty.org.uk/summary/contact.htm, users can also request to have automatic notification of updates sent to them by email. While the reports come out annually, the graphs on the website are updated within a few weeks of the data being published. The data behind every graph is also available on the website.

The geographical scope of the report

Wherever data sources permit, the scope of this report is the United Kingdom, that is England, Wales, Scotland and Northern Ireland. In some cases, however, only analysis at a Great Britain level (i.e. not including Northern Ireland) is possible. Furthermore, in a few cases, even the data from England, Scotland and Wales is not comparable and, in such cases, the analysis is either for England and Wales or for England only.

Commentary

This is the tenth edition of *Monitoring poverty and social exclusion*. The first, published in 1998 and subtitled *Labour's Inheritance*, documented the poverty and social exclusion that confronted the government that came to office the year before. Last year's, which gave an account of the position in 2006, in effect documented Mr Blair's legacy.

In looking back at that 2006 commentary, it is striking how little it seems necessary to alter what we wrote then. In one sense it is not surprising that a judgement based on a ten-year view should differ little from one based on nine. In another sense, though, this continuity of view reflects something more substantial, namely, that our judgement that little had changed in the immediate period up to 2006 has been reinforced this year – little has changed since then either. Indeed, the change that has been visible in the past year has usually served to darken the mood rather than lighten it.

The greater part of this commentary is devoted to a selection of what we believe to be the most interesting key points from the 50 indicators in the main body of the report. The inclusion of a fair number of points on the differences between men and women reflects the special theme of this year's report.

A summary judgement: an exhausted strategy?

Before listing the detailed key points, however, the following ten points are offered as a summary of, and some substantiation for, our principal conclusion, namely that the strategy against poverty and social exclusion pursued since the late 1990s is now largely exhausted. The momentum that was certainly there in the last years of the 1990s and the first few years of this decade has now gone. 'Doing nothing new' no longer means, as it did a few years ago, slow but steady progress. Instead, it essentially now means that nothing changes.

In his speech to his party's annual conference in September 2007, the Prime Minister reaffirmed the commitment to abolish child poverty, describing it as a 'goal for this generation'. In that speech, he went on to say that the next steps towards that goal would be set out in the Pre-Budget report. Yet when that report and the three-year Comprehensive Spending Review for 2008 to 2011 were published a fortnight later, those steps were revealed to be modest: an extra £1 a week (in addition to the previously announced £3 a week) on Child Tax Credit by 2010; the national roll-out of the In-Work Credit for lone parents returning to work; an increase in the amount of child maintenance a parent can receive before starting to lose Income Support; and an increase in the benefit rates for 16- and 17-year-olds to bring them into line with those for 18- to 24-year-olds. Though welcome in themselves, these measures are nowhere near enough to create an approach commensurate with the scale of the challenge. The question that must now be asked, for the first time since 1999 when the then Prime Minister committed the Government to ending child poverty in a generation, is whether that commitment is now much more than just rhetoric.

Progress stalled?

A. The period of slow but steady progress in reducing poverty has now come to an end, arguably around three or four years ago. In particular, overall poverty levels in 2005/06 were the same as they were in 2002/03. Child poverty in 2005/06 was still 500,000 higher than the target set for 2004/05.

B. The unemployment rate among the under 25s has been rising since 2004 while the rate for those 25 and over stopped falling in 2005. The proportion of working-age people who are economically inactive but want work (a group not classified as 'unemployed', a majority of whom are disabled) also appears to have stopped falling.

Policy undermined?

C. Tax credits are taking greater numbers of children out of poverty – around a million in each of the last three years – but the number of children in working families whose earnings and Child Benefit are insufficient by themselves to escape poverty is also rising. Half the children in poverty belong to working families.

D. While inequality in the lower half of the pay distribution is narrowing, and women are catching up with men (but are still well behind), pay inequality in the upper half of the pay distribution is growing. Overall earnings inequalities are widening and the beliefs that sustain them remain unchallenged.

Rhetoric unmatched by action?

E. At least a quarter of 19-year-olds lack the minimum levels of qualification that are likely to be needed in order to acquire sufficient, well-enough paid work to avoid poverty in working life.

F. Continuing fear of going out alone, coupled with still high proportions of people lacking access to a car, leaves women in general, and lower income women especially, unable to participate fully in society, including easy access to important services.

Problems ignored?

G. Not all those who want to work can do so, and disability rather than lone parenthood is the factor most likely to leave a person workless. As the value of social security benefits for working-age adults without dependent children continues to fall ever further behind earnings, the ten-year-old question of 'what security for those who can't (work)' remains unanswered.

H. Half the poorest households lack home contents insurance, the same as in the late 1990s when a government action team first identified this as a priority. Yet over the same period, official pressure has seen the proportion of households without bank accounts cut by three-quarters.

As well as opportunities missed?

I. 1.5 million children in poverty – almost half of all children in poverty – and 3.5 million working-age adults in poverty belong to households that pay full Council Tax. Yet the flexibility to help such people that is contained in Council Tax Benefit remains unexplored and unexploited.

J. The public sector is the largest employer of low-paid workers aged 25 or over – yet the public sector as an employer has no role in the current anti-poverty strategy. The stress on globalisation obscures the fact that only a small minority of low-paid jobs could be relocated abroad.

The measurement of income poverty

A household is defined as being in income poverty ('poverty' for short) if its income is less than 60 per cent of the contemporary UK median household income. In 2005/06, the latest year for which data is available, this was worth £108 per week for a single adult, £186 per week for a couple with no dependent children, £223 per week for a lone parent with two dependent children and £301 per week for a couple with two dependent children.

These sums of money are measured after Income Tax, Council Tax and housing costs have been deducted, where housing costs include rents, mortgage interest, buildings insurance and water charges. The sum of money left over is therefore what the household has available to spend on everything else it needs, from food and heating to travel and entertainment.

Key points from the indicators

In each case, the numbers in the brackets is the numbers of the relevant indicators in the main text.

Poverty in the whole population (1 and 2)

1. The number of people living in poverty rose between 2004/05 and 2005/06 by around three-quarters of a million, to almost 13 million. As this is the only occasion on which the number has risen since 1996/97, it is premature to conclude that poverty is now on a rising trend. But with poverty in 2005/06 at the same level as it was in 2002/03, it is clear that progress on poverty reduction has stalled.
2. Over the last decade, the proportion of both children and pensioners in poverty has fallen while the proportion of working-age adults in poverty has remained unchanged. As a result, the pensioner poverty rate is now lower than the poverty rate for working-age adults – an historic shift – and more than half of the people now in poverty are working-age adults.

Child poverty (3, 7 and 12)

3. 3.8 million children were living in poverty in 2005/06. This fall, of some 600,000 compared with the government's 1998/99 baseline, leaves the overall number of children still 500,000 above the government's 2004/05 target. To achieve the government's 2010 target, the required annual fall over the next five years (i.e. to 2010/11) is about twice what has been achieved over the previous seven.
4. Among children in poverty in 2005/06, half lived in working families and half in workless ones. Three-fifths lived in couple families while two-fifths lived with a lone parent. Of those in in-work poverty, four-fifths lived with both parents and one fifth with one. Conversely, of those in workless poverty, two-thirds lived with just one parent.
5. 1.5 million young adults aged 16 to 24 were in poverty in 2005/06. Though no longer counted as children, most were when the Prime Minister first pledged to abolish child poverty in 1999. Two-thirds of them (one million people) are single and without dependent children, many still living at home with their parents (and who are therefore also in poverty themselves).

Lone parent poverty (12)

6. Lone parents under the age of 25 account for just one in eight of all young adults in poverty and just a fifth of all the lone parents in poverty. The stereotypical image of a lone parent in poverty as a young, even teenaged, mum, is therefore quite wrong. Rather, most of lone parents in poverty are aged 25 or over and there are, in fact, as many over 40 as there are under 25.

The gender poverty 'gap' (10 and 11)

7. Some five million women (20 per cent) and four million men (18 per cent) belong to households in poverty. By definition, differences in household poverty between men and women are to do with single adult households. Single women in poverty are divided almost equally between pensioners, lone parents and working-age without children. By contrast, almost all single men in poverty are working-age without children. Men (whether single or not) in the 60 to 64 age group have a higher poverty rate than men in any other age group from 25 to 80.

8. The gap of two percentage points between the poverty rates for men and women is half what it was in the mid-1990s. The fall between then and now reflects the decline in the poverty rates for two kinds of single adult households in which women are predominant: single pensioners, for whom the poverty rate among women fell from nearly 40 per cent in the mid-1990s to 20 per cent in the three most recent years; and lone parents, for whom the rate fell from 60 per cent to 50 per cent over the same period.

Poverty and disability (4 and 38)

9. At 30 per cent, the poverty rate among those aged 25 to retirement who are disabled is twice the rate for those who are not disabled. Though steady in recent years, this 'excess' risk for disabled people compared with non-disabled people is larger than it was a decade ago.

10. Three-quarters of those in long-term receipt of out-of-work benefits are sick or disabled. Among those receiving disability benefits for two years or more, the largest category are the 40 per cent with mental or behavioural disorders. Musculoskeletal disorders, the second largest, account for 20 per cent. Around a third are aged 55 to retirement, a further third are aged 45 to 54, and the final third are aged under 45. Long-term disability is therefore by no means confined to older working-age adults.

Poverty and tax credits (8)

11. In each of the last three years, around a million children were in working families where the income exceeded the poverty line by less than the tax credits received. Since they would have been in poverty without them, this means that tax credits are now lifting a million children out of poverty. In the early years of the decade, the comparable figure was 0.6 million; in the late 1990s, with Family Credit, it was 0.3 million.

12. At the same time, however, the number of children in working households who need tax credits to avoid poverty has risen steadily, from around 2 million in the mid-1990s, to around 3 million in 2005/06. So, as the number of children helped by tax credits to escape poverty has increased, so too has the number needing tax credits to do so. The net result is that the number of children who are both in working families and in poverty is similar to a decade ago.

Poverty and Council Tax (9)

13. In 2005/06, some 6 million people in England and Wales belonged to households in poverty which paid full Council Tax. Of these, 1.5 million were children. Put another way, nearly half of all children in poverty were in households paying full Council Tax.

The overall distribution of income (6)

14. With the exception of the top and bottom tenths of the income distribution, the percentage rises in incomes for households in the lower half of the income distribution over the period 1996/97 to 2005/06 were greater than the rises for those in the upper half. But measured in absolute rather than percentage terms, three-quarters of the total extra income went to households in the upper half of the income distribution. Fully one third of it went to those in the richest 10 per cent.

Unemployment and worklessness (14, 17 and 18)

15. At 11.5 per cent in 2006, the unemployment rate for young adults has been rising since 2004, when it stood at 9.5 per cent, a level at which it had held since 2001. The recent rise in the rate for young adults has exceeded the smaller rise in the rate for adults aged 25 and over. As a result, the young adult rate is now three times the rate for older adults.

16. Taking a longer term perspective, over the last decade, the number of unemployed adults aged 25 and over has almost halved, from 1.6 million in 1996 to 0.9 million in 2006, with particularly large falls in long-term unemployment. The number of economically inactive people wanting work has also fallen but much more slowly, down 15 per cent, from 1.8 million in 1996 to 1.5 million in 2006. The combined effect of this smaller fall with the much larger falls for unemployment is that the economically inactive wanting work now substantially outnumber the unemployed; a decade ago by contrast they were about equal in size. 'Unemployment' is therefore nowadays only a small part of the overall picture of worklessness.

17. Almost half of all those aged 25 to retirement not in work have a work-limiting disability.

18. Single adult households, both with and without children, are far more likely than two adult ones to be workless. Among households without children, a quarter of single adult households are workless, around four times the rate for couple households.

Work, disability, lone-parenthood and gender (19)

19. Since the late 1990s, the work rate for people aged 25 to retirement who are neither disabled nor lone parents has remained largely unchanged at around 87 per cent. Over the same period, the rate for people with a work-limiting disability (and who are not lone parents) has risen, but only slightly, from just under to just over 40 per cent. By contrast, the work rate for non-disabled lone parents has risen considerably, from around 55 per cent in the mid/late 1990s to just under 70 per cent in 2006.

20. Broken down by gender, among those aged 25 to retirement, around 80 per cent of women and 90 per cent of men who are neither lone parents nor disabled have jobs. 65 per cent of non-disabled female lone parents also have jobs. By contrast, work rates for disabled people are about 40 per cent for both non lone-parent men and women and around 25 per cent for disabled female lone parents. So while lone parenthood reduces the female work rate by 15 percentage points (from 80 per cent to 65 per cent), disability reduces the work rate for both female lone parents and female non-lone parents by much more (around 40 percentage points in both cases). In other words, disability is a much greater risk factor for worklessness than lone parenthood.

Low pay (22, 23, 24 and 25)

21. Since 2000, the proportion of both men and women who are low paid has come down, with the decrease for women being much larger than the decrease for men. Despite this, it is still the case that a much larger proportion of women than men are low paid. Half of those who were paid less than £6.50 per hour in 2006 were full-time employees and half were part-time employees. The proportion of part-time employees who were paid less than £6.50 per hour in 2006 was, at just over 40 per cent, the same for both men and women.

22. Over the past decade, the gap between low-paid, full-time employees and the male median has stayed the same for men and has come down for women. Despite this, a gap still remains (50 per cent of male median pay for women at the 10th percentile compared with 55 per cent of the median for men). By contrast, the gap between highly-paid, full-time employees and the male median has increased for both men and women. As a result, overall pay inequality in the lower half of the pay distribution has come down slightly while overall pay inequality in the upper half of the pay distribution has increased slightly.

23. Thanks to its size, the public sector is now the largest employer of low-paid workers aged 25 or over, accounting for more than a quarter of all such low-paid employees. It should be stressed that these are people who are employed directly by the public sector, not those working in the public sector but employed by contractors. The next largest employer of low-paid workers over the age of 25 is the retail sector, with a quarter of the total. Only a minority of low-paid workers are in sectors that face international competition and the consequent threat that the job could move abroad.

Lacking minimum qualifications (28, 29, 30 and 31)

24. In 2005/06, 11 per cent of 16-year-olds in England and Wales obtained fewer than five GCSEs, the same proportion as in 1999/00. This lack of progress is in stark contrast to the continued progress on the higher 'headline' measure of five GCSEs at grade C or above, the proportion failing to reach that level having come down 50 per cent in 1999/00 to 42 per cent in 2005/06. 33 per cent of white British boys eligible for free school meals failed to obtain at least five GCSEs at any level, a far higher proportion than for any other combination of ethnic group, gender and free school meal entitlement.

25. Throughout the past decade, around a quarter of 19-year-olds have not been qualified at NVQ2 level or above. If people have not reached NVQ2 by age 19, they are unlikely to have gone on to do so in the next few years.

Health inequalities (39, 40, 41 and 42)

26. Where data exists, it shows substantial inequalities in health between income levels or proxies thereof, such as social class. For example, among men aged 45 to 64, 45 per cent of those in the poorest fifth report a limiting long-standing illness or disability, compared with 25 per cent for men on average incomes and barely more than 10 per cent for men in the richest fifth. The figures for women show a similar gradient, although rather less pronounced, from 40 per cent among those in the poorest fifth, to around 15 per cent for those in the richest fifth. The rate of infant death among social classes 1 to 4 is around 4 per 1,000 live births, compared to 5½ for those in social classes 5 to 8.

Households newly classified as homeless (44 and 45)

27. The number of households newly recognised as homeless in England has fallen sharply in recent years, down from 200,000 in 2004 to just over 100,000 in 2006. This latter level is also now substantially below the level in the late 1990s, when it was running at around 150,000 a year. By contrast, the number of homeless households placed in temporary, as opposed to permanent, accommodation has doubled over the last decade. Loss of accommodation with family or friends is the most common immediate cause of homelessness.

Access to services (47)

28. Households without a car are much more likely to report difficulties accessing local services than households with a car. In 2006, 15 per cent of men and 20 per cent of women lived in households that did not have car. A quarter of men and two-fifths of women either lack a car in their household or do not have a driving licence.

Feeling unsafe walking at night (48)

29. In 2005/06, 25 per cent of women aged 60 and over reported feeling very unsafe walking alone at night, four times the figure for men. In lower income households, 30 per cent of women and 10 per cent of men reported feeling very unsafe walking alone at night.

Financial exclusion (49 and 50)

30. In recent years, the proportion of households without a bank account has come down sharply, to just 6 per cent for households in the poorest fifth and 3 per cent for households with average incomes. By contrast, 50 per cent of households in the poorest fifth lack home contents insurance, nearly three times the level for households with average incomes and the same as a decade ago. In 2005/06, 7 per cent of households without home contents insurance suffered a burglary, compared with just 2 per cent for those with this insurance.

Relevant 2007 public service agreements

On 9 October 2007, alongside its *Pre-budget report for 2008/09*, the Government published its *Comprehensive Spending Review* containing its spending plans for the three years 2008-2011. As part of this, it includes a set of *public service agreements*, which are effectively agreements between the spending departments and the Treasury on the key objectives that will be delivered over the next few years.

Of the 30 overall aims in the public service agreements, the 12 that are clearly relevant to poverty and social exclusion are summarised overleaf.

Each overall aim has a number of indicators of progress associated with it. Some of these indicators also have specific national targets for achievement. Where there is no specific national target, government's expectation is that the indicator will improve against baseline trends over the next few years. These two types of indicator are distinguished in the material below as follows:

- Indicators with national targets: grouped under the heading 'national targets' and listing the target only (the indicator itself not being necessary).
- Indicators without national targets: grouped under the heading 'other indicators of progress'.

In addition, for each aim, there are brief comments about how the material compares with its equivalent from the previous (2004) comprehensive spending review. The overall conclusion is that the 2007 material is very similar to the 2004 material. Note that, as in 2004, the child poverty target is in terms of relative low income.

Overall aim	National targets	Other indicators of progress	Compared to the 2004 targets
Overall aim 2: Improve the skills of the population, on the way to ensuring a world-class skills base by 2020.	597,000 people of working age to achieve a first level 1 or above literacy qualification, and 390,000 to achieve a first entry level 3 or above numeracy qualification. 79 per cent of working age adults qualified to at least full Level 2. 56 per cent of working age adults qualified to at least full Level 3. 130,000 apprentices to complete the full apprenticeship framework in 2010/11. 36 per cent of working age adults qualified to Level 4 and above by 2014, with an interim milestone of 34 per cent by 2011. Increase participation in Higher Education towards 50 per cent of those aged 18 to 30 with growth of at least a percentage point every two years to the academic year 2010/11.		A more extensive set of targets than in 2004, reflecting the Leitch report.
Overall aim 8: Maximise employment opportunity for all.	None.	Overall employment rate taking account of the economic cycle. Narrow the gap between the employment rates of the following disadvantaged groups and the overall rate: disabled people; lone parents; ethnic minorities; people aged 50 and over; those with no qualifications; and those living in the most deprived Local Authority wards. Number of people on working-age out-of-work benefits. Amount of time people spend on out-of-work benefits.	Similar in scope and focus.
Overall aim 9: Halve the number of children in poverty by 2010-11, on the way to eradicating child poverty by 2020.	Reduce by a half the number of children living in relative low income by 2010-11.	Number of children in absolute low-income households. Number of children in relative low-income households and in material deprivation.	Similar in scope and focus. The target is still in terms of the numbers in relative low income households. Still no indicators or targets for working-age poverty.
Overall aim 10: Raise the educational achievement of all children and young people.	Increase the proportion of young children achieving a total points score of at least 78 across all 13 Early Years Foundation Stage Profile (EYFSP) scales – with at least 6 in each of the communications, language and literacy and language (CLL) and personal, social and emotional development (PSED) scales – by an additional 4 percentage points from 2008 results, by 2011. Increase the proportion achieving Level 4 in both English and maths at Key Stage 2 to 78 per cent by 2011. Increase the proportion achieving Level 5 in both English and maths at Key Stage 3 to 74 per cent by 2011. Increase the proportion achieving 5A*-C GCSEs (and equivalent), including GCSEs in both English and maths, at Key Stage 4 to 53 per cent by 2011. Increase the proportion of young people achieving Level 2 at age 19 to 82 per cent by 2011. Increase the proportion of young people achieving Level 3 at age 19 to 54 per cent by 2011.		Similar in scope and focus. Still no targets or indicators for GCSE thresholds below the 5A*-C headline measure.

Overall aim	National targets	Other indicators of progress	Compared to the 2004 targets
Overall aim 11: Narrow the gap in educational achievement between children from low-income and disadvantaged backgrounds and their peers.	Improve the average (mean) score of the lowest 20 per cent of the Early Years Foundation Stage Profile (EYFSP) results, so that the gap between that average score and the median score is reduced by an additional 3 percentage points from 2008 results, by 2011. Increase the proportion of pupils progressing by 2 Levels in English and maths at each of Key Stages 2, 3 and 4 by 2011: ■ KS2: English 9 percentage points, maths 11 percentage points. ■ KS3: English 16 percentage points, maths 12 percentage points. ■ KS4: English 15 percentage points, maths 13 percentage points. Increase the proportion of children in care at Key Stage 2 achieving level 4 in English to 60 per cent by 2011, and level 4 in mathematics to 55 per cent by 2011. Increase the proportion of children in care achieving 5A*-C GCSEs (and equivalent) at Key Stage 4 to 20 per cent by 2011.	Achievement gap between pupils eligible for Free School Meals and their peers at Key Stages 2 and 4. Proportion of young people from low-income backgrounds progressing to higher education.	The subject has a higher prominence in 2007 than in 2004.
Overall aim 14: Increase the number of children and young people on the path to success.	Reduce the proportion of young people not in education, employment or training by 2 percentage points by 2010. Reduce the under-18 conception rate by 50 per cent by 2010 as part of a broader strategy to improve sexual health.	Young people participating in positive activities. Young people frequently using drugs, alcohol or volatile substances. First-time entrants to the Criminal Justice System aged 10-17.	Similar in scope and focus.
Overall aim 15: Address the disadvantage that individuals experience because of their gender, race, disability, age, sexual orientation, religion or belief.	None.	Gender gap in hourly pay. Level of choice, control and flexibility to enable independent living. Participation in public life by women, ethnic minorities, disabled people and young people. Discrimination in employment. Fairness of treatment by services.	More extensive in scope than in 2004 and more specific.
Overall aim 16: Increase the proportion of socially excluded adults in settled accommodation and employment, education or training.	None.	Care leavers at 19 in suitable accommodation. Offenders under probation supervision and in settled and suitable accommodation. Adults in contact with secondary mental health services in settled accommodation. Adults with learning disabilities in settled accommodation. Care-leavers at 19 in education, training and employment. Offenders under probation supervision in employment. Adults in contact with secondary mental health services in employment. Adults with learning disabilities in employment.	More extensive than in 2004.
Overall aim 17: Tackle poverty and promote greater independence and well-being in later life.	None.	Employment rate age 50-69: percentage difference between this and overall employment rate. Pensioner poverty. Healthy life-expectancy at age 65. Over 65s satisfied with home and neighbourhood. Over 65s supported to live independently.	Similar in scope and focus but with pensioner poverty mentioned for the first time.

Overall aim	National targets	Other indicators of progress	Compared to the 2004 targets
Overall aim 18: Promote better health and well-being for all.	By 2010, increase the average life expectancy at birth in England to 78.6 years for men and to 82.5 years for women monitored using mortality rates as a proxy. Reduce health inequalities by 10 per cent by 2010 as measured by life expectancy at birth. To reduce adult (16+) smoking rates to 21 per cent or less by 2010, with a reduction in prevalence among routine and manual groups to 26 per cent or less.	Proportion of people supported to live independently. Access to psychological therapies.	Less specific than in 2004.
Overall aim 20: Increase long-term housing supply and affordability.	Increase the number of net additional homes provided per annum to 240,000 by 2016. Increase the number of gross affordable homes provided per annum to 70,000 by 2010-11 including 45,000 social homes. Halve the number of households in temporary accommodation to 50,500 households by 2010. By March 2011, 80 per cent of local planning authorities to have adopted the necessary Development Plan Documents, in accordance with their agreed Local Development Scheme.	Trends in affordability. Efficiency rating of new homes.	Reflecting the Barker report, focuses on affordability whereas the 2004 targets mostly focused on quality.
Overall aim 25: Reduce the harm caused by alcohol and drugs.	None.	Percentage change in the number of drug users recorded as being in effective treatment. Rate of hospital admissions per 100,000 for alcohol-related harm. Rate of drug-related offending. Percentage of the public who perceive drug use or dealing to be a problem in their area. Percentage of the public who perceive drunk and rowdy behaviour to be a problem in their area.	Broader but less specific than in 2004.

Chapter 1 **Low income**

The definition and measurement of income poverty

Poverty at the household level

Throughout this report, poverty is defined and measured for the *household* as a whole rather than for the *individuals* in it. This is in line with long-established practice, reflected in the official statistics from which all our poverty measures are drawn. This is a particularly important point to bear in mind when reading the section of the report on differences in the poverty rates between men and women.

While most households consist of one or two adults, with or without dependent children, one in eight also include other adults, usually other family members but not always so. A major part of this 'other adult' group is made up of those aged 16+ (or 18+ if still in full-time education) who are still living at home with their parents.

Note that, in this report and again in line with long-established practice, analysis of poverty by work status is undertaken by 'family' rather than by 'household'. Whereas a household is everyone living in the dwelling, a family comprises an adult plus their spouse (if applicable) plus any dependent children they are living with. So, a young adult living with their parents would count as one household but two families, as would two unrelated and non-cohabiting adults.[2]

Poverty measured relative to median income

Almost all measures of poverty in this report are based on income. A household is considered to be in income poverty (or poverty for short) if its income is less than 60 per cent of *median* household income for the year in question. The median is the income of the average UK household (that is, half of UK households have an income below this level). UK government targets for child poverty use 60 per cent of median income as the threshold against which to measure progress.

Unlike *mean* income, median income is not affected by the income of the very rich: if the Duke of Westminster's income were suddenly to go up, mean income would rise but median income would stay the same. Note that, while it must always be the case that half of households have an income less than the median, it is not in any sense arithmetically necessary that there should be any households with an income less than 60 per cent of the median.

The value of the poverty line 'after deducting housing costs'

In calculating household income, an adjustment (following an internationally agreed scale) is made for the number of adults and children it contains.[3] In the most recent year, 2005/06, the 60 per cent threshold was worth:

- £108 per week for a single adult;
- £186 per week for a couple with no dependent children;
- £223 per week for a single adult with two dependent children;
- £301 per week for a couple with two dependent children.

These sums of money are after Income Tax, Council Tax and housing costs have been paid. Housing costs comprise rent, mortgage interest (but *not* the repayment of principal), buildings insurance and water charges. They therefore represent what the household has available to spend on everything else it needs, from food and heating to travel and entertainment.

The value of the poverty line 'before deducting housing costs'

In recent years, a gap has opened up on the question of whether poverty should be measured before housing costs have been deducted (BHC) or after (AHC). If there is to be one measure only, we strongly prefer the AHC one, chiefly because the BHC measure counts Housing Benefit as a part of income even though it actually only manifests itself as a reduction in rent. On its own, the BHC measure is therefore misleading, causing households with high rents but receiving Housing Benefit to look much better off than they really are.

Since the UK Government's 2010 child poverty target is pitched explicitly in terms of BHC, the values of that threshold for the same household types as given above are:

- £145 per week for a single adult;
- £217 per week for a couple with no dependent children;
- £260 per week for a single adult with two dependent children;
- £332 per week for a couple with two dependent children.

Different income poverty thresholds

A weakness in the poverty measures used here is in the identification of the 60 per cent threshold with poverty. While it has now long been the convention, in the UK and more widely across the European Union, to do this, it is still only a convention. In part to address this, the main income poverty indicator in this report also shows the numbers of people with household incomes below 50 per cent and 40 per cent of median income.

But while the focus on 60 per cent is open to question, there is nothing to suggest that it is badly wrong. Furthermore, the acceptance of the convention has provided anti-poverty policy – and the public discussion of it – with a stability that has been essential to clarity.

Why this is not just 'relative' poverty

In our view, one of the worst things that has happened to the discussion of poverty in recent years is the way in which the poverty measured in this report is now often referred to as 'relative' poverty.

This is wrong in principle and betrays a misunderstanding of what poverty is: in short, poverty is measured relative to average income because poverty itself is *inherently* relative, that is, when someone is so short of resources that they are unable to attain the minimum norms for the society in which they live. So what is being measured is not some lesser thing called 'relative poverty' but poverty itself.

It is perfectly possible – and one of our indicators does this – to measure progress relative to a fixed poverty line, that is, one that does not change from year to year. In the statistics for the latest year, for the first time in many years, the fixed threshold measure has important information to impart. But it is not in any sense an 'absolute' poverty measure and it plays only a supporting role.

Poverty and material deprivation

In its modern formulation, the idea that poverty is inherently relative goes back to the pioneering work of Peter Townsend in the 1960s and 1970s. On this view, poverty is when 'resources are so seriously below those commanded by the average individual or family that they are, in effect, excluded from ordinary living patterns, customs and activities'.

While this provides a rationale for relative income measures of poverty, the Townsend approach also leads in a rather different direction, towards attempts to measure material deprivation directly. The government has now decided that there should be an official measure of material deprivation for child poverty and the survey that is used to gather data on household incomes has now been extended to acquire information on 'essential items' too.[4] But as this data has only been collected for the last two years (rather than the three years which is the minimum used in this report for any poverty breakdowns), no indicator on this aspect of poverty is included in this year's report.[5]

Income poverty

This theme presents the key statistics for the numbers of people living in income poverty in the UK. The graphs are a mix of the *change over time* in the number of people in income poverty, the *proportion* of different groups in income poverty (which are also the poverty *rates* or *risks* of poverty), and the *share* of the total number of people in income poverty accounted for by different groups.

1 Numbers in low income

(The number of people in income poverty)

The first indicator shows how the number of people living in income poverty has changed over time, with annual figures going back to 1979.

The main definition of income poverty used in this indicator, as elsewhere in this report, is a household income below 60 per cent of same-year, median household income after deducting housing costs (a threshold which rises as the country becomes richer). In addition:

- The first graph also shows the number of people living in households below 50 per cent and below 40 per cent of same-year median household income;
- The second graph shows the number of people living in households with incomes below the 1996/97 60 per cent threshold (adjusted only for inflation) in each year since 1996/97; it also shows the numbers below half the average 1979 income (again adjusted only for inflation) in each year up to 1994/95 (up until 1994/95, poverty thresholds were defined in terms of half-average income rather than 60 per cent of median income, but these were similar amounts of money).

Key points:

- The number of people living in income poverty rose between 2004/05 and 2005/06 by around 0.75 million, to almost 13 million people. This, the first rise in the number since 1996/97, is large enough to be statistically significant. The rise takes the overall number of people in poverty back to where it was three years earlier, in 2002/03. That number is, however, still 1.5 million below the peak level recorded in 1996/97. It is also still around 5 million more than the number of people in poverty in the early 1980s.
- The number of people with incomes below the *fixed* 1996/97 income poverty threshold also went up in 2005/06, by some 500,000 to 7.5 million. This rise, the first since 1996/97, is particularly striking since the number of people with incomes below this fixed threshold had been coming down at the rate of around 1 million a year up to 2004/05.
- One implication of the rise in the numbers below the fixed threshold is that the overall increase in income poverty in 2005/06 did *not* come about because median income rose quickly (that is, everyone is better off but those at the bottom rather less so). In fact, over the period since 1996/97, poverty rates have usually fallen fastest when median income went up more quickly – and fallen more slowly when median incomes rose more slowly.

- The number of people living in households with an income below 40 per cent of (same-year) median income has not changed since 1996/97, remaining at around 5 million people a year. On that basis, the criticism that the government's anti-poverty policies have done nothing to reduce 'deep poverty' is a fair one. However, the suggestion that this is because policies have only benefited those nearest the poverty line is not correct. Rather, the biggest fall – about 1 million people between 1996/97 and 2005/06 – has been among those with incomes between 40 per cent and 50 per cent of same-year median income, rather than among those just below the poverty line with incomes between 50 per cent and 60 per cent of the median.
- In line with long-established practice, all the statistics above relate to household income in a given year. Clearly, however, the effects of low income are more severe if that low income persists over a number of years. Of those in income poverty in any given year, around four-fifths will have been in poverty in at least one of the preceding three years, three-fifths in at least two of the preceding three years and two-fifths in all three of the preceding three years.[6]

2 Low income by age group

(Income poverty rates for children, working-age adults and pensioners)

This indicator shows what has happened to poverty among children, adults of working-age, and pensioners. The first graph shows the proportions of each of these groups in poverty for each year since 1994/95. The supporting graph shows the change in the number of people in each group in poverty comparing 2005/06 with 1994/95. In this second graph, working-age adults are split according to whether they are living with dependent children while all groups are split according to whether there are one or two adults in the family.

Key points:

- Over the full eleven-year period, the proportion of both children and pensioners in poverty has fallen while the proportion of working-age adults in poverty has remained unchanged. In more detail, child and pensioner poverty rates both started falling in about 1999/00, with pensioner poverty falling more sharply from 2003/04.
- In the most recent year, the pensioner poverty rate continued to fall slightly, while both the child and working-age adult rates rose. But neither the rise in child poverty nor the fall in pensioner poverty in the latest year are sufficiently large to be statistically significant.
- Comparing the latest year with 1994/95, the numbers of pensioners, children and working-age adults with children who are in poverty are all down, by about 1 million, 400,000 and 200,000 respectively. The fall in both child and working-age poverty has been concentrated in two-adult rather than one-adult families. By contrast, the fall in pensioner poverty has been concentrated among single pensioners.
- By contrast, the numbers of working-age adults without children living in poverty has gone up, by about 500,000. Note that this increase, which is concentrated among single adult households, reflects a rise in the size of the underlying population group rather than a rise in the proportion of such people living in poverty.

3 Children in low-income households

(The number of children in income poverty)

The first graph in this indicator shows the number of children in income poverty for each year since 1994/95. It does so on both the after deducting housing costs (AHC) measure (used elsewhere throughout this report) and the before deducting housing costs (BHC) one. The BHC measure is shown here because this is the basis for the government's 2010 child poverty target. In addition to this target, the graph also shows AHC and BHC targets that were due to be met in 2004/05.

The supporting graph shows how the risk of a child being in income poverty varies according to the work status of its family, from fully working to unemployed, and how these risks differ in the three most recent years compared with the 1998/99 year, which is the baseline for the government's child poverty targets.

Key points:

- 3.8 million children were living in income poverty in 2005/06, a rise of some 200,000 on the previous year. The fall in child poverty since the government's baseline year of 1999 is now just 600,000. This means that the number of children in poverty in the latest year is still some 500,000 *above* the targeted 25 per cent reduction that was set for 2004/05.
- On the BHC measure, the number of children living in income poverty also rose by some 100,000 in 2005/06, to 2.8 million. On this measure, the fall in child poverty since the government's baseline year of 1999 is also 600,000. 2.8 million is around 250,000 *above* the 2004/05 target and some 1.1 million above the target set for 2010. To set this 2010 target in context, the required fall over the next five years is about twice what has been achieved over the previous seven.
- A child's risk of being in income poverty depends to a large extent on how much work is being done by their family, the risk varying from around 5 per cent for those families where all adults are working (at least one of whom is working full-time) to upward of 80 per cent for workless families counted as unemployed. Of note is the fact that, for part-working families (families with either one of the couple not working or no one working full-time), the risk of poverty is 30 per cent.

4 Low income and disability

(Income poverty rates for disabled and non-disabled working-age adults)

This indicator contrasts the situation of disabled and non-disabled adults (age 25 to retirement) as far as income poverty is concerned. The first graph shows the income poverty rate for non-disabled adults along with the 'excess' rate for disabled adults for each year since 1994/95. The supporting graph shows how the proportion varies between disabled and non-disabled adults according to whether there are one or two adults in the family and whether there are dependent children or not.

Key points:

- Since the late 1990s, while the poverty rate for non-disabled working-age adults has fluctuated around 15 per cent, the rate for disabled adults has been around double that, fluctuating around 30 per cent. While there has been no real change in this pattern over this period, the poverty rates in the mid-1990s did look rather different, with a markedly smaller 'excess' for disabled adults (around 12 per cent then compared with 15 per cent now).

- For all family types, a disabled working-age adult's risk of being in poverty is between 10 and 20 percentage points higher than that for their non-disabled counterparts. Except for lone parents (where the non-disabled rate is already very high), this means a doubled risk for a disabled adult.

5 Low income by ethnicity

(The proportion of people in income poverty by ethnic group)

This indicator shows how poverty rates vary between ethnic groups; the groups being white, Indian, Pakistani, Bangladeshi, black Caribbean and black African. The first graph shows how the rates for the different groups have changed between the mid-1990s and the latest three years. The supporting graph shows how the poverty risks for working-age families vary according to its economic status and whether it is white or belonging to an ethnic minority (that is, all ethnic minority groups treated as one).

Key points:

- Poverty rates for all ethnic groups are now lower than they were in the mid-1990s, the falls being similar in proportional terms for all ethnic groups and thus largest in absolute terms for groups with the highest poverty rates to start with. Nevertheless, every ethnic minority group's poverty rate is still markedly higher than that for whites, with the rates for both Bangladeshi and Pakistani households remaining above 50 per cent.
- For every work status, people living in ethnic minority households are more likely to be in poverty than people living in white households. The 'excess' poverty risk for ethnic minorities is particularly high – double the white British rate – for part-working families: 40 per cent compared with 20 per cent.

A more detailed analysis of income poverty by ethnicity can be found in our 2007 report entitled *Poverty among ethnic groups: how and why does it differ?*[7]

6 Income inequalities

(Change in the extent of income inequality over time)

As it is measured in relation to *median* income, income poverty can be seen as being about inequality in the *lower* half of the income distribution only. In looking at what has happened to the *whole* of the income distribution, the last indicator in this section is therefore moving beyond poverty to look at income inequality more widely.

The first graph shows how incomes (after adjusting for inflation) have changed between 1996/97 and 2005/06 in percentage terms for each level of household income. The supporting graph shows where the extra income available in the latest year compared with the start year has gone – that is, how the extra cake has been divided up between the different parts of the income distribution. To represent this distribution, households are divided into ten equal sized groups (deciles), the first having the lowest income and the last having the highest.

Key points:

- The average income of households in the lowest decile of the income distribution in 2005/06 was 12 per cent higher than the average for the lowest decile in 1996/97. This increase is the smallest for any of the ten deciles. The largest increases – around 35 per cent – were recorded for households in the second, third and tenth (top) deciles. With the exception of the top and bottom deciles, the percentage rises in incomes for those in the lower deciles were greater than the rises for those in the upper deciles.

- By contrast, measured in absolute rather than percentage terms, three-quarters of the total extra income generated in 2005/06 compared with 1996/97 went to households in the upper half of the income distribution. Fully one-third of it went to those in the top decile and a half went to those in the top two deciles.

Selected relevant research

Some recent research has looked at the possibility, and likely costs, of achieving the government's target of reducing child poverty by half by 2010 and eradicating it completely by 2020.

- A report by Hirsch (2006) concludes that tax and benefit changes alone will not be enough to hit the target unless more parents also enter work. Drawing on work by the Institute for Fiscal Studies (Shaw, 2006), the report looks at two distinct phases, the 2010 and the 2020 target. The first target could potentially be achieved by raising child tax credit, though the second would require substantial rises in the level of income support. The report estimates that eliminating child poverty will require a doubling in real terms of both child tax credits and income support for parents.

Other research has looked at children in particularly high-risk groups.

- Bradshaw *et al.* (2006) found that around two-fifths of all children in poverty live in families of three or more children but that the benefit system does not adequately support larger families. For example, childcare costs covered by tax credits only cover a maximum of two children.
- Preston and Robinson (2006) cite recent figures showing that one million children living in a household where at least one person, adult or child, is disabled are in the poorest fifth of the population. The report points out that increased access to, and take up of, disability benefits, such as Disability Living Allowance, can substantially increase a household's income and so reduce the level of child poverty.

Numbers in low income

1A: The number of people on low incomes rose in 2005/06 following falls in each of the six previous years.

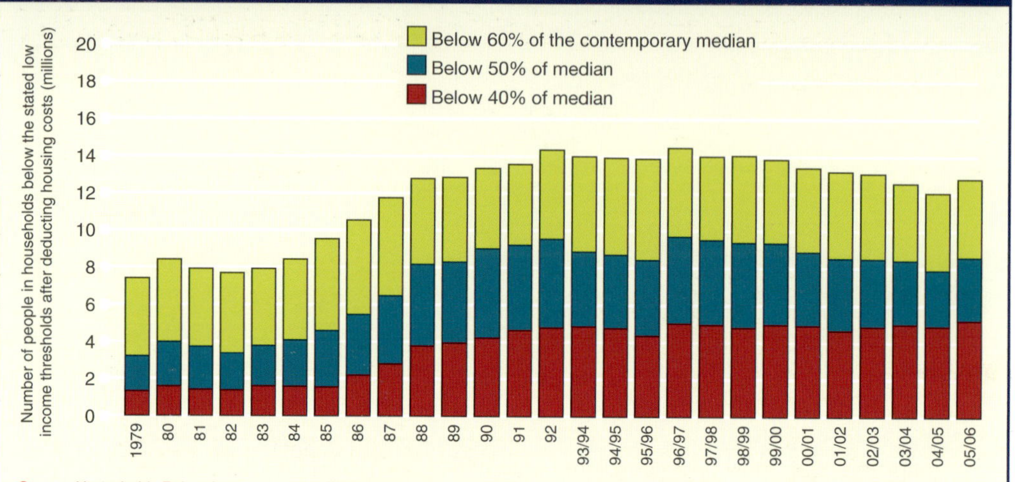

Source: Households Below Average Income, DWP (1994/95 onwards) and the IFS (earlier years); UK

1B: As real incomes have risen, the number of people below a fixed 1996/97 low-income threshold has halved, from 14 million to 7 million.

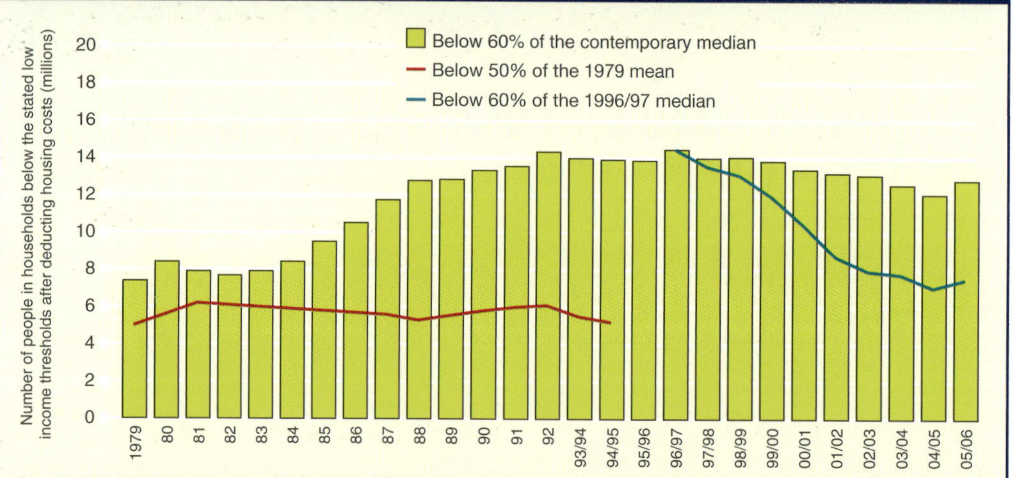

Source: Households Below Average Income, DWP (1994/95 onwards) and the IFS (earlier years); UK

The first graph shows the number of people living in households below 40 per cent, 50 per cent and 60 per cent of the contemporary British median household income for each year since 1979.

The second graph provides three measures of low income. The bars show the number of people in households below 60 per cent of contemporary median income for each year since 1979 (i.e. they are the same in each year as the bars in the first graph). The line from 1996/97 onwards shows the number of people below a fixed threshold of 60 per cent of 1996/97 median income (adjusted for price inflation). The line from 1979 to 1994/95 shows the number of people below a fixed threshold of 50 per cent of 1979 mean income (adjusted for price inflation) – 50 per cent of mean rather than 60 per cent of median being used because this was the threshold of low income commonly used at the time.

The data source for both graphs is Households Below Average Income, based on the Family Resources Survey (FRS) since 1994/95 and the Family Expenditure Survey (FES) for earlier years. The analysis of the FES dataset was undertaken by the IFS. The data relates to the United Kingdom, although this has required Great Britain figures for the years 1994/95 to 2001/02 to be scaled up as Northern Ireland was not included in the survey for these years. Income is disposable household income after deducting housing costs. All data is equivalised (adjusted) to account for variation in household size and composition. The self-employed are included in the statistics. Note that in 2007 the Department for Work and Pensions (DWP) made some technical changes to how it adjusted household income for household composition (including retrospective changes) and, as a result, the data is slightly different than previously published figures.

Overall adequacy of the indicator: high. The FRS and FES are both well-established annual government surveys, designed to be representative of the population as a whole.

Low income by age group

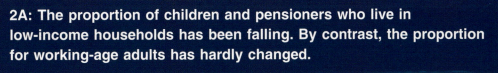

2A: The proportion of children and pensioners who live in low-income households has been falling. By contrast, the proportion for working-age adults has hardly changed.

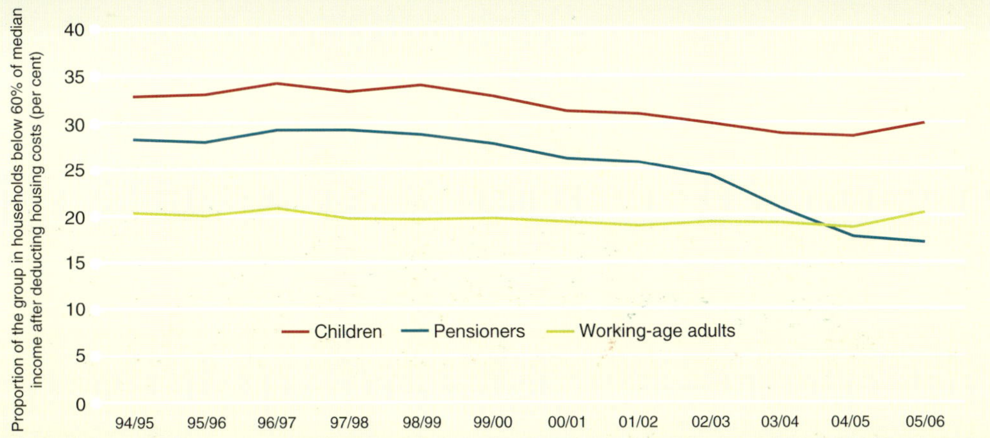

Source: Households Below Average Income, DWP; UK

2B: The only group where the number of low-income people is higher than a decade ago is working-age adults without dependent children.

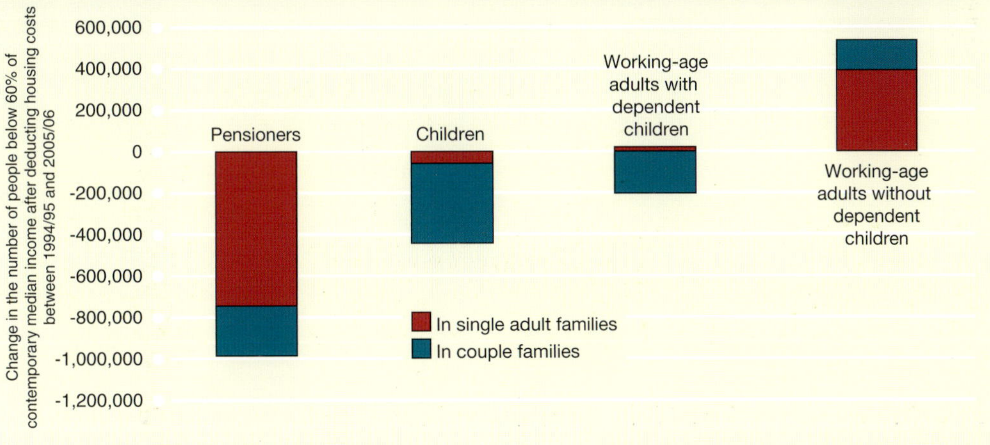

Source: Households Below Average Income DWP; Great Britain

The first graph shows the risk of a person being in a low-income household, with the data shown separately for children, pensioners and working-age adults.

The trends are somewhat different when considered in terms of absolute numbers rather than percentage risks. To illustrate this, the second graph shows the numbers of people in low-income households by type of person (children, pensioners and working-age adults with or without dependent children) and family type (single adult or couple), showing the change in the numbers between 1994/95 and 2005/06.

The data source for both graphs is Households Below Average Income, based on the Family Resources Survey (FRS). A child is defined as an individual who is either under 16 or is an unmarried 16- to 18-year-old on a course up to and including A level standard (or Highers in Scotland). For 2002/03 onwards, the data relates to the United Kingdom while the data for earlier years is for Great Britain (FRS did not cover Northern Ireland until 2002/03) and, given this, the data in the second graph relates to Great Britain. Income is disposable household income after deducting housing costs and the low-income threshold is the same as that used elsewhere, namely 60 per cent of contemporary median household income. All data is equivalised (adjusted) to account for variation in household size and composition. The self-employed are included in the statistics. Note that in 2007 the Department for Work and Pensions (DWP) made some technical changes to how it adjusted household income for household composition (including retrospective changes) and, as a result, the data is slightly different than previously published figures.

Overall adequacy of the indicator: high. The FRS is a well-established annual government survey, designed to be representative of the population as a whole.

Indicator 3

Children in low-income households

3A: The number of children in low-income households is still well above the Government's target for 2004/05.

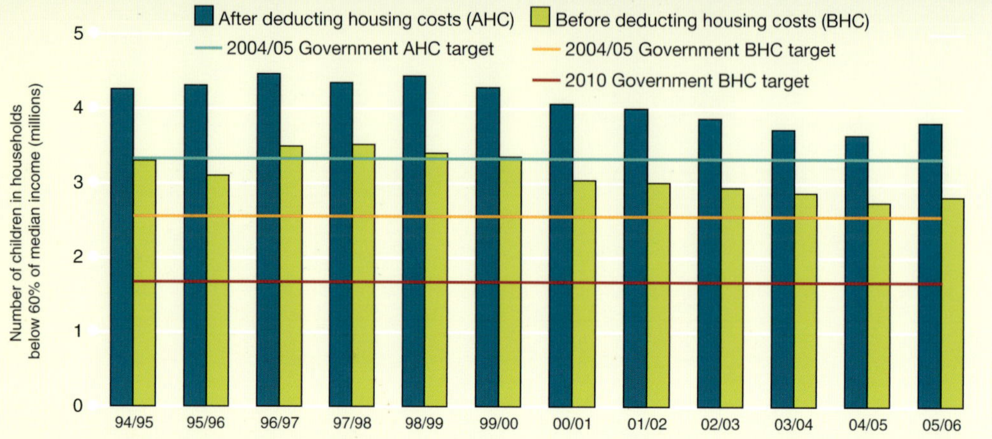

Source: Households Below Average Income, DWP; UK

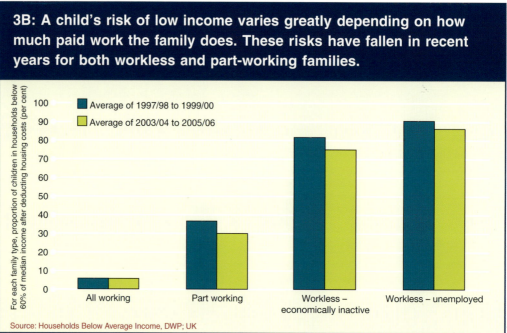

3B: A child's risk of low income varies greatly depending on how much paid work the family does. These risks have fallen in recent years for both workless and part-working families.

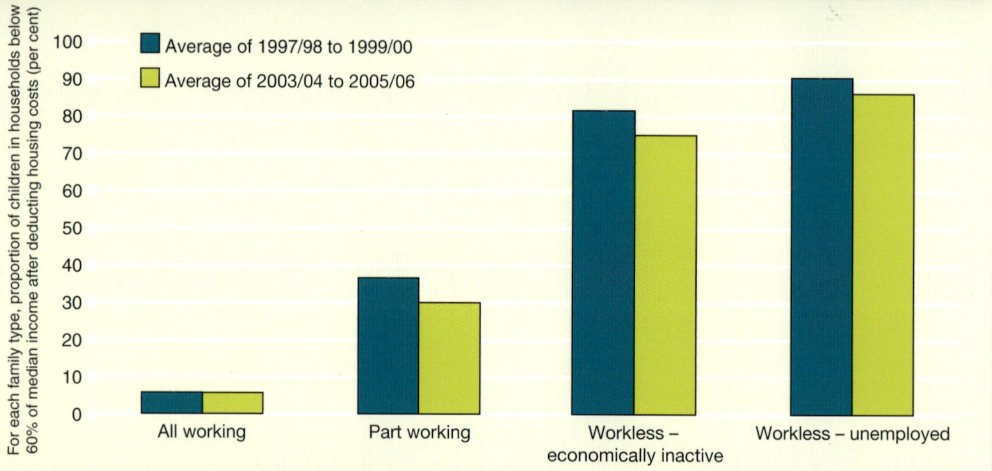

Source: Households Below Average Income, DWP; UK

The first graph shows the number of children living in low-income households, both before and after deducting housing costs. It also shows the government's target to reduce the number of children in poverty by a quarter by 2004/05 compared to the number in 1998/99, again both before and after deducting housing costs – the government's child poverty target for 2004/05 was ambiguous about which it was using. Finally, it shows the government's target to reduce the number of children in poverty by a half by 2010 compared to the number in 1998/99 – this measure being shown on a before deducting housing costs basis only as that is the basis for the official government target.

The second graph shows the risk of a child being in a low-income household, with the data shown separately by family work status. The work statuses shown are: all working (single or couple, with one in full-time work and the other – if applicable – also working); part-working (couples where one is working and the other is not plus singles or couples where no one is working full-time but one or more are part-time); workless – unemployed (head or spouse unemployed) and workless – economically inactive (includes long-term sick/disabled and lone parents).

The data source for both graphs is Households Below Average Income, based on the Family Resources Survey (FRS). For 2002/03 onwards, the data relates to the United Kingdom while the data for earlier years is for Great Britain and, given this, the data in the first graph prior to 2002/03 has been scaled up to put it onto a comparable UK basis to that for later years. The low-income threshold, adjustment to household incomes for their size and composition, and definition of children are all as for indicator 2.

Overall adequacy of the indicator: high. The FRS is a well-established annual government survey, designed to be representative of the population as a whole.

Low income and disability

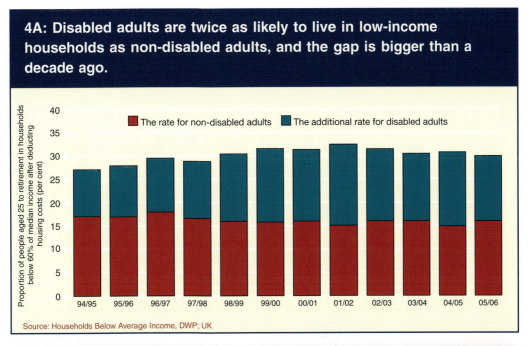

4A: Disabled adults are twice as likely to live in low-income households as non-disabled adults, and the gap is bigger than a decade ago.

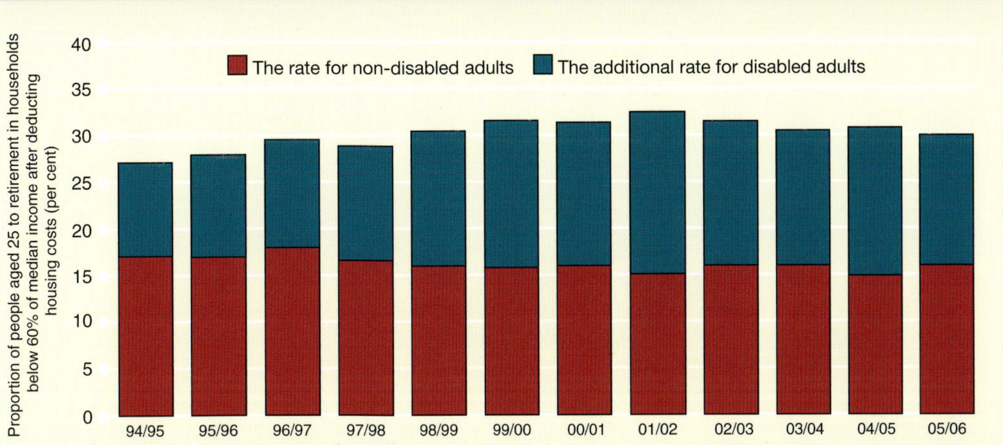

Source: Households Below Average Income, DWP; UK

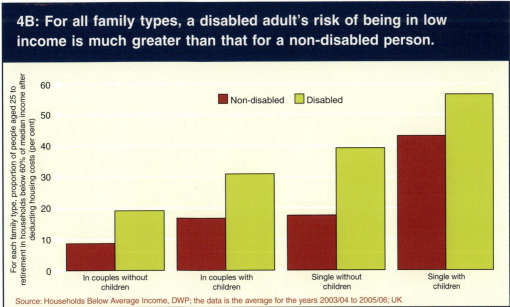

4B: For all family types, a disabled adult's risk of being in low income is much greater than that for a non-disabled person.

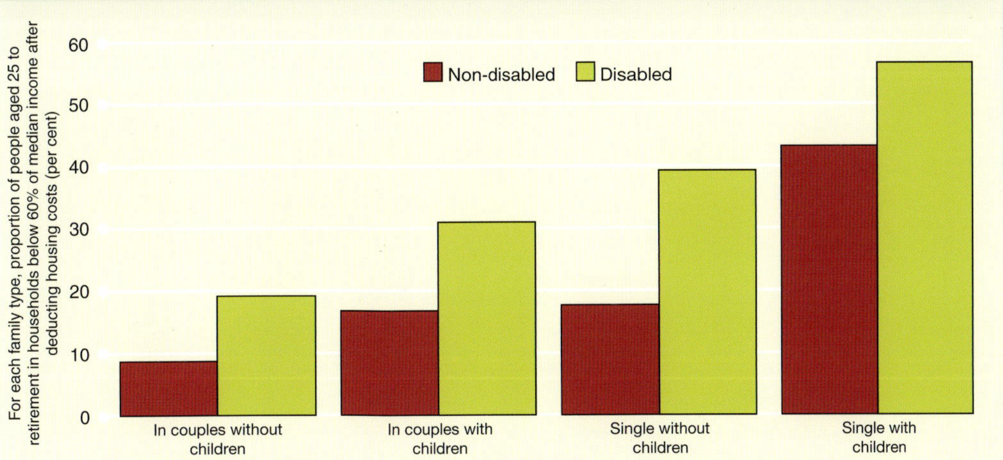

Source: Households Below Average Income, DWP; the data is the average for the years 2003/04 to 2005/06; UK

The first graph shows the proportion of adults aged 25 to retirement living in low-income households, with the data shown separately for disabled and non-disabled adults.

The second graph shows how the risks of being in low income vary by family type, with the data shown separately for disabled and non-disabled adults aged 25 to retirement.

The data source for both the graphs is Households Below Average Income, based on the Family Resources Survey (FRS). For 2002/03 onwards, the data relates to the United Kingdom while the data for earlier years is for Great Britain (FRS did not cover Northern Ireland until 2002/03). The low-income threshold and adjustment to household incomes for their size and composition are both as for indicator 2.

Where the household contains two adults, one disabled but the other not, and one in the 25 to retirement age group but the other not, it is not possible to tell from the data which of the two adults is disabled. In such cases, the assumption has been made that half of the disabled adults are in the 25 to retirement age group.

Overall adequacy of the indicator: high. The FRS is a well-established government survey, designed to be representative of the population as a whole.

Low income by ethnicity

5A: While rates have been falling for all ethnic groups, more than half of people from Bangladeshi and Pakistani ethnic backgrounds still live in low-income households.

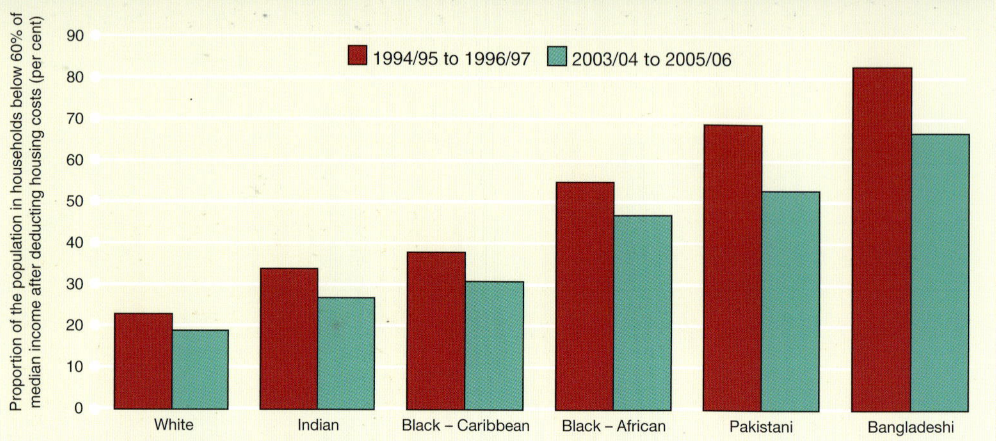

Source: Households Below Average Income, DWP; UK

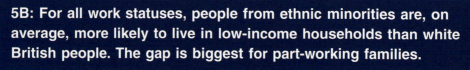

5B: For all work statuses, people from ethnic minorities are, on average, more likely to live in low-income households than white British people. The gap is biggest for part-working families.

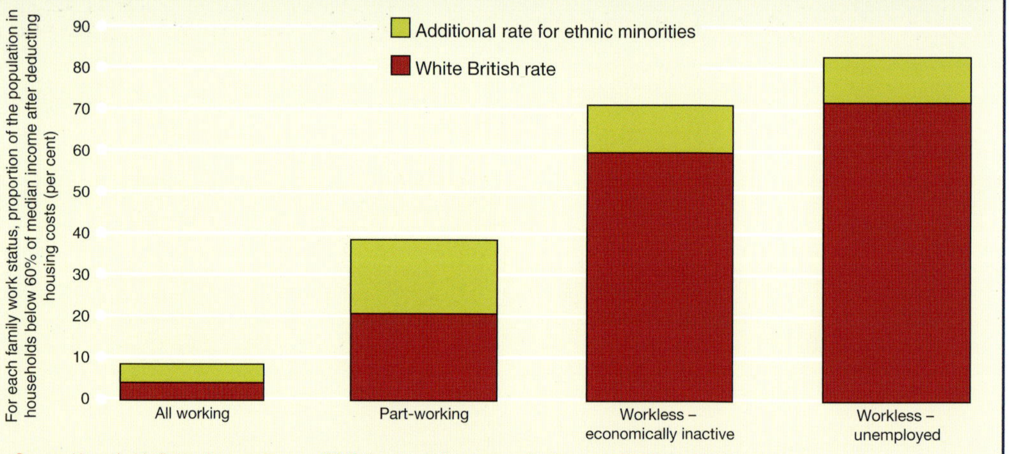

Source: Households Below Average Income, DWP; the data is the average for the years 2003/04 to 2005/06; UK

The first graph shows how the proportion of people living in low-income households varies by different ethnic groups, with the ethnic groups shown being those for which sufficient data exists to derive a reasonably reliable estimate.

The second graph shows how the proportion of people living in low-income households varies by family work status, with the data shown separately for those from ethnic minorities and white British people.

The data source for both graphs is Households Below Average Income, based on the Family Resources Survey (FRS). For 2002/03 onwards, the data relates to the United Kingdom while the data for earlier years is for Great Britain (FRS did not cover Northern Ireland until 2002/03). The low-income threshold and adjustment to household incomes for their size and composition are both as for indicator 2. The definitions of family work statuses are as for indicator 3.

Both the definition of 'ethnic minority' and the division between different ethnic minority groups is driven by the data. In the first graph, the white grouping includes both 'white British' and 'white other' as the data prior to 2001/02 does not distinguish between the two. In the second graph, 'white other' are included in the ethnic minority figures.

Overall adequacy of the indicator: medium. The FRS is a well-established annual government survey, designed to be representative of the population as a whole, but both the ethnic classification and sample sizes limit what analyses can be undertaken.

Income inequalities

6A: Except for those at the top and bottom of the income distribution, households with below-average incomes have enjoyed bigger proportional increases over the last decade than households with above-average incomes.

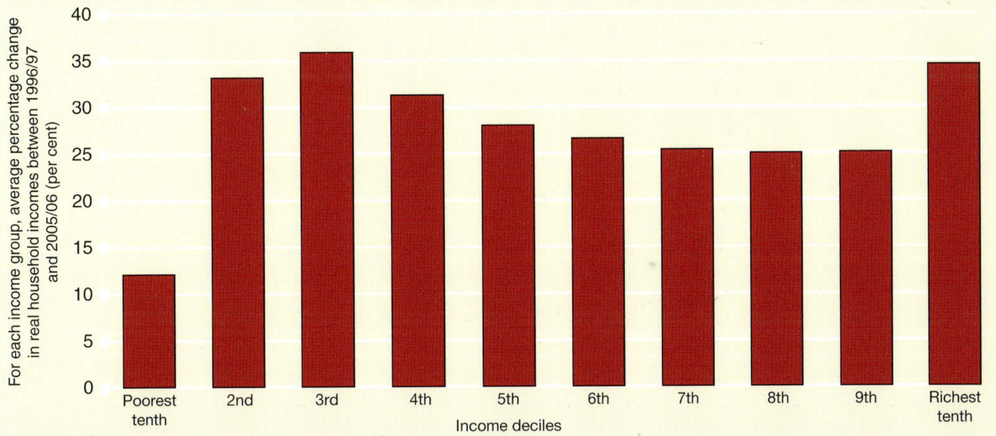

Source: Households Below Average Income, DWP; UK

6B: Three-quarters of the total increase in incomes over the last decade has gone to those with above-average incomes and a third has gone to those in the richest tenth.

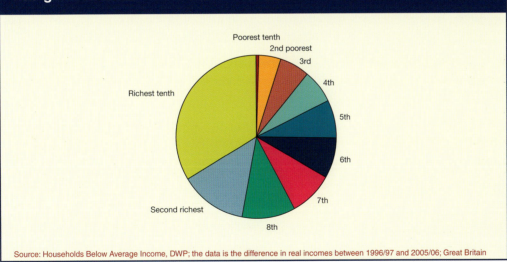

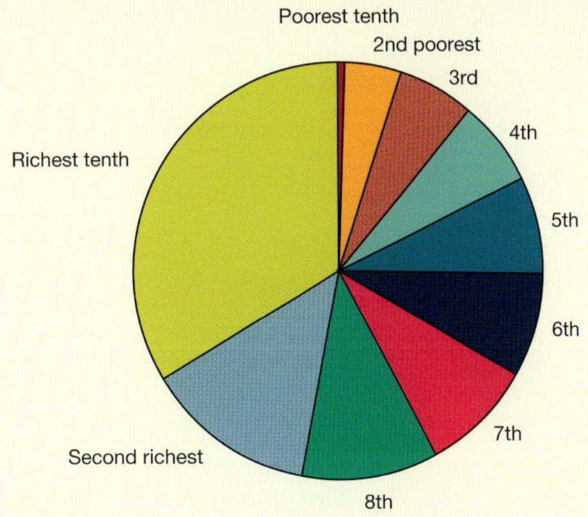

Source: Households Below Average Income, DWP; the data is the difference in real incomes between 1996/97 and 2005/06; Great Britain

The two graphs focus on the change in real incomes by income decile.

The first graph shows the average percentage change in real (i.e. after adjusting for inflation) incomes for each income decile over the period 1996/97 to 2005/06.

The second graph shows the shares of the total change in real incomes since 1996/07 by income decile.

The data source for both graphs is Households Below Average Income, based on the Family Resources Survey (FRS). The data relates to Great Britain (FRS did not cover Northern Ireland until 2002/03). Income is disposable household income after deducting housing costs. All data is equivalised (adjusted) to account for variation in household size and composition. The self-employed are included in the statistics.

Overall adequacy of the indicator: high. The FRS is a well-established annual government survey, designed to be representative of the population as a whole.

In-work poverty

At the heart of the government's drive to reduce child poverty lies the idea that work is the route out of poverty. Nothing that has been said or done by government ministers suggests any weakening in, or even qualification of, that core belief. This section is, therefore, concerned with those people who, despite either working themselves or having at least one working member of their family, continue to find themselves in poverty: 'in-work poverty' for short.

7 Low income and work

(The number of people in working households in income poverty)

This indicator counts the number of people in in-work poverty and compares them with the number in poverty but in workless families. The first graph does this for those aged 25 to retirement, showing the numbers in in-work and out-of-work poverty for each year from 1994/95 to 2005/06. The supporting graph focuses on children, showing how the 3.8 million children in income poverty in 2005/06 are divided up according to whether they live in working or workless families, and whether they are living with one or two parents.

Key points:

- Up to the late 1990s, a majority of people aged 25 to retirement who were in poverty belonged to workless rather than working families: for example, in 1996/97, some 2.8 million belonged to workless families compared with 2.4 million who belonged to working families. By contrast, over the last two years, the position has been reversed, some 2.2 million compared with 2.8 million (average for 2004/05 and 2005/06).
- Among children in poverty in 2005/06, half live in working families and half in workless ones. Three-fifths live in couple families while two-fifths live with a lone parent.
- Among children in poverty in working families in 2005/06, four-fifths live with both parents. Conversely, of those in workless poverty, two-thirds live with just one parent.

8 In receipt of tax credits

(The number of children in households receiving tax credits)

This indicator, counting the number of children in working families, looks at the connections between the receipt of tax credits and the family's poverty status.

The first graph shows the number of children in working families who are (a) in poverty and not receiving tax credits; (b) in poverty and receiving tax credits; and (c) not in poverty thanks to the tax credits they receive. This graph goes back to the mid-1990s, using the numbers receiving Family Credit before 1999 when the first version of tax credits was introduced.

The second graph, for the latest year 2005/06, shows how many children are lifted above the poverty line by tax credits, comparing this with the number still below it despite receiving tax credits, and the number who would not be below it even if they did not receive tax credits. Children whose families receive only the family element of the child tax credit (to which all but the 10 per cent or so of families with incomes above £50,000 are entitled) are excluded from both graphs.

Key points:

- In each of the last three years, around 1 million children have belonged to working families whose incomes exceed the poverty line by an amount less than the tax credits they receive. As this means that they would have been in poverty without those credits, it can be said that tax credits have been lifting a million children a year out of poverty since 2003/04. The comparable figure for the early years of the decade was around 0.6 million a year. In the late 1990s, the predecessor benefit Family Credit lifted about 0.3 million a year above the poverty line.
- Over the same period, the number of children in working families who were in poverty and not receiving tax credits averaged around 0.8 million in the three most recent years, down from well above 1 million a year in the period up to 2002/03.
- At the same time, however, the number of children in working families who either are, or would be, in poverty but for tax credits, has risen steadily, from around 2 million in the mid-1990s, to 2.5 million in the early years of this decade, to around 3 million in the most recent year. In short, as the number of children helped by tax credits to escape poverty has increased, so too has the number needing tax credits in order to do that. One result of this is that the number of children in working families who are in poverty is similar to a decade ago.
- The around 1 million children not in poverty thanks to tax credits represent a quarter of all the children in families receiving the credits. Another quarter is made up of children whose families receive tax credits but are still in poverty despite that. The other half are the children who would not be in poverty even if their families did not receive tax credits.

9 Low income and Council Tax

(The proportion of people in income poverty paying Council Tax)

This indicator counts the people in households who are in income poverty yet paying full Council Tax. The first graph shows the proportion of people in such households in England and Wales for each year since the mid-1990s. The supporting graph breaks those numbers down, for the latest year, between children, working-age adults and pensioners.

Key points:

- In 2005/06, nearly 60 per cent of people in poverty belonged to households paying full Council Tax. This proportion is nearly a third higher than it was in the late 1990s, having risen steadily from around 45 per cent in 1998/99.
- In 2005/06, some 6 million people in England and Wales belonged to households that were in poverty yet paid full Council Tax. Of these, around one-and-a-half million were children: in other words, almost half of all children in poverty were in households paying full Council Tax. A further one million were pensioners. Dwarfing both, however, was the number of working-age adults in poverty and paying full Council Tax – around 3.5 million.

Selected relevant research

In-work poverty is often related to low pay, but the two are not synonymous – low pay is an individual measure, whereas poverty relates to household income. Some recent research has looked at the intersection of the two.

- Work by the New Policy Institute and the Bevan Foundation (Kenway and Winkler, 2006) found that, in 2003/04, 65 per cent of families in in-work poverty were low-paid while 23 per cent of low-paid families were in poverty. This second statistic is largely explained by two factors. First, the income of low-paid families can be topped up by tax credits, lifting the family out of poverty. Second, around a quarter of low-paid families have very low housing costs, either because they share accommodation or own properties with very small or non-existent mortgage repayments.
- The same piece of work showed that 87 per cent of low-paid men lived in a low-paid family (that is, one where the average hourly rate for all earning adults was under £6 an hour), compared with to 60 per cent of women. As Miller and Gardiner (2004) state, low-paid women are more likely to have partners who are employed and not low-paid than low-paid men, who often have either non-employed partners or partners who are also low-paid.

Low income and work

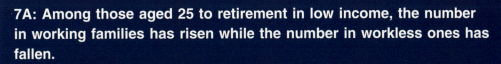

7A: Among those aged 25 to retirement in low income, the number in working families has risen while the number in workless ones has fallen.

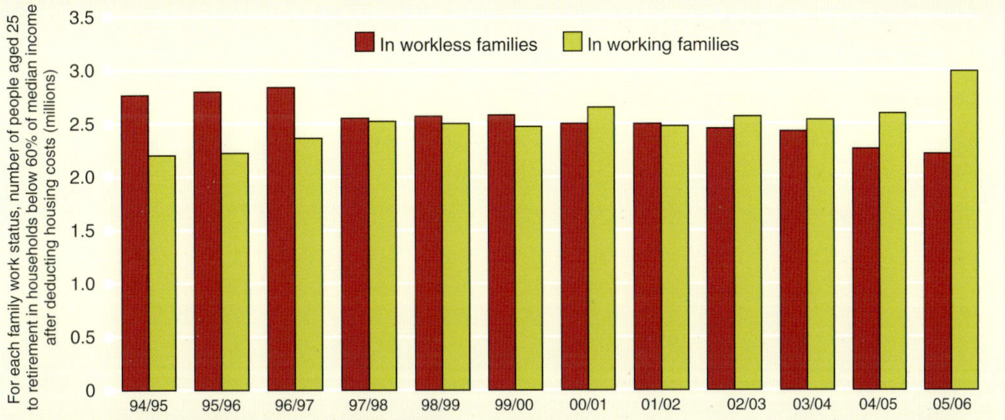

Source: Households Below Average Income, DWP; Great Britain

7B: Half of the children in low-income households live in families where at least one of the adults is in paid work.

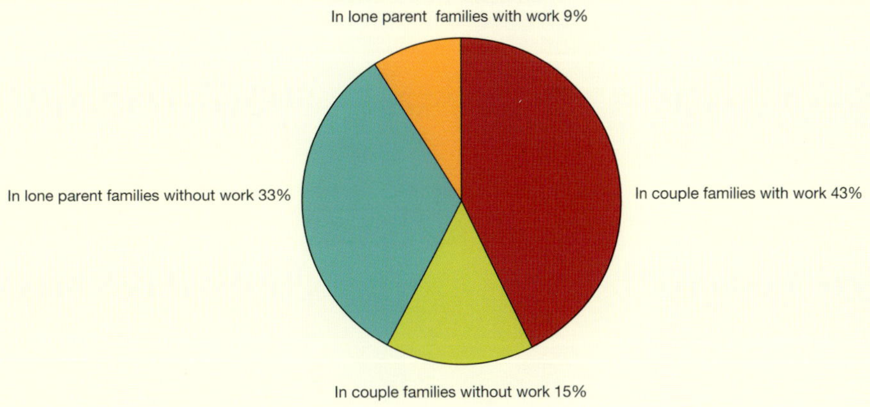

Source: Households Below Average Income 2005/06, DWP; UK

The first graph shows, over time, the number of adults aged 25 to retirement who are in low-income households, with the data shown separately for families where someone is in paid work and for workless families.

The second graph shows, for the latest year, a breakdown of the children who were in low-income households by family type (couple or lone parent) and work status (workless or someone in paid work).

The data source for both graphs is Households Below Average Income, based on the Family Resources Survey (FRS). The data relates to Great Britain in the first graph and to the United Kingdom in the second graph. The low-income threshold and adjustment to household incomes for their size and composition are both as for indicator 2.

Note that the term 'family' is used to cover an adult and their spouse (if applicable) whereas the term 'household' is used to cover everyone living in a dwelling. So, a young adult living with their parents would count as one 'household' but two 'families'. In analysing low income by work status, the work status is analysed by family whereas the income is analysed by household. Note that an alternative – and more technically correct – term for 'family' is 'benefit unit'.

Overall adequacy of the indicator: high. The FRS is a well-established annual government survey, designed to be representative of the population as a whole.

Indicator 8

In receipt of tax credits

8A: Tax credits now take around 1 million children in working families out of low income – but a million more children need this support than a decade ago.

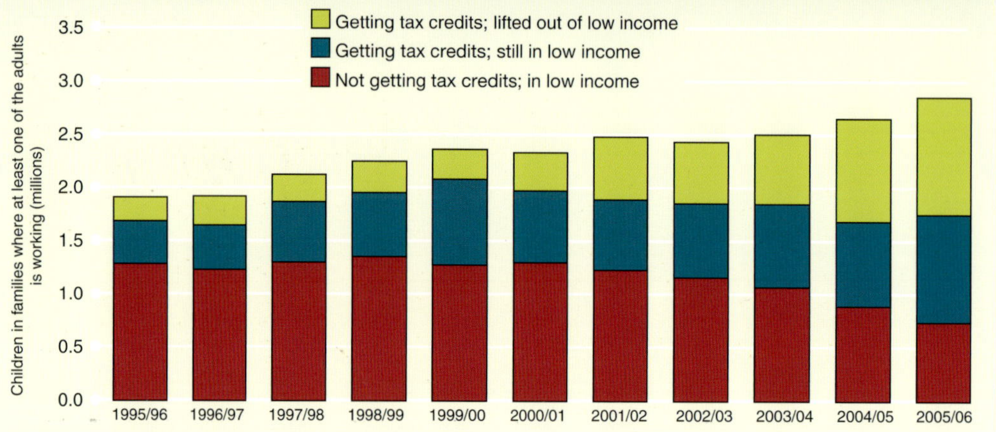

Source: Households Below Average Income, DWP; Great Britain

8B: Only a quarter of the children in working families in receipt of tax credits are no longer in low income because of the tax credit monies received.

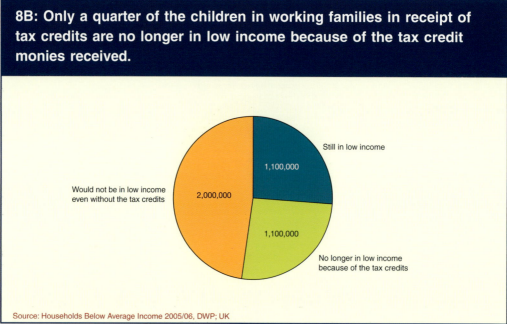

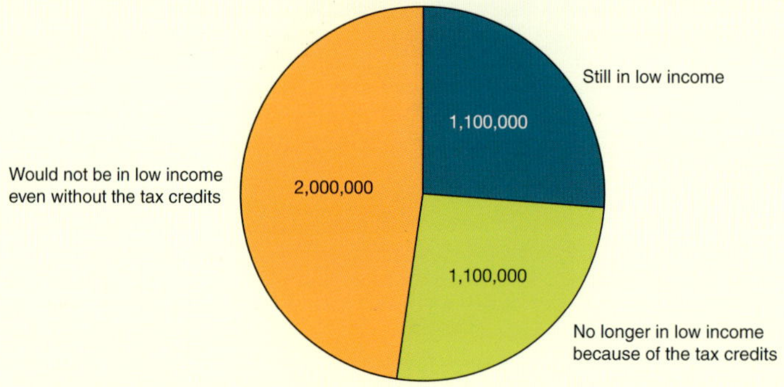

Source: Households Below Average Income 2005/06, DWP; UK

The first graph provides an analysis of the number of children in working families where, excluding tax credits (and their predecessors), the household is in low income. For each year, it shows the number of children in three categories, namely: not in receipt of tax credits; in receipt of tax credits (over and above the family element) but still in low income; and in receipt of tax credits and, as a result, no longer in low income. Note that the restriction to working families only is important as the child supplements of some out-of-work benefits (although not the base benefits themselves) are now considered by the government to be tax credits rather than benefits, so their inclusion would have made the data non-comparable over time.

The second graph provides, for the latest year, an analysis of the children in working families in receipt of tax credits over and above the family element. The first two categories – those who are still in low income and those who, as a result of tax credits, are no longer in low income – are the same as in the first graph. The third category is children whose household would not be in low income even without tax credits.

The data source for both graphs is Households Below Average Income, based on the Family Resources Survey (FRS). The data in the first graph relates to Great Britain while that in the second graph relates to the United Kingdom (FRS did not cover Northern Ireland until 2002/03). The low-income threshold and adjustment to household incomes for their size and composition are both as for indicator 2. To ensure comparability over time, the data for 1998/99 and earlier includes recipients of Disability Working Allowance as well as Family Credit while the data for 2003/04 onwards excludes those just receiving the family element of Child Tax Credit.

Overall adequacy of the indicator: medium. All the data is considered to be reliable and provides reasonable estimates. However, the extensive changes in the system from year to year make the data somewhat difficult to interpret.

Low income and Council Tax

9A: More than half of all low-income households are paying full Council Tax, noticeably higher than a decade ago.

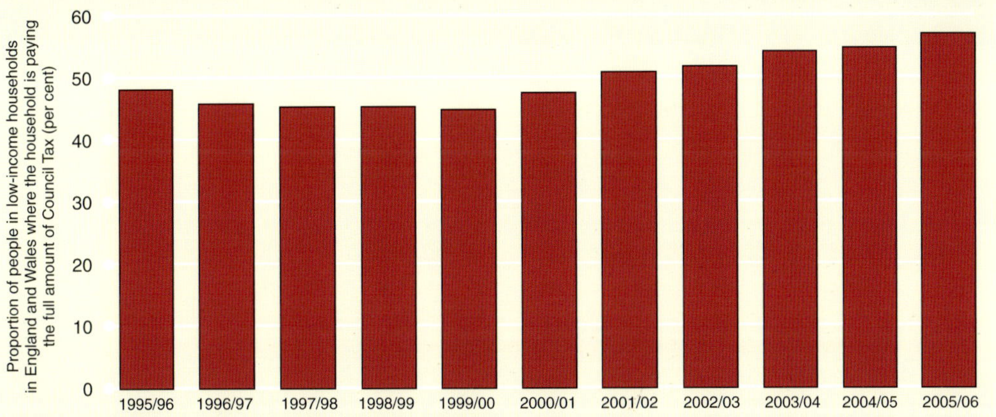

Source: Households Below Average Income, DWP; England and Wales

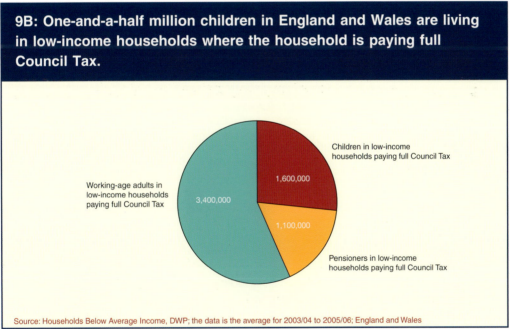

9B: One-and-a-half million children in England and Wales are living in low-income households where the household is paying full Council Tax.

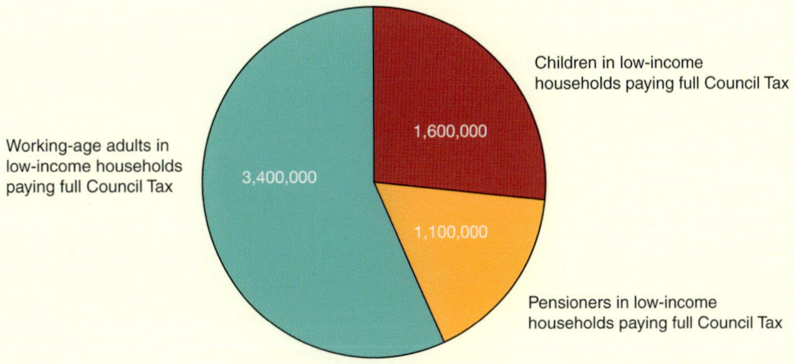

Source: Households Below Average Income, DWP; the data is the average for 2003/04 to 2005/06; England and Wales

The first graph shows, for each year, the proportion of people living in low-income households where the household is paying the full amount of Council Tax (i.e. is not in receipt of any Council Tax Benefit).

The second graph shows how the people living in low-income households where the household is paying full Council Tax divide by age group.

The data source for both graphs is Households Below Average Income, based on the Family Resources Survey (FRS). The data relates to England and Wales (in Scotland, Council Tax and water charges are paid as part of the same bill so it is not possible to distinguish people who are paying no Council Tax and the Northern Ireland system is different again). The low-income threshold and adjustment to household incomes for their size and composition are both as for indicator 2.

Overall adequacy of the indicator: medium. The FRS is a well-established annual government survey, designed to be representative of the population as a whole. However, the Council Tax data relates to a survey of what people said they were paying rather than to their actual bills.

Income poverty by age and gender

The indicators in this section have been created specifically for this year's report, with its theme on differences by gender and age. It is worth repeating here the point made earlier, in the discussion of the definition of poverty, that poverty is defined at the household, rather than the individual, level. In what follows, therefore, it should always be remembered that a phrase such as 'women in (income) poverty' is a shorthand for 'women in *households* in (income) poverty'. For households with just one adult, there is no ambiguity about this. But for households with two or more adults, it is possible that the distribution of resources between the adults within the household could be so uneven as to mean that one would be in poverty if they lived alone, while the others would not. This, however, is not measured and, without a widely agreed definition of 'individual' poverty, cannot be.

10 Adults in low-income households by gender

(The proportion of men and women in income poverty)

The first graph shows the poverty rates for men and women separately, for each of the years since 1994/95, with the rate for women shown as an 'excess' above that for men. The supporting graph shows the number of both men and women in poverty in 2005/06, broken down according to whether they are part of a couple or, if they are single, whether they are a pensioner, a lone parent or a single working-age adult without dependent children.

Key points:

- In the mid-1990s, around 24 per cent of women were in households in poverty, a rate four percentage points in excess of the 20 per cent rate for men. Since then, the gap between men and women has declined steadily, to reach a point where, with a 20 per cent poverty rate for women and 18 per cent poverty rate for men averaged over the three most recent years (2003/04 to 2005/06), the excess has halved.
- Over the three most recent years, an average of 4 million men and nearly 5 million women were in poverty at any one time. The composition of the two groups is, however, very different. Those in couples account for the same number of men and women, of course, but they represent a greater proportion of the men in poverty (more than half) than of the women (less than half). The real difference between men and women concerns the single adults in poverty. For men, almost all of these, and therefore nearly half of all the men in poverty, are single working-age without children with whom they are living. So for men, the vast majority (95 per cent) are either in couples or are single working-age without children with whom they are living. By contrast, the single women in poverty are divided almost equally between pensioners, lone parents and single working-age without children.

11 Single adults in low-income households by gender

(The proportion of single men and women in income poverty)

Given that poverty is measured at the household level, differences in the poverty rates between men and women can only reflect differences in the poverty rates for different groups of single men and single women. Changes in the overall excess poverty rate for women in the previous indicator therefore reflect changes in the *rates* for single men, single women and couples, as well as changes in the *proportions* in each of these groups.

The first graph in this indicator shows the poverty rates for single men and women separately, for each of the years since 1994/95. The supporting graph compares the poverty rates for various groups of adults for the three years 1994/95 to 1996/97 with those for the three years 2003/04 to 2005/06. The groups shown are single pensioners, lone parents, single working-age without dependent children, and couples.

Key points:

- In the mid-1990s, around 36 per cent of single women were in poverty, a rate eleven percentage points in excess of the 25 per cent rate for men. This excess has now fallen to around four percentage points, a fall of two-thirds over the last decade.
- The most important reason for this fall in the gap between women and men is that the two groups which have seen the biggest fall in poverty rates over the past decade are both dominated by women.
- The first of these groups is single pensioners, for whom the poverty rate among women fell from around 40 per cent in the mid-1990s to 20 per cent in the three most recent years. While poverty rates for single male pensioners are only slightly lower than for single female ones, the fact that three-quarters of single pensioners are women means that falls in the poverty rate for this group have a big impact on the overall difference in male and female poverty rates.
- The second of the two groups to see a big fall in poverty rates are lone parents, for whom the rate fell from 60 per cent in the mid-1990s to 50 per cent in the most recent three years. Again, because most lone parents are women, this fall has an impact on the extent to which poverty rates overall among women exceed those among men.
- By contrast, the poverty rates for single working-age adults without children do not show any appreciable difference between men and women; nor has there been any marked fall in these poverty rates over the past decade.
- Although there is too little reliable data to allow the 'excess' poverty rate for women to be tracked year-by-year prior to the mid-1990s, the evidence[8] suggests that at the end of the 1970s, there was no such excess, or gap, to speak of. This was because the two groups who 'cause' the gender gap, namely lone parents and single pensioners, were either very few in number then (lone parents) or had average, as opposed to high, poverty rates at that time (single pensioners).

12 Working-age composition

(The characteristics of working-age adults in income poverty)

This indicator offers more detail about the half of the population in poverty who are neither children (that is, dependent children) nor pensioners; in other words, the 6.5 million working-age people in poverty. The first graph breaks that population down into four age groups, 16 to 24 ('young adults'), 25 to 37, 38 to 50 (both 'prime working age') and 51 to 59 ('older working age') and then breaks it down again, variously by: single/couple status and whether with dependent children (young adults); family work status and whether a couple with dependent children or not (prime working age); and family work and disability status (older working age).

The supporting graph shows the age range of female lone parents in poverty, comparing it with the age range of women in couples with dependent children who are in poverty. In what follows, the term 'mother' should be understood as applying to any women living with their dependent children.

Key points:

- Two-thirds of all young adults (16 to 24) in poverty are single adults *without* dependent children. The great majority of this group of one million people (who were all, of course, classified as 'children' when Prime Minister Blair first pledged to eradicate child poverty in 1999) are still living at home with their parents. The remaining half million or so young adults in poverty are divided almost equally between lone parents, couples with children and couples without children. That means that lone parents account for just one in eight of all young adults living in poverty.
- A third of all the adults of 'prime' working age (25 to 50) in poverty belong to *working* couples with dependent children, some 1.3 million adults. A further 0.9 million belong to other working families, either as single adults (both with and without children) or as couples without dependent children. Taken together, this means that nearly 60 per cent of the prime working-age adults who are in poverty belong to working families. Only 10 per cent belong to two-adult, *workless* families with dependent children.
- Among the 1 million or so older working-age adults (51 to 59) in poverty, about half are in working families and half in workless ones. Among those who are workless, some two-thirds have someone disabled in the family; among those who are working, some two-thirds have no one disabled in the family.
- A fifth of lone mothers in poverty are under the age of 25, three-fifths are between 25 and 40 and the final fifth are aged over 40. Young lone mothers in poverty therefore represent just a small proportion of all lone mothers in poverty.

13 Low income by detailed age bands

(The proportion of people in income poverty by age)

The last indicator in this section provides a breakdown of poverty rates by age, from birth to age 85 and above. For those aged 25 and over, the analysis is in five-year age bands. For those aged under 25, the bands have been chosen by grouping years with similar risks together, noting that there is a marked change in risk around the age of 21. The supporting graph shows a detailed breakdown of poverty rates among pensioners by gender, age (under 75 and 75 and above) and whether single or in a couple.

Key points:

- Among children there is little difference in poverty rates by age; whatever the age, the poverty rate is well in excess of the rate for working-age adults. However, the higher poverty rate for children does not end when childhood ends (at age 16, or age 18 for those in full-time education) but continues undiminished through to age 21. By contrast, the poverty rate for those aged 22 to 24 is much lower, only a little above the rate for working-age adults as a whole.
- Poverty rates are at their lowest for those aged between about 45 and 54, rising thereafter, though with a marked spike for those aged 60 to 64. More detailed analysis shows that this is associated with a higher poverty rate for men at that age. As a result, the poverty rate for men aged 60 to 64 is higher than the rate for men in any other age group from 25 to 80.
- Among pensioners, the poverty rate for single women of all ages, and for couples aged 75 and above, is about five percentage points higher than the poverty rate for either single male pensioners or for couples aged under 75.

Selected relevant research

The research reviewed in this area falls into three parts – individual incomes for men and women, the different way in which men and women experience low income, and vulnerability to adverse events.

- The Individual Income Series, produced by the Department for Work and Pensions from 1996/97 to 2004/05, breaks down household income according to whether it accrues to the woman or the man. In doing so, it focuses on the money coming in to a household, not how it is then shared between members of the household and this limits its value. However, it does allow an investigation of how individual incomes of men and women within households have changed over time. The most recent – and final – report (Johnson and Semmence, 2006) showed that, on average, women's individual incomes had risen relative to men's over the eight years that data were analysed. Whereas in 1996/97, women's average individual income was 46 per cent of men's (£127 compared to £276), in 2004/05 it was 55 per cent (£173 compared to £315, all figures given in 2004/05 prices).
- The table below shows male and female individual incomes in the lower half of the (household) income distribution for 1996/97 and 2004/05 for three different 'couple' families, namely pensioner, and working-age without, and then with, dependent children.

Year	***Women***	***Men***	***Women as % of men***
		Pensioner couple	
1996/97	*£49*	*£134*	*37%*
2004/05	*£66*	*£165*	*40%*
		Couple without children	
1996/97	*£57*	*£151*	*38%*
2004/05	*£90*	*£200*	*45%*
		Couple with children	
1996/97	*£78*	*£257*	*30%*
2004/05	*£125*	*£304*	*41%*

- In pensioner couples, the gap between female and male individual income has narrowed slightly, with women's incomes now 40 per cent of men's, compared to 37 per cent in 1996/97.
- More noticeable changes have occurred in working-age families, where the incomes of women in couples without children are now around 45 per cent of men's, compared to 38 per cent in 1996/97. This increase of seven percentage points could be due to the closing pay gap between men and women and/or to the increasing number of women in couples who work.
- An even larger relative change has occurred in couples with children. Whereas women's incomes were 30 per cent of men's in 1996/97, they are now 41 per cent. Again, this may reflect the narrowing gender pay gap and/or the increasing number of women in couples who work. As well as this, though, new benefits such as Child Tax Credit are paid directly to the mother. Goode *et al.* (1998) observed that, where benefits are paid to the woman in the couple, the resulting distribution of individual incomes is more even.

Some recent research has looked into how the burden of poverty affects men and women and suggests that the experiences of men and women in poverty are not necessarily the same.

- Bradshaw *et al.* (2003) argue that women within two-adult families often experience poverty differently, and carry a heavier burden. This is because they (i) tend not to receive their fair share of resources coming into the household; (ii) tend to carry more than an equal responsibility for managing what money is coming into the family and for managing debt; and (iii) tend to forgo their own consumption in order to support the living standards of children.
- Middleton *et al.* (1997) found that, when women are in charge of a family's finances, they often felt that they should go without in order to ensure the health and wellbeing of other members of the family. Bradshaw *et al.* (2003) found this to be especially prevalent among low-income single mothers.
- Gordon *et al.* (2000), analysing their Poverty and Social Exclusion Survey, looked at whether people go without essential items because they cannot afford them. They found that women were slightly more likely to go without than men (also cited in Pantazis and Rospini, 2006).

One of the arguments made as to why poverty affects women more than men is that they are more vulnerable to adverse events. Research suggests that savings play a part in this.

- McKay's research for the Fawcett Society (2007) found that women's median savings are lower than men's: £2,000 compared with £3,000. Again, the way in which resources enter the household might not match the distribution within the household, but the real issue here is that, due to their lower savings rates, women are typically more financially reliant on their partners than men are. Lone mothers have a lower savings rate than either lone fathers or mothers or fathers in couples.
- McKay also showed that women's saving rates are more vulnerable to changes in life circumstances than men's. On entering the workforce, women's pension saving rates are typically as high as men's if not higher. On having children, though, they often drop, whereas fatherhood appears to act as a trigger for pensions saving. Pensions saving rates of mothers with occupational pensions typically do not catch up with those of childless women until shortly before retirement.
- A survey by the Citizens Advice Bureau (Edwards, 2003) showed that women, tenants of social landlords and the unwaged were the most likely to have debts associated with poverty. Such debts typically included catalogue debts and loans to home-collected credit providers. Interest rates associated with these types of borrowing are significantly higher than for so-called mainstream sources of credit.
- However, Pantazis and Rospini (2006) show that, while women are more susceptible to changes in circumstance caused by divorce, birth or widowhood, men are more at risk of changes caused by unemployment or the onset of ill-health.

Adults in low-income households by gender

10A: Women are a bit – but only a bit – more likely to live in low-income households than men.

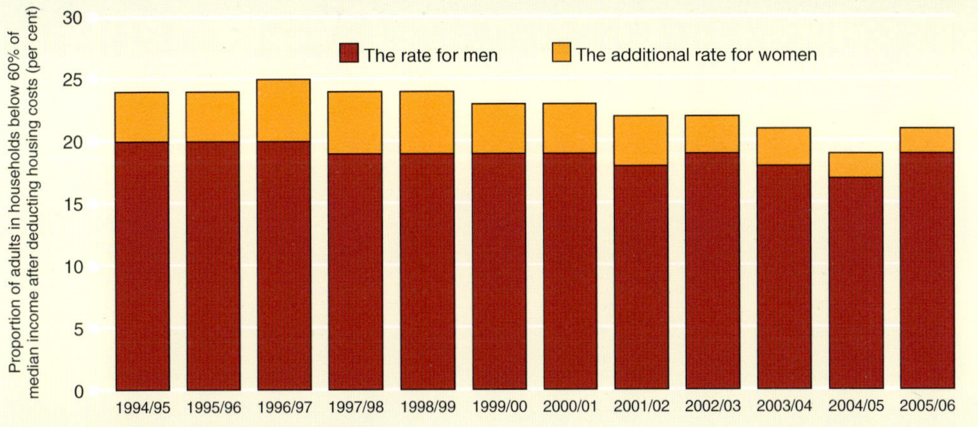

Source: Households Below Average Income, DWP; UK

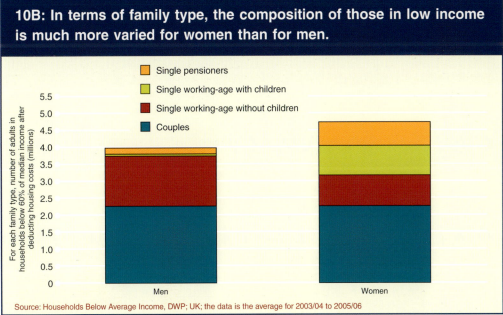

10B: In terms of family type, the composition of those in low income is much more varied for women than for men.

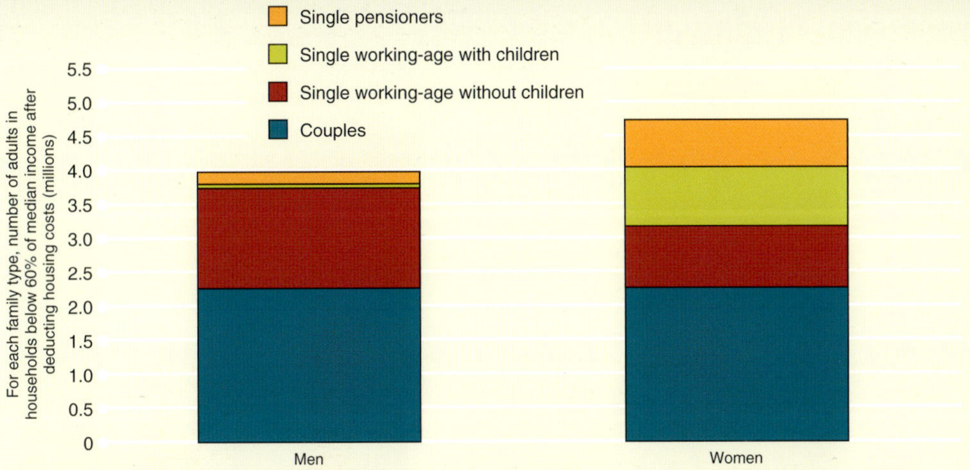

Source: Households Below Average Income, DWP; UK; the data is the average for 2003/04 to 2005/06

The first graph shows how the risk of an adult being in a low-income household has changed over time, with the data shown separately for men and women.

The second graph shows the division of the adults in low-income households by family type, with the data again shown separately for men and women.

The data source for both graphs is Households Below Average Income, based on the Family Resources Survey (FRS). For 2002/03 onwards, the data relates to the United Kingdom while the data for earlier years is for Great Britain (FRS did not cover Northern Ireland until 2002/03). The low-income threshold and adjustment to household incomes for their size and composition are both as for indicator 2.

Overall adequacy of the indicator: high. The FRS is a well-established annual government survey, designed to be representative of the population as a whole.

Indicator 11

Single adults in low-income households by gender

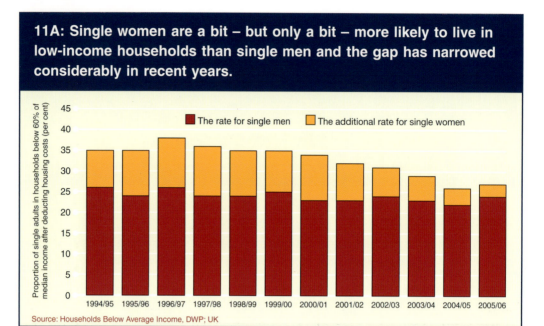

11A: Single women are a bit – but only a bit – more likely to live in low-income households than single men and the gap has narrowed considerably in recent years.

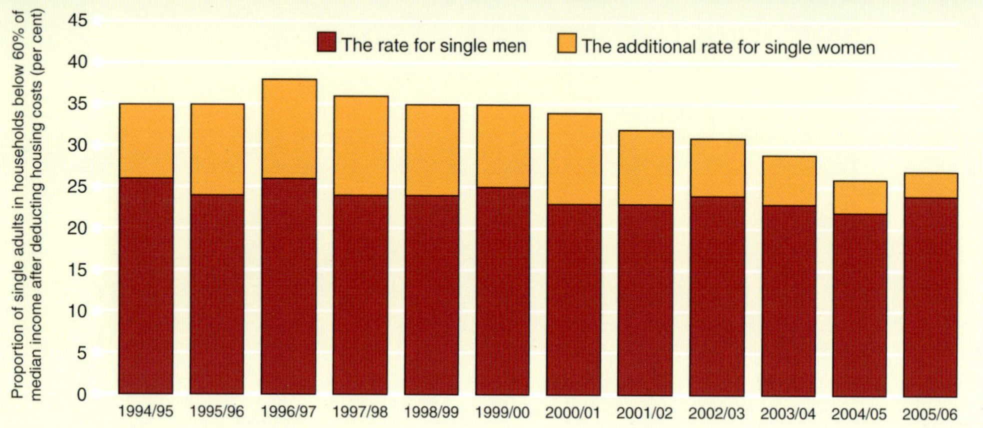

Source: Households Below Average Income, DWP; UK

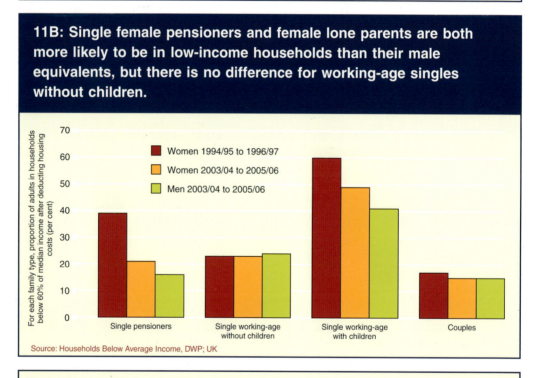

11B: Single female pensioners and female lone parents are both more likely to be in low-income households than their male equivalents, but there is no difference for working-age singles without children.

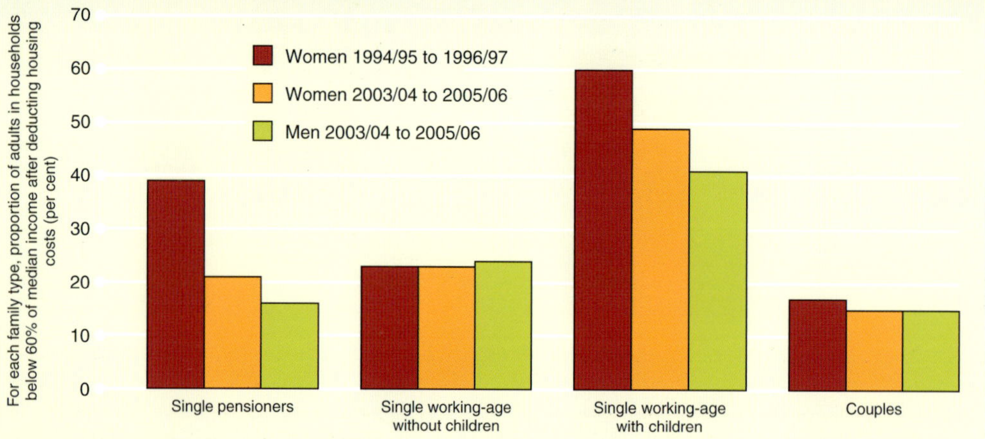

Source: Households Below Average Income, DWP; UK

The first graph shows how the risk of a single adult (i.e. excluding couples) being in a low-income household has changed over time, with the data shown separately for men and women.

The second graph shows, for each family type, the risk of an adult being in a low-income household, with the data again shown separately for men and women. For women, it also shows how, for each family type, the risk of an adult being in a low-income household has changed over time (the equivalent over-time data for men is not shown for presentational reasons).

The data source for both graphs is Households Below Average Income, based on the Family Resources Survey (FRS). For 2002/03 onwards, the data relates to the United Kingdom while the data for earlier years is for Great Britain (FRS did not cover Northern Ireland until 2002/03). The low-income threshold and adjustment to household incomes for their size and composition are both as for indicator 2.

Overall adequacy of the indicator: high. The FRS is a well-established annual government survey, designed to be representative of the population as a whole.

Working-age composition

12A: One million young adults aged 16 to 24 with no dependent children and living without a partner are in low-income households.

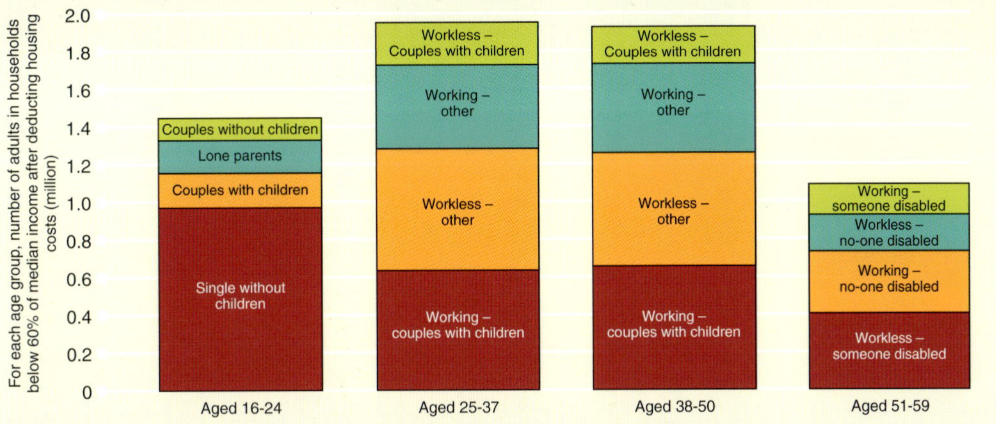

Source: Household Below Average Income, DWP; the data is the average for 2003/04 to 2005/06; UK

12B: Four-fifths of lone parents in low-income households are aged 25 or older.

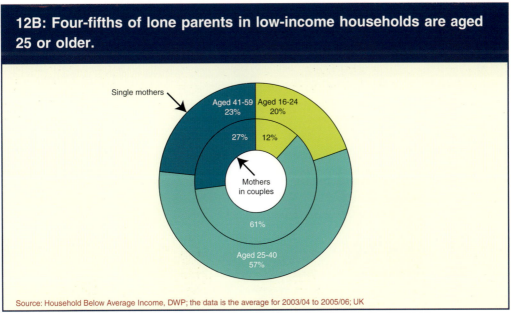

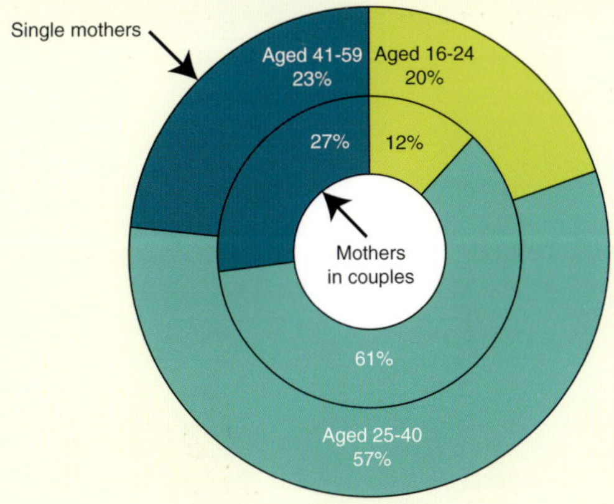

Source: Household Below Average Income, DWP; the data is the average for 2003/04 to 2005/06; UK

The first graph shows the number of working-age adults who are living in low-income households, with the data broken down into four age groups, namely 16-24, 25-37, 38-50 and 51-59. For each age group, the data is further broken down by family characteristics, where, for each age group, these characteristics have been chosen to best illustrate the composition of that age group. More specifically: for the 16-24 age group the division is by family type (i.e. whether the family is a couple or single and whether or not there are dependent children); for the 25-37 and 38-50 age groups, the division is by family work status (i.e. whether or not anyone is working) and whether or not the family is a couple with dependent children; and for the 51-59 age group, the division is by family work status and family disability status (i.e. whether or not any of the adults is disabled).

The second graph shows the proportions of lone parents who are living in low-income households by age group. For comparison purposes, the equivalent data for mothers in couples is also shown.

The data source for both graphs is Households Below Average Income, based on the Family Resources Survey (FRS) and the data relates to the United Kingdom. All data is the average for the years 2003/04 to 2005/06. The low-income threshold and adjustment to household incomes for their size and composition are both as for indicator 2. The definition of 'family' is as for indicator 7.

Overall adequacy of the indicator: high. The FRS is a well-established government survey, designed to be representative of the population as a whole.

Indicator 13

Low income by detailed age bands

13A: The proportion of people who live in low-income households only begins to fall from the age of 21.

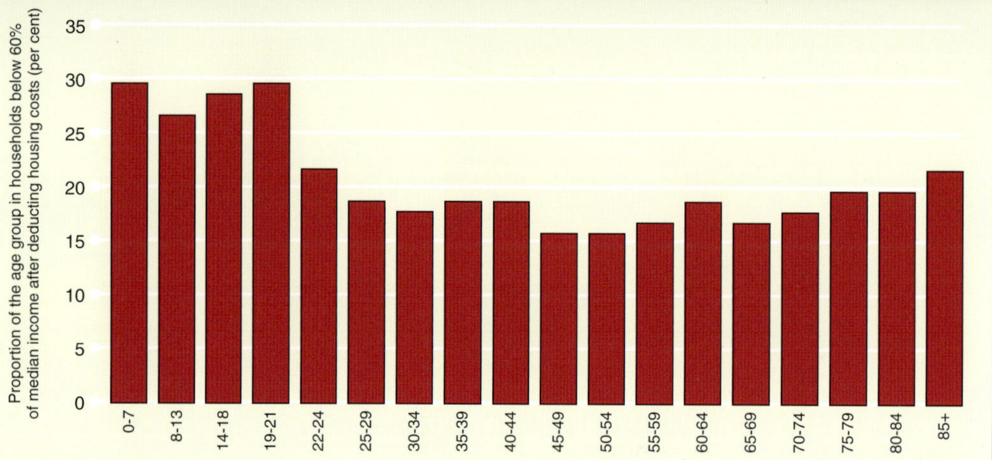

Source: Household Below Average Income, DWP; the data is the average for 2003/04 to 2005/06; UK

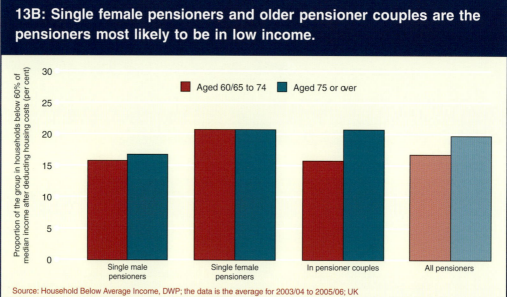

13B: Single female pensioners and older pensioner couples are the pensioners most likely to be in low income.

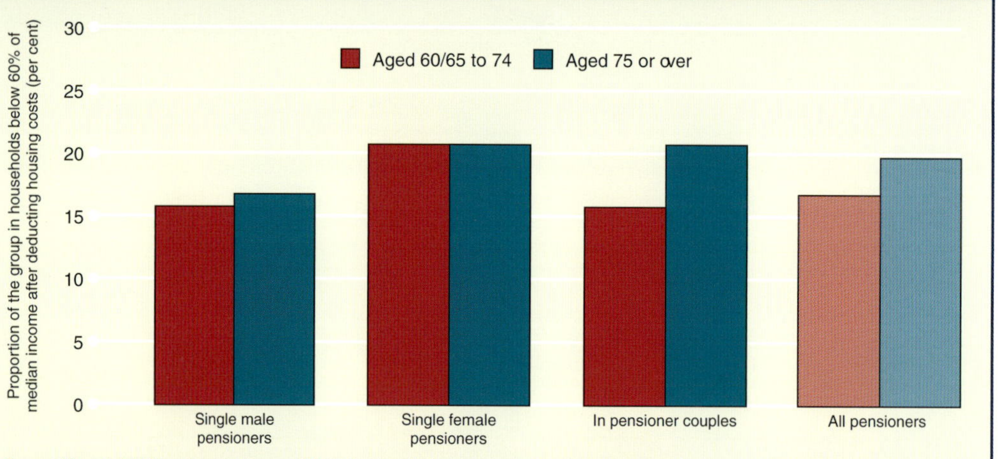

Source: Household Below Average Income, DWP; the data is the average for 2003/04 to 2005/06; UK

The first graph shows the risk of a person being in a low-income household by age. The ages are banded in five-year age bands from 25 onwards but, for those under the age of 25, the bands have been chosen by grouping years with similar risks together, noting that there is marked change around the age of 21.

The second graph shows the proportion of pensioners living in low-income households for different combinations of age group (less than 75 and 75 and over) and family type (pensioner couple, single female pensioner and single male pensioner).

The data source for both graphs is Households Below Average Income, based on the Family Resources Survey (FRS) and the data relates to the United Kingdom. All data is the average for the years 2003/04 to 2005/06. The low-income threshold and adjustment to household incomes for their size and composition are both as for indicator 2.

Overall adequacy of the indicator: medium. The FRS is a well-established annual government survey designed to be representative of the population as a whole. However, the sample sizes are relatively small in the first graph and the second graph does not include people in residential institutions (such as nursing homes) as FRS only covers people living in private households.

Chapter 2 **Lacking work**

Workless households

This section focuses on working-age households in which no one (of working age) is in paid work.

14 Workless households

(The proportion of different types of household who are workless)

This indicator is concerned with the proportion of workless households of different types, that is, whether the household contains one or more working age adults and whether there are dependent children or not. The first graph shows, for each of these four types, the proportion who were workless year by year over the past decade. The second graph, for the latest year, divides the total number of workless households according to which of the four types they are.

Key points:

- Single adult households, both with and without children, are far more likely than two adult ones to be workless. So among households with children, two-fifths of lone parent households are workless, around seven times the rate for couple households. Among households without children, a quarter of single adult households are workless, around four times the rate for couple households.
- The proportion of households who are workless has come down for each of the four household types over the past decade. In proportional terms, the falls have been somewhat greater for households with children than for those without children. In absolute terms, however, the falls have been greater for single-adult households than for couple households (because their starting proportion was so much higher).
- Overall, half of all workless working-age households are single adults without dependent children and a further fifth are lone parent households.

15 Children in workless households

(The number of children in workless households)

The second indicator focuses on children in workless households. The first graph shows how the number of children living in workless households has changed year by year over the past decade. The second graph shows how the proportion of children in workless households in the UK compares with the proportions in each of the other 26 European Union member states.

Key points:

- In 2006, some 1.8 million children were living in workless households, half a million fewer than a decade earlier. Most of this fall took place in the first half of this ten-year period, up to about 2000.
- In 2006, some 1.2 million children were living in workless, lone parent households, between 0.1 and 0.2 million lower than ten years earlier. This means that most of the fall in the overall number of children in workless households has taken place among couple, rather than lone parent, households.

Despite the falls in the number of children in workless households, the UK still has the highest proportion of its children living in workless households in any European Union country, its 16 per cent rate (in 2006) exceeding that of the next worst three (Bulgaria, Belgium and Hungary) by at least 2 percentage points and being around two-thirds higher than the rates in both France and Germany.

Selected relevant research

Some other research on workless households has further explored their characteristics.

- Analysis by Bivand (2005) for the Centre for Social Inclusion showed that there are substantial differences in the prevalence of workless households by ethnicity. Further analysis of the Labour Force Survey by the New Policy Institute brings this up to date: in 2006, one third of Bangladeshi and black African households were workless, twice the rate for white British households.[9]
- Bivand also looked at the proportion of children in workless households by ethnicity. Around 40 per cent of black African children lived in workless households, compared to around 10 per cent of Indian children. The rate of worklessness among black African households varies substantially between Christian and Muslim households, with the latter being higher. Bivand suggests that this is mainly because the immigration status of many black African Muslim families makes it harder for them to find work.
- Among workless households, the vast majority are classified as 'inactive', rather than 'unemployed' (ONS, 2007). In the last decade, while the proportion of households described as unemployed or mixed unemployed and inactive has decreased from around 5 per cent to around 3 per cent, the proportion of inactive households has stayed at around 13 per cent.

Indicator 14

Workless households

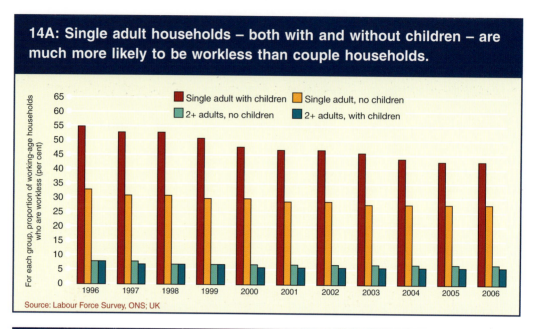

14A: Single adult households – both with and without children – are much more likely to be workless than couple households.

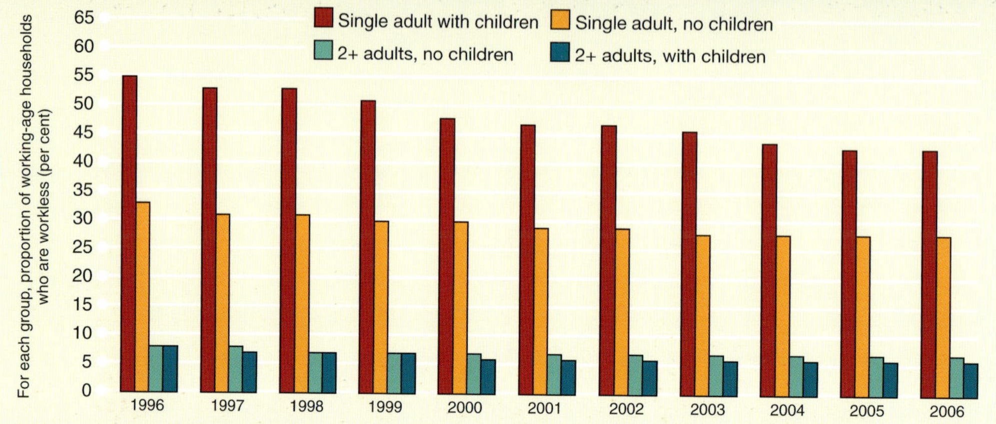

Source: Labour Force Survey, ONS; UK

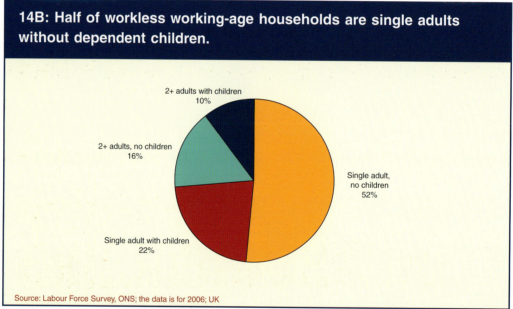

14B: Half of workless working-age households are single adults without dependent children.

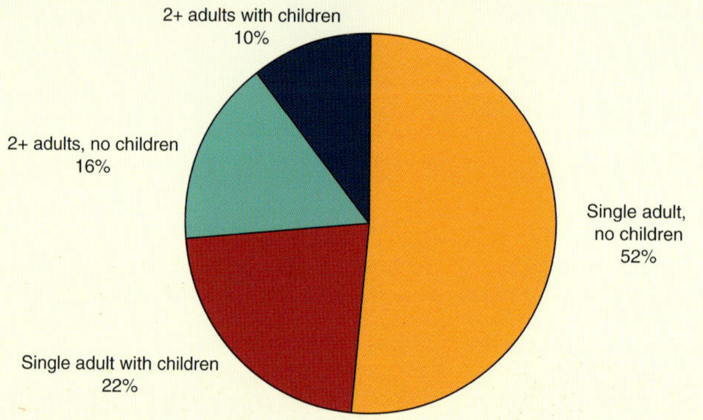

Source: Labour Force Survey, ONS; the data is for 2006; UK

For each of a number of working-age household types, the first graph shows the proportion of the households who are workless (i.e. households where none of the adults are working). The four household types shown are lone parent households, single adults without dependent children, households with two or more adults but no dependent children, and households with two or more adults and one or more dependent children.

The second graph shows, for the latest year, the proportion of all workless working-age households who are in each household type.

The data source for both graphs is the Labour Force Survey (LFS) and relates to the United Kingdom. The data for each year is the average for the 2nd and 4th quarters, analysis by household type not being available for the 1st and 3rd quarters (noting that prior to 2006, the four quarters ran from December to November).

In both graphs, households which are entirely composed of full-time students have been excluded from the analysis, as have households where their economic status is not known. Full-time students have also been excluded from the calculations to decide whether the household has one or more than one adult. So, for example, a household comprising one full-time student and one other working-age adult has been allocated to the 'one adult' household type. In line with ONS methods, children comprise all those under the age of 16 (i.e. not including dependent children aged 16-18).

Overall adequacy of the indicator: high. The LFS is a well-established, quarterly government survey designed to be representative of the population as a whole.

Children in workless households

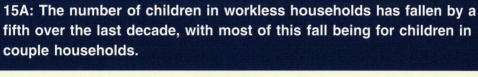

15A: The number of children in workless households has fallen by a fifth over the last decade, with most of this fall being for children in couple households.

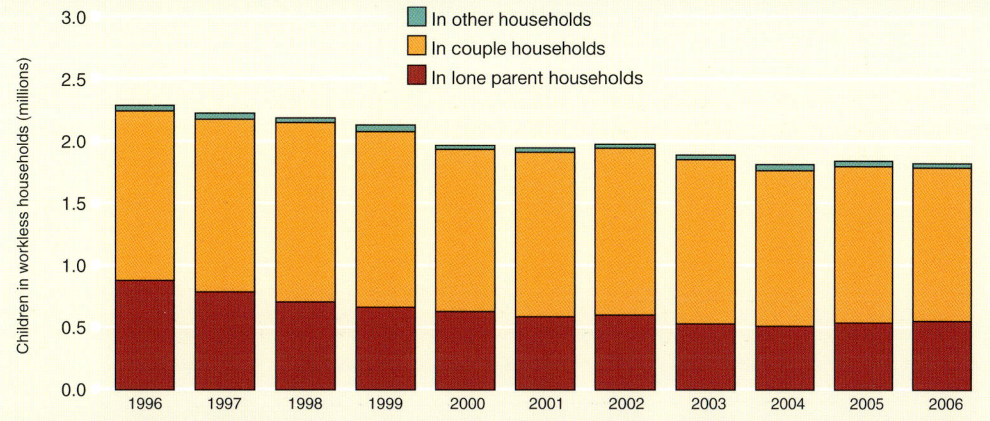

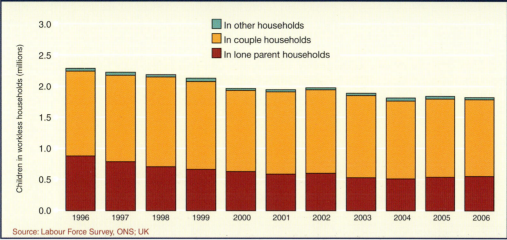

Source: Labour Force Survey, ONS; UK

15B: The UK has a higher proportion of its children living in workless households than any other EU country.

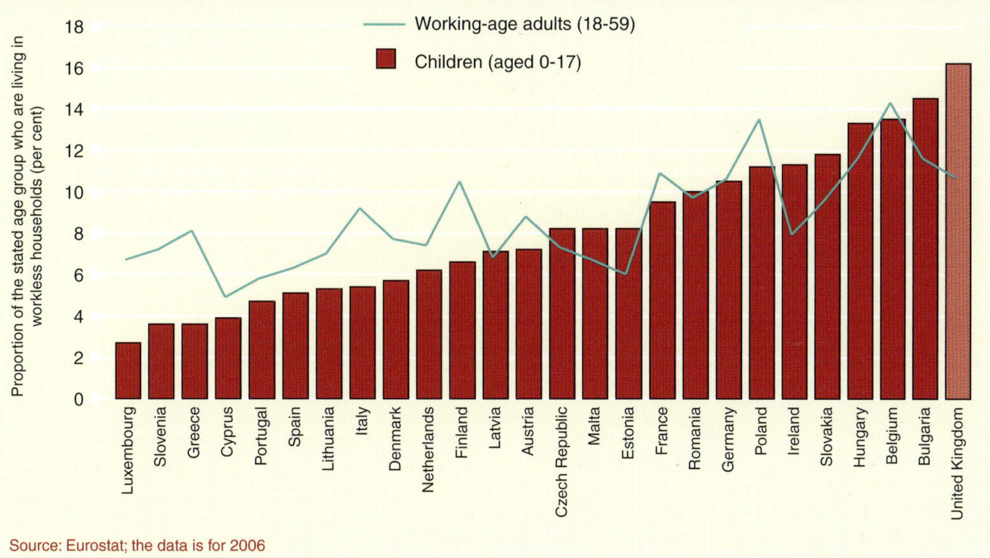

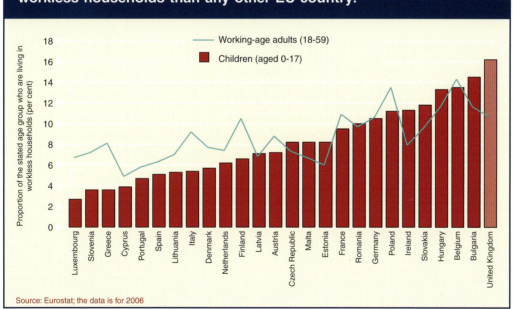

Source: Eurostat; the data is for 2006

The first graph shows the number of children living in households in which none of the working-age adults is in paid work. The data is separated by household type, namely couple households, lone parent households and other households. The data source is the Labour Force Survey (LFS) and the data relates to the United Kingdom. The data for each year is the average for the 2nd and 4th quarters, analysis by household type not being available for the 1st and 3rd quarters (noting that prior to 2006, the four quarters ran from December to November). In line with ONS methods, children comprise all those under the age of 16 (i.e. not including dependent children aged 16-18).

The second graph shows the proportion of children aged 0-17 in each EU country who live in workless households. For comparison purposes, the equivalent data for 18-59-year-olds is also shown. The data source is Eurostat, which in turn draws its data from the Labour Force Surveys in each country. The data is for the year 2006. Note that there is no data available for Sweden.

Overall adequacy of the indicator: high. The LFS is a large, well-established, quarterly government survey, designed to be representative of the population as a whole.

Unemployed and workless individuals

In contrast to the previous section, which looked at workless households, this section looks at workless individuals.

Those who are counted as unemployed are at the core of this group but they are by no means the only members. The official definition of unemployment is based upon the ILO (International Labour Organization) standard, namely, jobless people who (a) want to work, (b) are available to start work in the next two weeks, and (c) have been actively seeking work in the last four weeks, or who have just found a job and are waiting to start. This group goes wider than those who are claiming the relevant social security benefit (Jobseeker's Allowance). People who are (ILO) unemployed, along with those who are working, are described as 'economically active'.

But many members of the 'economically inactive' group also want to work. The reason why they are not counted as unemployed is because they are either not actively seeking work or are not immediately available for work. Disabled people and lone parents are likely to be in this category, rather than the unemployed, if they lack but want work.

16 Not in education, employment or training

(The proportion of 16- to 18-year-olds not in education, employment or training)

This indicator focuses on a group who have long been a cause for official concern, namely those teenagers above the compulsory school age who are not in education, employment or training. The first graph shows the proportion of 16- to 18-year-olds in this situation for each year over the last decade. The second, for 2006, shows the status of 16-year-olds according to whether they are in full-time education, training, employment (with or without training), not settled or unknown. These results are shown separately for boys and girls.

Key points:

- At 11 per cent, the proportion of 16- to 18-year-olds not in employment, education or training in 2006 was no better than it was ten years earlier, and higher than it was five years earlier. This is around 200-300,000 16- to 18-year-olds at any point in time.
- The main difference between boys and girls relates to the proportions in full-time education – more than 80 per cent for girls but less than 75 per cent for boys – with this difference then reflected in the higher proportion of boys than girls in employment with training: 10 per cent compared with 5 per cent.

17 Young adult unemployment

(The proportion of young adults who are unemployed)

This indicator focuses on the important subject of unemployment among young adults, defined here as those aged 19 to 24. The first graph shows the unemployment rate for young adults for each year over the last decade, comparing it with the rate for those aged 25 to retirement. The second graph shows the rate for young adult men and women separately, again compared with the rates for older men and women. In both cases, the unemployment rate expresses the numbers unemployed as a proportion of the economically active population, that is, those in jobs plus those unemployed. People who are economically inactive are not included in the statistic.

Key points:

- At 11.5 per cent in 2006, the unemployment rate for young adults has been rising since 2004, when it stood at 9.5 per cent, a level at which it had held since 2001. This in turn followed a period in the late 1990s when the rate had fallen sharply, from around 14 per cent in 1996.
- The recent rise in the rate of young adult unemployment has exceeded the smaller rise in the rate for adults aged 25 and over. As a result, the 11.5 per cent young adult rate in 2006 was three times the rate for older adults. By contrast, a decade earlier, the young adult rate at 14 per cent was just twice the older adult rate.
- The unemployment rate for young adult men is around one third higher than the rate for young adult women: 12 per cent over the period 2004 to 2006 for men, compared with 9 per cent for women. Both these rates are about three times the comparable rates for older male and female workers.

18 Wanting paid work

(The number of adults aged 25 to retirement who lack but want paid work)

This indicator extends the focus on people lacking but wanting paid work to include those who are economically inactive but wanting paid work as well as those who are unemployed. Attention is restricted to those aged 25 to retirement. The first graph shows the number of adults in this age group lacking but wanting work for each year over the last decade, with separate figures for those who have been unemployed for less than a year, those who have been unemployed for more than a year, and those who are economically inactive but wanting paid work. The supporting graph provides a breakdown of the proportions who are unemployed and economically inactive but wanting paid work by age (25 to 34, 35 to 49 and 50 to retirement) and gender. It should be noted that the proportions here are of the whole male/female population and that this 'unemployment rate' is therefore not comparable with the unemployment rate (expressed as a proportion of the economically active population) in the previous indicator.

Key points:

- Over the last decade, the number of unemployed adults aged 25 and over has almost halved, from 1.6 million in 1996 to 0.9 million in 2006. The fall has been especially large among those unemployed longer than a year: down from 0.75 million to 0.25 million. The number unemployed for less than a year has also fallen but by much less, down from 0.85 million to 0.65 million.
- The number of economically inactive people wanting paid work has also fallen but much more slowly, down 15 per cent from 1.8 million in 1996 to 1.5 million in 2006. The combined effect of this smaller fall with the much larger falls for unemployment is that the economically inactive wanting paid work now outnumber the unemployed by almost two to one; a decade ago by contrast they were about equal in size.

- In terms of proportions rather than absolute numbers, the proportion of adults aged 25 and over who were unemployed fell from 5.5 per cent in 1996 to 3 per cent in 2001 and then remained at 3 per cent through to 2006. The proportion who were economically inactive but wanting paid work fell from 6 per cent in 1996 to 5 per cent in 2004 and then remained at 5 per cent through to 2006.
- Differences in the relative size of the two 'lacking but wanting work' groups becomes even sharper when broken down by age and gender. Thus for women in every age group, and for men aged over 50, there are around twice as many economically inactive wanting paid work as there are unemployed. Men aged 25 to 34 are the only group where the unemployed clearly outnumber the inactive wanting paid work, by about two to one. Even among men aged 25 to 49, the two categories are about equal in size. For all except younger men, therefore, 'unemployment' is only a small part of the overall picture.

19 Work and disability

(Work rates among those aged 25 to retirement by disability and lone parent status)

The final indicator focuses on the work rates for people aged 25 to retirement according to whether or not they have a work-limiting disability and/or are a lone parent. The first graph shows the proportions in work for each year since 1998 for four groups, namely those neither disabled nor a lone parent; non-disabled lone parents; people who are disabled but are not lone parents; and disabled lone parents. The second graph, for 2006, shows how gender alters the picture (although data limitations mean that male lone parents are not shown).

Key points:

- Since the late 1990s, the work rate for people aged 25 to retirement who are neither disabled nor lone parents has remained largely unchanged, at around 87 per cent. Over the same period, the rate for people with a work-limiting disability (and who are not lone parents) has risen but only slightly, from just under to just over 40 per cent. By contrast, the rate for non-disabled lone parents has risen considerably, from around 55 per cent in the mid/late 1990s to just under 70 per cent in 2006. The rate for disabled lone parents has risen but only very slightly, and remains below 30 per cent.
- Looked at in terms of who is not working, almost half of all those aged 25 to retirement not in work have a working-limiting disability.[10]
- When broken down by gender, among those aged 25 to retirement, work rates for those who are neither disabled nor a lone parent are around 80 per cent for women and 90 per cent for men. In both cases, a further 5 per cent lack but want paid work.
- By contrast, work rates for disabled, non-lone parents are around 40 per cent for both men and women. Not only, therefore, does disability massively reduce the work rate but it also does so in a way to remove the gender gap apparent among non-disabled, non-lone parents.

- Disability also dramatically reduces the work rate among female lone parents, 65 per cent among those non-disabled compared with just 25 per cent for those who are disabled. So while lone parenthood reduces the female work rate by 15 percentage points (from 80 per cent to 65 per cent), disability reduces the work rate for both female lone parents and female non-lone parents by 40 percentage points (from 65 per cent to 25 per cent and 80 per cent to 40 per cent respectively).

Selected relevant research

Relating to young adults not in education, employment or training (NEETs):

- Rennison *et al.* (2005) found that children in the NEET category were more likely to come from workless households, with parents who had low educational qualifications. The study also found that truancy and caring responsibilities were more common in this group.
- They further observe that half of those who are NEET at 17 were also NEET at 16. The majority of those who join the NEET group at age 17 come from full-time education. Those who leave the NEET group at that age are equally likely to go into work, education or training.
- Field and White (2007) point to the fact that the number of young people on the New Deal has fallen relative to the number of young people on benefits. Moreover, around one third of young people on the New Deal are now people who have been through the New Deal before.

Relating to work and disability:

- Rigg (2005) found that disabled people were far more likely to exit work – that is quit, retire, be sacked or made redundant – than non-disabled people. Disabled men were around three times as likely to exit as non-disabled men, with disabled women about twice as likely as non-disabled women. This propensity to exit increases with the severity of the disability.

Indicator 16

Not in education, employment or training

16A: One in ten 16- to 18-year-olds is not in education, employment or training, the same as a decade ago.

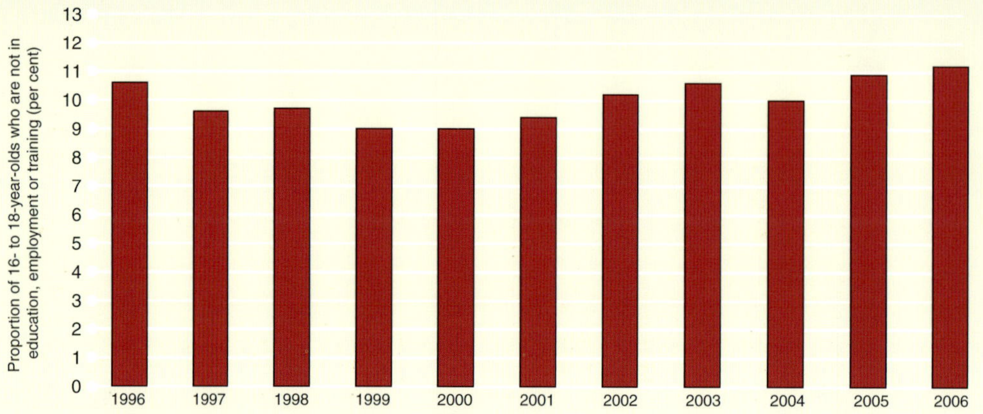

Source: Labour Force Survey, ONS; UK

16B: For pupils who have completed year 11 – proportion in each destination.

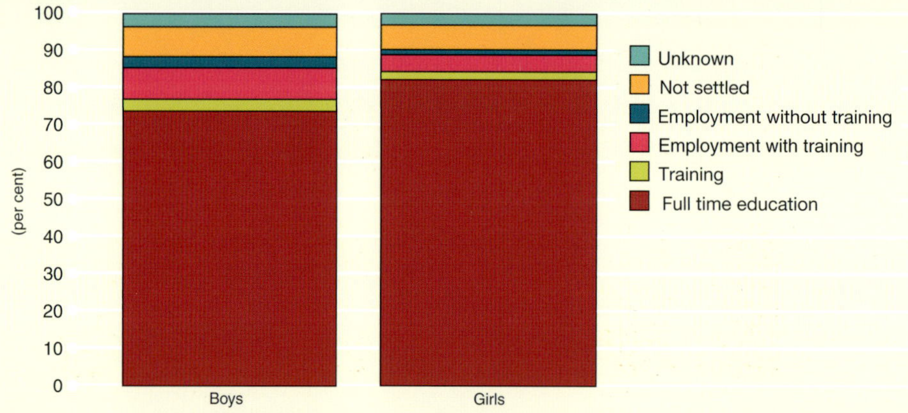

Source: Careers Service Activity Survey, Connexions; the data is for 2006; England

The first graph shows the proportion of 16- to 18-year-olds who are not in education, employment or training (sometimes referred to as NEETs). The data source is the Labour Force Survey (LFS) and relates to the United Kingdom. The figures for each year are the average for the four quarters of the relevant year (noting that prior to 2006, these four quarters ran from December to November). Note that the figures are not precisely the same as those in official government publications, mainly because those publications are based on analysis of the fourth quarter data for each year only.

The second graph shows, for the latest year, how the destinations of pupils who have completed year 11 vary by gender. The data source is the Connexions Careers Service Activity Survey and the data relates to England only.

Overall adequacy of the indicator: limited. The LFS is a large, well-established, quarterly government survey designed to be representative of the population as a whole but nevertheless the sample sizes are small. Furthermore, LFS may not always capture all types of education or training that a person is engaged with.

Young adult unemployment

17A: The unemployment rate for 19- to 24-year-olds has been rising since 2004 and is now three times the rate for older workers.

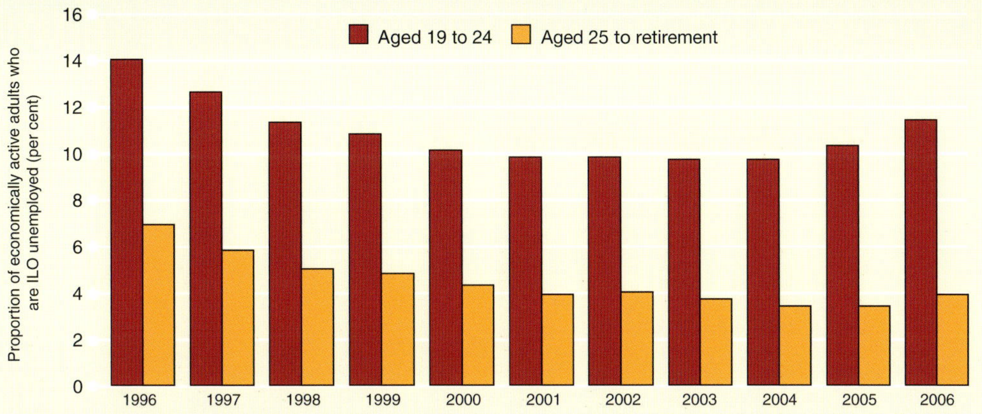

Source: Labour Force Survey, ONS; UK

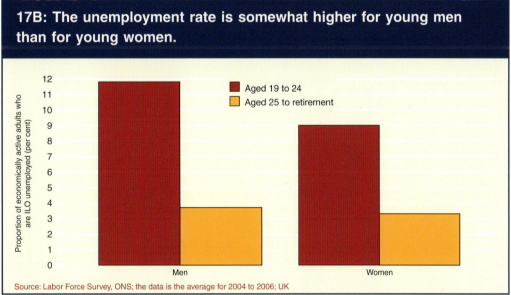

17B: The unemployment rate is somewhat higher for young men than for young women.

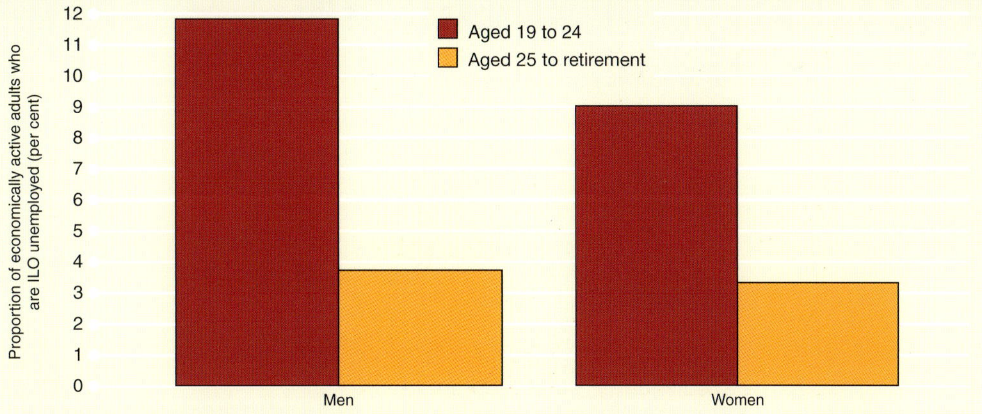

Source: Labor Force Survey, ONS; the data is the average for 2004 to 2006; UK

The first graph shows the unemployment rate for those aged 19 to 24, compared with those aged 25 and over (up to retirement).

The second graph shows how the unemployment rate for 19- to 24-year-olds varies by gender, with the equivalent data for those aged 25 to retirement also shown. To improve its statistical reliability, the data is the average for the latest three years.

'Unemployment' is the ILO definition, which is used for the official government unemployment numbers. It includes all those with no paid work in the survey week who were available to start work in the next fortnight and who either looked for work in the last month or were waiting to start a job already obtained. The ILO unemployment rate is the percentage of the economically active population who are unemployed on the ILO measure (i.e. the total population for the relevant age group less those classified as economically inactive).

The data source for both graphs is the Labour Force Survey (LFS) and relates to the United Kingdom. The figures for each year are the average for the four quarters of the relevant year (noting that prior to 2006, these four quarters ran from December to November).

Overall adequacy of the indicator: high. The LFS is a large, well-established, quarterly government survey designed to be representative of the population as a whole.

Indicator 18

Wanting paid work

18A: Official unemployment has almost halved over the last decade, with particularly large falls in long-term unemployment. The number who are economically inactive but want work has fallen much more slowly.

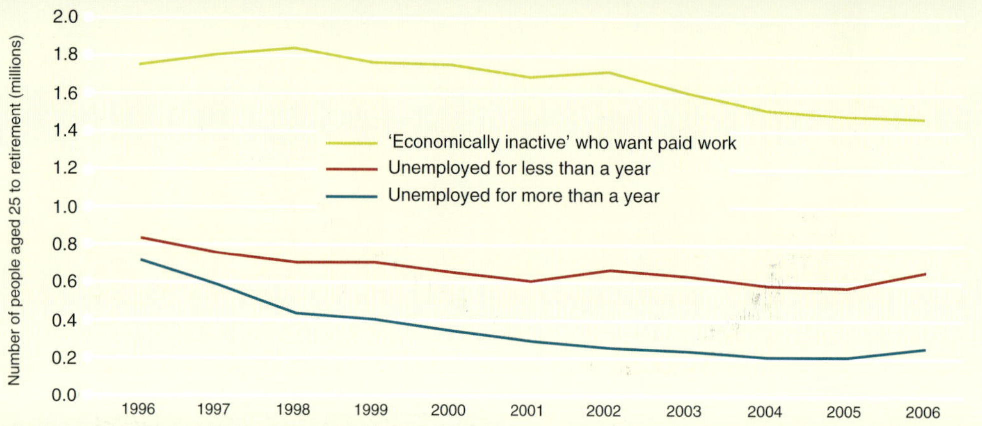

Source: Labour Force Survey, ONS; UK; updated April 2007

18B: For all women of all ages, and for older men, those who are economically inactive but wanting paid work substantially outnumber the officially unemployed.

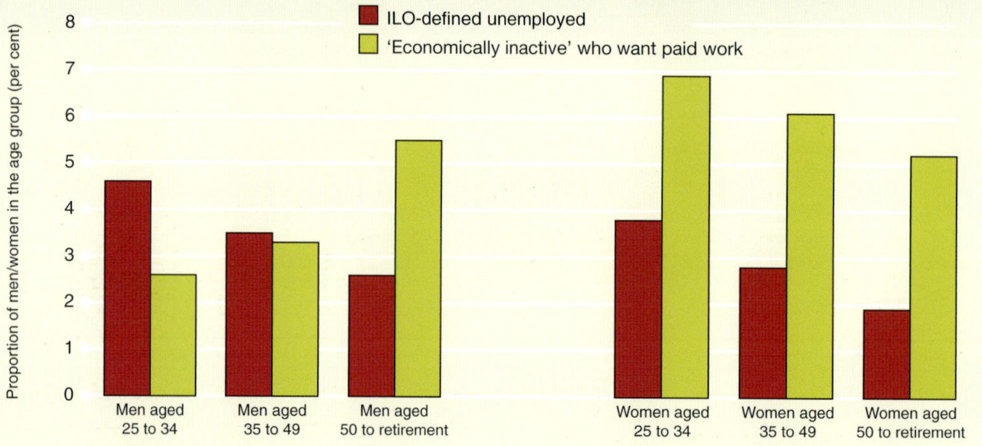

Source: Labour Force Survey, ONS; the data is for 2006; UK

The first graph shows the number of people aged 25 to retirement lacking but wanting paid work. It is divided between the long-term unemployed, the short-term unemployed, and those counted as 'economically inactive' who nevertheless want paid work.

'Unemployment' is the ILO definition, which is used for the official UK unemployment numbers. It includes all those with no paid work in the survey week who were available to start work in the next fortnight and who either looked for work in the last month or were waiting to start a job already obtained. The economically inactive who want paid work includes people not available to start work for some time and those not actively seeking work. The data is based on a question in LFS asking the economically inactive whether they would like paid work or not.

The second graph shows, for the latest year, how the proportions of people aged 25 to retirement lacking but wanting paid work, vary by age and gender.

The data source for both graphs is the Labour Force Survey (LFS). The data relates to the United Kingdom and is not seasonally adjusted. To improve statistical reliability, the figures for each year are the average for the four quarters of the relevant year (noting that prior to 2006, these four quarters ran from December to November).

Overall adequacy of the indicator: high. The LFS is a well-established, quarterly government survey designed to be representative of the population as a whole.

Work and disability

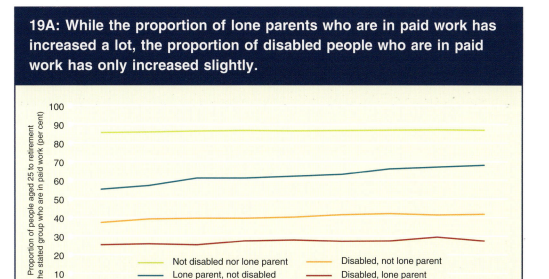

19A: While the proportion of lone parents who are in paid work has increased a lot, the proportion of disabled people who are in paid work has only increased slightly.

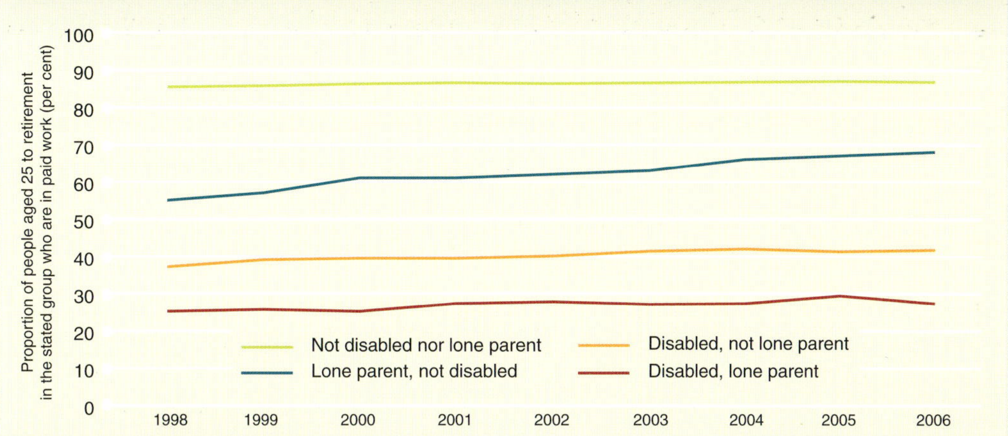

Source: Labour Force Survey, ONS; UK

19B: Disability affects work status much more than gender or even lone parenthood.

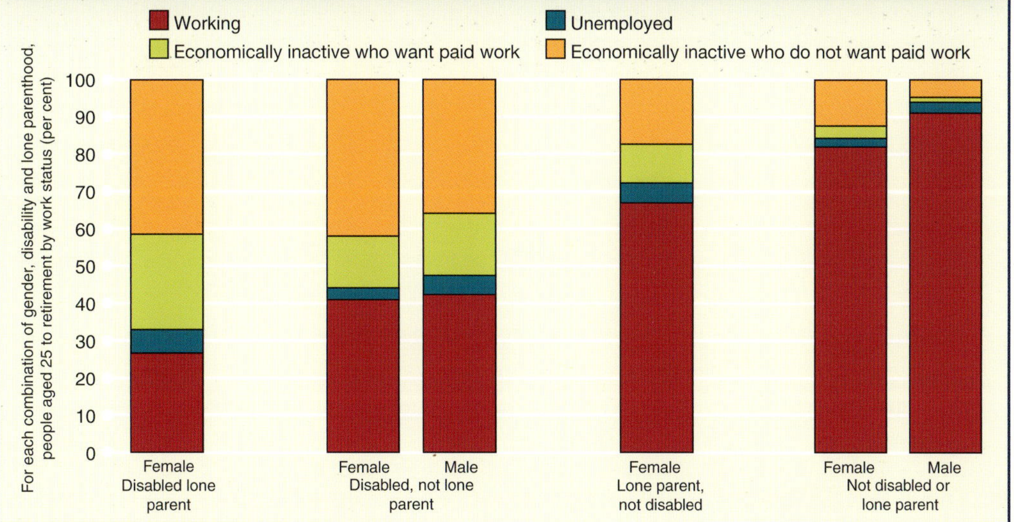

Source: Labour Force Survey, ONS; the data is for 2006; UK

The first graph shows the proportion of people aged 25 to retirement who are in paid work, with the data shown separately for four groups of people, namely disabled lone parents, non-disabled lone parents, disabled people who are not lone parents, and people who are neither disabled nor lone parents.

The second graph shows, for the latest year, the proportion of people aged 25 to retirement in each work status, with the data shown separately for each combination of gender, disability (disabled or not) and lone parenthood (lone parent or not). Note that male lone parents are not shown as the sample sizes are not sufficient to derive reliable estimates.

The data source for both graphs is the Labour Force Survey (LFS) and relates to the United Kingdom. The figures for each year are the average for the 2nd and 4th quarters (data on household type not being available for the other two quarters).

The definitions of 'unemployment' and the 'economically inactive' are as for indicator 18. 'Work-limiting disability' is an LFS classification and comprises those people who stated that they have had health problems for more than a year and that these problems affect either the kind or amount of work that they can do. This classification, rather than whether or not someone is disabled in terms of the Disability Discrimination Act (DDA), has been used as it results in greater differences in the 'disabled or not' categories. Note that there is a high overlap between the two groups and that both are of similar size.

Overall adequacy of the indicator: high. The LFS is a large, well-established, quarterly government survey, designed to be representative of the population as a whole.

Out-of-work benefits

The two indicators in this section look at out-of-work benefits both for pensioners and for those of working age. Increases in the value of these benefits for both families with children and pensioners have formed an integral part of the government's anti-poverty policies. By contrast, raising the value of benefits for working-age people without dependent children has formed no part of that strategy. This section therefore looks at the value of such benefits, at who receives them and where they live, in the sense of whether they are concentrated in particular areas or more evenly spread out.

20 Benefit levels

(The value of state benefits relative to earnings)

The first graph shows what has happened to the value of out-of-work benefits for various household types, relative to earnings since 1997. All the household types shown here are couples: pensioners, and working-age with none, one and two dependent children respectively. The shapes of the lines, relative to one another, are similar for the equivalent one adult households. In essence, the graph plots the value of Income Support. Jobseeker's Allowance also follows the value of Income Support for working-age households. For pensioners, Income Support is nowadays badged as (Guarantee) Pension Credit.

The supporting graph shows the relative sizes of the different groups of adults in receipt of state benefits (not just Income Support), namely pensioners, lone parents, couples with dependent children and working-age without dependent children. These figures are for 2007.

Key points:

- The value of Income Support for both pensioner couples and couples with two children is about 10 per cent higher relative to average earnings in 2007 than it was in 1997. By contrast, the value of this benefit for working-age adults with no dependent children is about 20 per cent lower relative to earnings in 2007 than it was in 1997. For couples with one dependent child, the value is about the same in 2007 as in 1997 relative to earnings. The reason for the difference in the trends for working-age families with differing numbers of children is that all the increases in benefit levels have been in the child element rather than the adult element, so the fewer the children in the family the lower the increase in the benefit level.
- These changes are a direct reflection of the policies pursued by the government. Increases in the value of benefits paid for children, echoing those brought in when tax credits were introduced (in 1999) and reformed and extended (in 2003), raised benefits for families with children. By 2004, the size of this boost lifted the relative value of benefits for those with two children by 15 per cent compared with 1997. Since then, it has fallen back somewhat. Large rises in what became known as Pension Credit lifted benefit values for pensioners sharply in 2001, and by further smaller amounts in 2002 and 2003. Since then it has been tied to earnings.

- The recent stagnation in the benefit levels for couples with children and pensioners pale into insignificance compared with what has happened to the value of Income Support for working-age couples without dependent children. Tied only to price inflation, these have fallen back steadily relative to earnings and are now 20 per cent lower than a decade ago. In essence, this group has not shared in any of the economic growth and resulting higher income created since Labour came to office in 1997.
- In 2007, this group – working-age adults without dependent children – constituted nearly half of all adults in receipt of state benefits. With 45 per cent of the total, this group comfortably exceeds the number of pensioners in receipt of such benefits (36 per cent of the total) and represents more than twice the number of those with children in receipt of such benefits.

21 Concentrations of low income

(The geographical concentration of working-age claimants of out-of-work benefits)

While the geographical pattern of poverty and other forms of disadvantage always appear to attract great interest, statistics that purport to summarise those patterns are not only often difficult to understand but are also matters of dispute among the experts. Such measures are also hampered by the fact that data on poverty as defined in this report is simply not available below the level of the English region, Wales, Scotland and Northern Ireland. This indicator, using out-of-work benefits data rather than poverty data (an important difference given that half of all child poverty is in working families) employs simple measures to answer two questions.

The first question is whether working-age people receiving out-of-work benefits have become more or less concentrated geographically over recent years. The first graph answers this by comparing the number of such recipients in the 10 per cent of small areas with highest levels of concentration with the number in the 50 per cent of small areas with the lowest levels of concentration for each year since 1999 (when such data first became available).

The second question is what proportion of such people live in the areas with the highest concentrations. The second graph answers this directly, for 2007.

Key points:

- In 1999, some 1.4 million working age-adults in receipt of out-of-work benefits lived in the 10 per cent of small areas with the highest concentration of such people. By 2007, this number had fallen to 1.2 million. This fall happened fairly steadily over the whole period.
- In 1999, a further 1.4 million working-age adults in receipt of out-of-work benefits lived in the 50 per cent of small areas with the lowest concentration of such people. By 2007, that number too had fallen to about 1.2 million. This fall was more rapid up to 2003 than it has been since.
- In other words, the overall level of geographical concentration of working-age people in receipt of out-of-work benefits has remained the same over the period between 1999 and 2007. In this sense at least, the policies of the last decade have not in general succeeded in reducing the gap between the most deprived areas of the country and the rest.

- In 2007, around 40 per cent of working-age recipients of out-of-work benefits lived in the fifth of small areas with the highest concentrations of such people, while the other 60 per cent lived outside of these areas. In other words, a majority of people receiving these benefits live outside of the high concentration areas.
- In 2007, there were 16 local authority areas where a majority of the small areas were in the fifth of small areas in Great Britain with the highest concentrations of out-of-work benefit recipients. These were:
  - five local authorities in the Welsh Valleys, namely Blaenau Gwent, Merthyr Tydfil, Neath, Port Talbot, Rhondda Cynon Taff and Caerphilly;
  - two local authorities in the central belt of Scotland, namely Glasgow City and Inverclyde;
  - two local authorities in London, namely Tower Hamlets and Hackney;
  - three urban local authorities in the North West of England, namely Liverpool, Knowsley and Manchester;
  - four urban local authorities in the North East of England, namely Easington, Hartlepool, South Tyneside and Middlesbrough.

Selected relevant research

Some other research has focused on attitudes to, and the adequacy of, sickness and disability benefits.

- Salway *et al.* (2007) show that attitudes and responses to long-term ill health vary by gender and ethnicity. For example Pakistanis, Bangladeshis and black African were less likely to receive Disability Living Allowance than white people of the same socio-economic and health status.
- Smith, Middleton, Ashton-Brooks, Cox and Dobson with Reith (2004) compared the costs of disability with out-of-work benefits paid to disabled people. It found that, in some cases, benefits were worth only around one third of the cost of living with a disability. The biggest difference was for people with high need disabilities.

Benefit levels

20A: While the level of Income Support/Jobseeker's Allowance for both pensioners and families with two or more children is higher, relative to earnings, than it was a decade ago, the level for working-age adults without children is much lower.

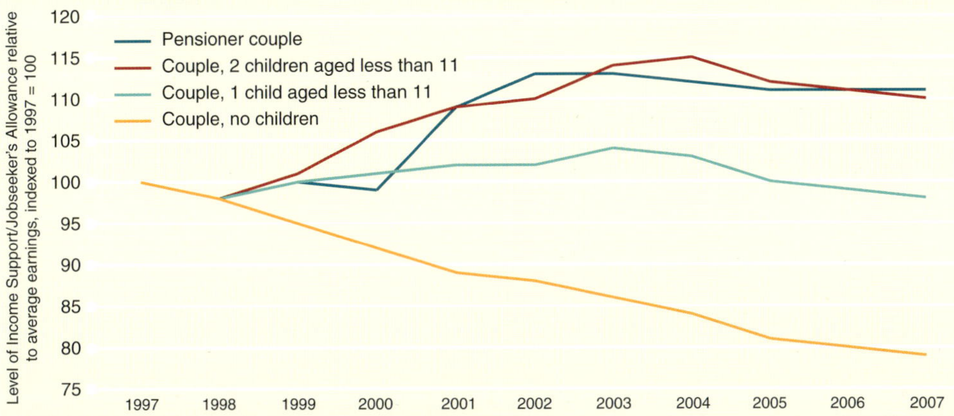

Source: Benefit levels from DWP and earnings indices from ONS; UK

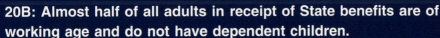

20B: Almost half of all adults in receipt of State benefits are of working age and do not have dependent children.

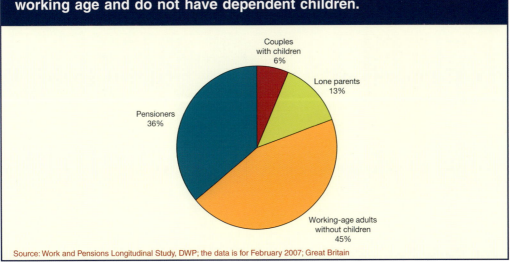

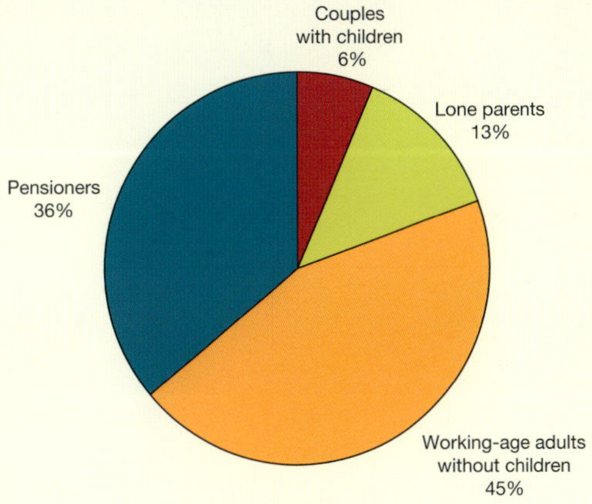

Source: Work and Pensions Longitudinal Study, DWP; the data is for February 2007; Great Britain

The first graph shows how the value of Income Support/Jobseeker's Allowance has varied over time for selected family types. The selected family types are pensioner couples, couples with two children aged under 11, couples with one child aged under 11 and couples with no children. In each case, the base year is 1997, at which point the value of the benefits is set to 100. The figures are deflated by the growth in average earnings in each year. So, for example, the value of Income Support/Jobseeker's Allowance for a couple aged 25 to 59 with no children was £92.80 in April 2007 and £77.15 in April 1997, a growth of 20 per cent in money terms; over the same period, average earnings grew by 53 per cent; so the figure on the graph for April 2006 is 79 (100* 1.20/1.53). The data source for the earnings data is the ONS Average Earnings Index, using the series which is seasonally adjusted. The family types were selected to best illustrate the differing trends over time. So, for example, single adults with no dependent children is not shown as it has followed similar trends to that for couples with no dependent children. No disability benefits have been included.

The second graph provides a breakdown of the recipients of one or more 'key out-of-work benefits' with a focus on with/without children. 'Key out-of-work benefits' is a Department for Work and Pensions (DWP) term which covers the following benefits: Jobseeker's Allowance, Income Support, Incapacity Benefit, Severe Disablement Allowance, Carer's Allowance and Pension Credit. The data source is the DWP Work and Pensions Longitudinal Study. The data has been analysed to avoid double-counting of those receiving multiple benefits by matching data from individual samples. The data relates to Great Britain and is for February 2007.

Overall adequacy of the indicator: high. The statistics in the first graph are factual and those in the second are considered to be very reliable.

Indicator 21

Concentrations of low income

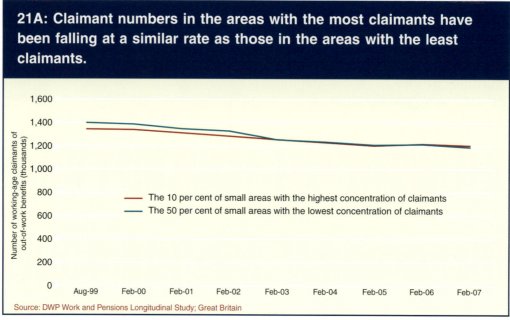

21A: Claimant numbers in the areas with the most claimants have been falling at a similar rate as those in the areas with the least claimants.

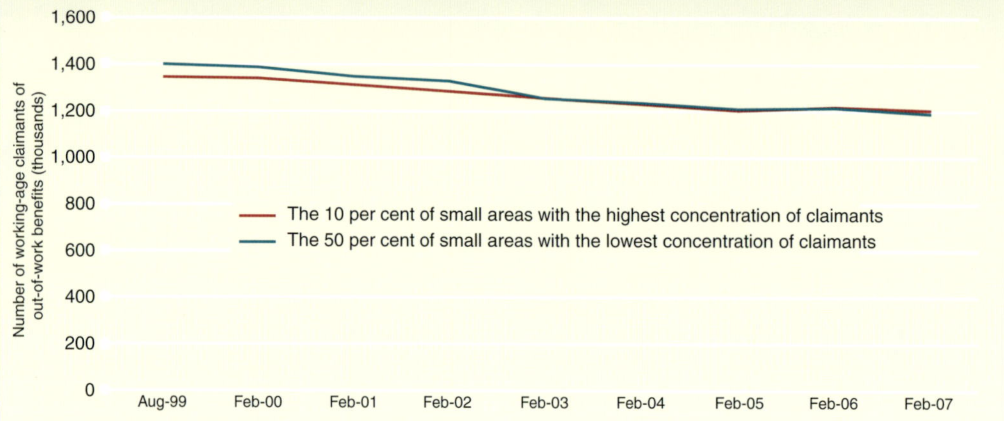

Source: DWP Work and Pensions Longitudinal Study; Great Britain

21B: A majority of recipients of out-of-work benefits live outside the one fifth of areas where such people are most likely to live.

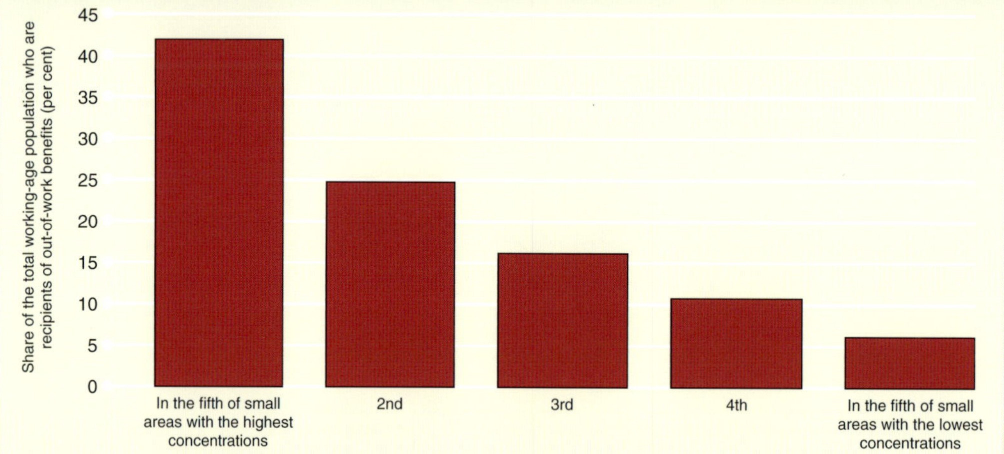

Source: DWP Work and Pensions Longitudinal Study; the data is for February 2007; Great Britain

This indicator examines how the pattern of recipiency of key out-of-work benefits by working-age people varies at a small area level and how these patterns have changed over time. It does so by placing the 40,000 small areas ('super output areas') in Great Britain into a number of equal groups according to the proportion of their working-age population who are in receipt of such benefits. The benefits included are Jobseeker's Allowance, Income Support, Incapacity Benefit, Severe Disablement Allowance and Carer's Allowance. If someone is receiving more than one of these benefits, they are only counted once.

The first graph shows how the levels of concentration have changed over time, comparing the number of recipients in the tenth of small areas with the highest levels of recipiency with the half of small areas with the lowest levels of recipiency (where high/low levels of recipiency are defined in terms of the proportion of the working-age population who are recipients).

The second graph shows the share of the total recipients who are in each group of small areas.

The data source for both graphs is the Department for Work and Pensions Longitudinal Study and relates to Great Britain. Note that August 1999 is the earliest date for which this data is available.

Overall adequacy of the indicator: medium. The underlying data is a full count and is considered to be very reliable. But the data is a count of people in receipt of key out-of-work benefits rather than a count of people in low income. So, for example, it excludes all people in low pay and includes all recipients of out-of-work benefits even if they have some private income.

Chapter 3 **Disadvantage in work**

Low pay

Here and elsewhere, 'low pay' is defined as £6.50 an hour or less in 2006. The justification for using this threshold is two-fold. First, at around two-thirds of the UK median hourly earnings, it is at a level commonly used in low pay research. Second, it is roughly what a two-earner couple, one full-time and one part-time, with two dependent children, would need to earn in order to have enough money (with child benefit and tax credits) to take them up to the poverty line. If, say, a threshold of £6 per hour or £7 per hour had been used instead, the findings in this section would still be similar. For the time trend analysis, the low pay thresholds for earlier years has been obtained by scaling the £6.50 figure down in proportion to the rate at which average earnings changed over the corresponding period.

22 Numbers in low pay

(The proportion of male and female employees who are low paid over time)

The first indicator shows the principal statistics on the extent of low pay among men and women between the ages of 18 and retirement. The first graph shows the proportion of male and female employees who were low paid each year since 1998 (the first year for which the data is available). The supporting graph shows the total number of low-paid employees (age 18+) broken down between men and women and whether the employment is full- or part-time.

Key points:

- Since 2000, the proportion of both men and women who are low paid has come down – but the decrease for women (down from 37 per cent to 28 per cent) has been much larger than the decrease for men (down from 18 per cent to 16 per cent). Despite these reductions – and the way that they have reduced the difference between men and women – it remains the case that a much larger proportion of women than men are low paid.
- Overall, using the £6.50 per hour threshold, around two-thirds of low-paid employees in 2006 were women.
- Half of those who were paid less than £6.50 per hour in 2006 were full-time employees and half were part-time employees. Among the low-paid *full-timers*, there were as many low-paid men as low-paid women. By contrast, among the low-paid *part-timers*, women predominate. So, the immediate reason why there are so many more low-paid women than low-paid men is that there are so many more low-paid part-time female workers than low-paid part-time male workers. We return to this issue in the last indicator in this section.

23 Low pay by age and gender

(The proportion of male and female employees who are low paid by age)

This indicator looks at how far low pay is concentrated among particular age groups, and in particular among those aged 21 and under. The first graph shows the proportion of employees who are low paid by age group, separately for full-time men, full-time women and all part-time workers together. The supporting graph shows how the total number of low-paid employees (age 18+) breaks down according to age and whether the employment is full- or part-time.

Key points:

- Low pay is the norm among young workers aged 18-21 where half of full-time men, half of full-time women and three-quarters of all part-timers were paid less than £6.50 an hour in 2006.
- Among full-time employees, there is a substantial difference by age in the proportions who are low paid, with typically no more than 15 per cent of full-timers aged over 21 being paid less than £6.50 per hour in 2006. But despite this much-reduced risk of low pay, it is still the case that some three-quarters of all low-paid full-time employees are aged over 21. Furthermore, while (per the previous indicator) there are as many low-paid full-time women as low-paid full-time men, the proportion of full-time women who are low-paid is, at every age, higher than for men.
- Among part-time employees, the risk of low pay is also reduced among those aged over 21 but to a much lesser extent, with 50 per cent of part-timers in their 20s, and 40 per cent in their 60s, being paid less than £6.50 per hour in 2006. The extent to which low-paid part-time work is common at every age can be seen in the observation that there are almost as many low-paid part-time employees aged over 50 as there are under 30.

24 Low pay by industry

(The proportion of male and female employees who are low paid by industry)

This indicator looks at both the risk and the share of low pay by industry sectors such as retail, the public sector and manufacturing. The first graph shows the proportions of all employees aged 25 and over in each industry sector who are low paid, with men and women shown separately. The supporting graph shows the share of the total number of low-paid employees employed in each sector.

Key points:

- 60 per cent of all employees aged 25 and over in the hotels and restaurants sector, and 40 per cent in the retail sector, earned less than £6.50 an hour in 2006. In both sectors, two-thirds of these low-paid employees are women. In other sectors, between 10 per cent and 20 per cent of employees aged 25 and over are low paid, the share accounted for by women varying between one third in manufacturing and four-fifths in the public sector.
- Thanks to its size, the public sector is now the largest employer of low-paid workers aged 25 or over, accounting for more than a quarter of all such employees. It should be stressed that these are people who are employed directly by the public sector, not those working in the public sector but employed by contractors. The next largest employer of low-paid workers over the age of 25 is the retail sector, with a quarter of the total.
- Only a minority of low-paid workers are in sectors that face international competition and the consequent threat that the job could move abroad. The jobs that are likely to be at risk in this way include manufacturing and some parts of banking/finance, other services, and transport and communication: perhaps a quarter of all low-paid jobs in total. Most low-paid jobs, therefore, are low paid for domestic, rather than international, reasons.

25 Pay inequalities

(Pay inequalities between men and women at the two ends of the pay scale)

Whereas the previous indicators in this section have focused on low pay, this last indicator looks at the difference between pay for men and women at the top and the bottom of the income scale. The first graph shows what has happened to full-time pay for men and women at the top (represented by the 90th percentile) and the bottom (the 10th percentile) of the pay scale every year since 1996. Pay here is expressed as a proportion of *male* median full-time earnings for the year in question.

The supporting graph shows the proportion of employees, separately for men and women and full- and part-time, who are paid less than £6.50 an hour, between £6.50 and £10 an hour, and more than £10 an hour.

Key points:

- Over the past decade, the gap between low-paid, full-time employees and the male median has stayed the same for men but has come down, by about 4 percentage points, for women. As a result, the gap between low-paid full-time men and low-paid full-time women has come down. Despite this, a gap still remains (50 per cent of male median pay for women at the 10th percentile compared with 55 per cent of the median for men).
- Over the past decade, the gap between high-paid, full-time employees and the male median has increased for both men and women, by about 10 percentage points in both cases. As a result, the gap between high-paid men and high-paid women (both at the 90th percentile) has remained roughly the same.
- For men and women together, overall pay inequality in the lower half of the pay distribution has come down slightly while overall pay inequality in the upper half of the pay distribution has increased slightly.
- The proportion of part-time employees who were paid less than £6.50 an hour in 2006 was, at just over 40 per cent, the same for both men and women. While women predominate in part-time employment, the equality in the low pay risks here suggests that the fundamental problem is the lowly status of part-time work *per se* rather than any disadvantage that part-time female employees face relative to part-time male ones.
- By contrast, the proportion of full-time female employees paid less than £6.50 an hour in 2006 was, at 15 per cent, markedly higher than the 10 per cent of full-time male employees. Thus, while there are as many low-paid full-time men as there are low-paid full-time women (see indicator 22 above), the difference in these low pay risks suggests that the fundamental problem here remains one of the disadvantages faced by full-time female employees compared with full-time male ones.

Selected relevant research

The gender pay gap referred to in official government reports is generally a comparison of average (median) full time hourly earnings for men and women. So, when, for instance, the Office of National Statistics said that the pay gap closed in 2006, they meant that the gap between male and female median incomes had closed. Much of the research follows this approach. The gap between part-time and full-time pay is not discussed very much in this literature, except as a possible explanation of the gender pay gap.

Some research has looked at the changing pay gap over time. In the UK, the gap between men's and women's pay for full-time workers has decreased over the last 25 years. The main reason given for the convergence in men's and women's full-time pay over this period is the closing of the gender gap in terms of educational qualifications. (Grimshaw and Rubery, 2007).

This pay gap still persists, though, and is composed of different factors. For example:

- Walby and Olsen (2002) and Olsen and Walby (2004) have carried out two studies attempting to break down the gender pay gap into its separate parts. In both studies, which included part- and full-time employees, they found that 'factors associated with being female' (which include discrimination, but also cover different preferences and motivations) accounted for the single largest proportion of the difference, though the precise amount varied between the two studies (around 30 per cent in the 2002 study, around 40 per cent in the 2004 study).
- Other factors found to be important were women's lower full-time work experience, women's *greater* part-time work experience, segregation (the prevalence of one particular gender in a particular profession), and interruptions due to family care. Education explained less than 10 per cent.
- Analysing women's lower full-time work experience, Manning and Swaffield (2005) found that the gender pay gap also widens as experience increases, this being because women's experience is often undervalued. Similarly, the gender pay gap is also higher in higher paying jobs. Purcell and Elias (2004) found that women in business, the highest paying sector, face the largest pay gap of all – on average around one-third. So, while an increasing number of women in high-paying jobs may close the pay gap on average, women who are in such jobs actually often face a bigger pay gap compared to men in the same jobs.
- Analysing women's greater part-time work experience, Olsen and Walby (2004) found that, for each year of part-time work experience a person has, their full-time hourly earnings decrease by 1 per cent on finding a full-time job. This wage penalty for working part-time was found to be much greater for women than for men. Furthermore, women who moved to full-time work after only one year of part-time work were earning up to 10 per cent less per hour some 15 years later (Manning and Petrongolo, 2005).
- Analysing segregation, Olsen and Walby (2004) found that for every 10 percentage points higher the proportion of men working in a particular occupation, the hourly wage rises by 1 per cent.
- Analysing the impact of family care, Joshi and Paci (1998) found that mothers who use only their maternity leave suffer a lower penalty, but those who move employers or come back to work part-time often suffer from lower wages.

Indicator 22

Numbers in low pay

22A: In 2006, 28 per cent of women employees aged 18 and over – and 16 per cent of men – were paid less than £6.50 per hour.

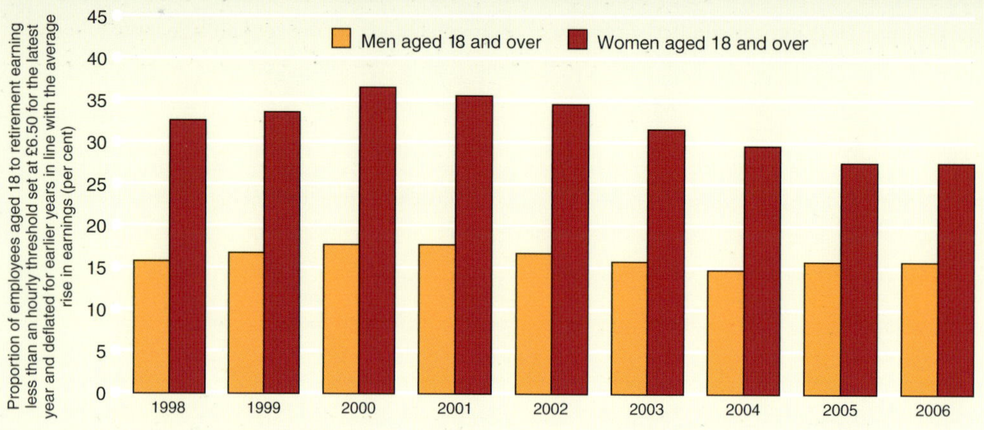

Source: NPI calculations based on ONS estimates; UK

22B: Around half of those paid less than £6.50 per hour are part-time workers, mainly women.

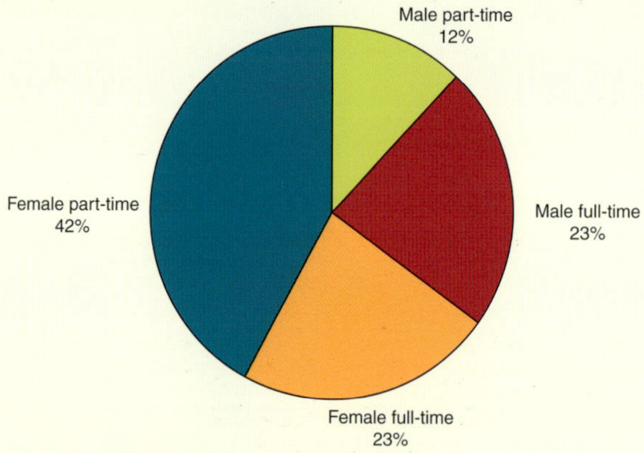

Source: Annual Survey of Hours and Earnings 2006, ONS; UK

The first graph shows the estimated proportion of employees aged 18 to retirement who were paid below an hourly pay threshold that rises in line with average earnings and reaches £6.50 in 2006. It is therefore £4.64 in 1998, £4.85 in 1999, £5.12 in 2000, £5.36 in 2001, £5.53 in 2002, £5.70 in 2003, £6.00 in 2004, £6.24 in 2005 and £6.50 in 2006. The data is shown separately for men and women. No data is available for years before 1998 and the available data only distinguishes between the 18-21 and 22+ age groups. The data is from published ONS statistics which were themselves derived from a combination of data from the Labour Force Survey (LFS) and Annual Survey of Hours and Earnings (ASHE), with adjustments by the ONS.

The second graph shows, for the latest year, the distribution of employees paid less than £6.50 per hour divided by male/female and full-time/part-time. The data source is the Annual Survey of Hours and Earnings (ASHE) and relates to the United Kingdom. The proportions have been calculated from the hourly rates at each decile using interpolation to estimate the consequent proportion earning less than £6.50 per hour.

Overall adequacy of the indicator: medium. The LFS and ASHE are well-established government surveys, designed to be representative of the population as a whole. However, the ONS methods for combining and adjusting the data are not available for public scrutiny, and the underlying dataset itself is not publicly available.

Low pay by age and gender

23A: At all ages, at least a third of part-time employees are paid less than £6.50 per hour. Except for the 18-21 age group, the proportion of full-time employees paid less than £6.50 per hour is much lower than this.

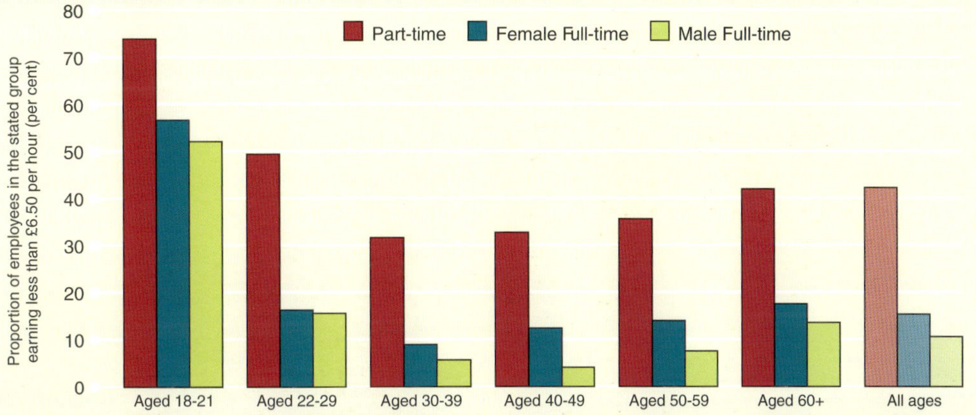

Source: Annual Survey of Hours and Earnings 2006, ONS; UK

23B: Around half of those paid less than £6.50 per hour are aged 40 or over.

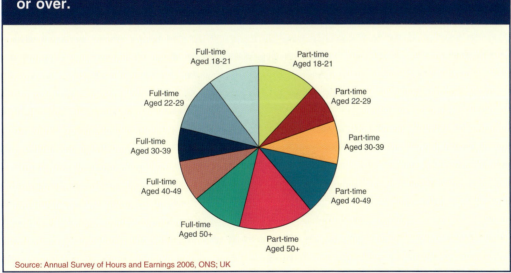

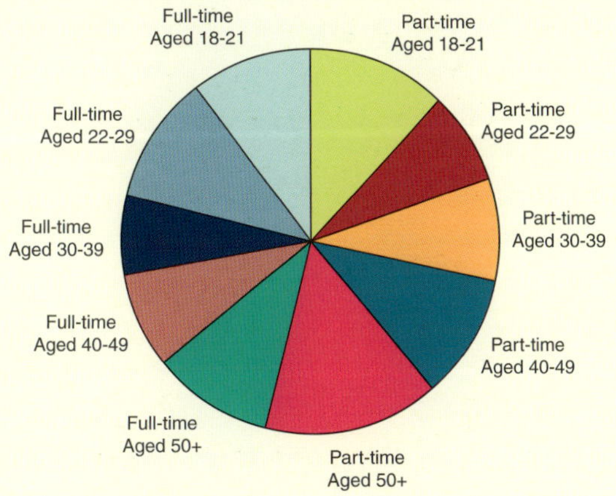

Source: Annual Survey of Hours and Earnings 2006, ONS; UK

The first graph shows, for the latest year and by age group, the proportion of employees paid less than £6.50 per hour, with the data shown separately for part-time workers, full-time working women and full-time working men.

The second graph shows, for the latest year, the distribution of employees paid less than £6.50 per hour, divided by age group and full-time/part-time.

The data source for both graphs is the Annual Survey of Hours and Earnings (ASHE) and relates to the United Kingdom. The proportions have been calculated from the hourly rates at each decile using interpolation to estimate the consequent proportion earning less than £6.50 per hour.

Overall adequacy of the indicator: medium. ASHE is a well-established government survey, designed to be representative of the population as a whole, and adjustments made to the survey methodology in 2004 mean that it is regarded by ONS as providing reliable estimates of low pay.

Low pay by industry

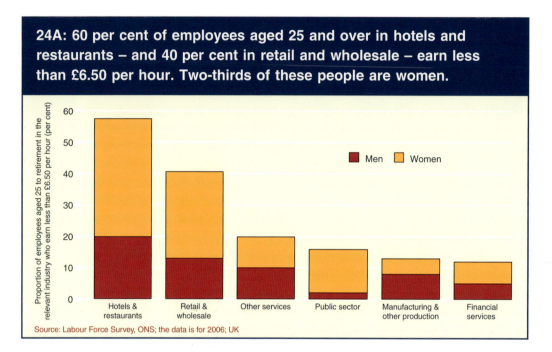

24A: 60 per cent of employees aged 25 and over in hotels and restaurants – and 40 per cent in retail and wholesale – earn less than £6.50 per hour. Two-thirds of these people are women.

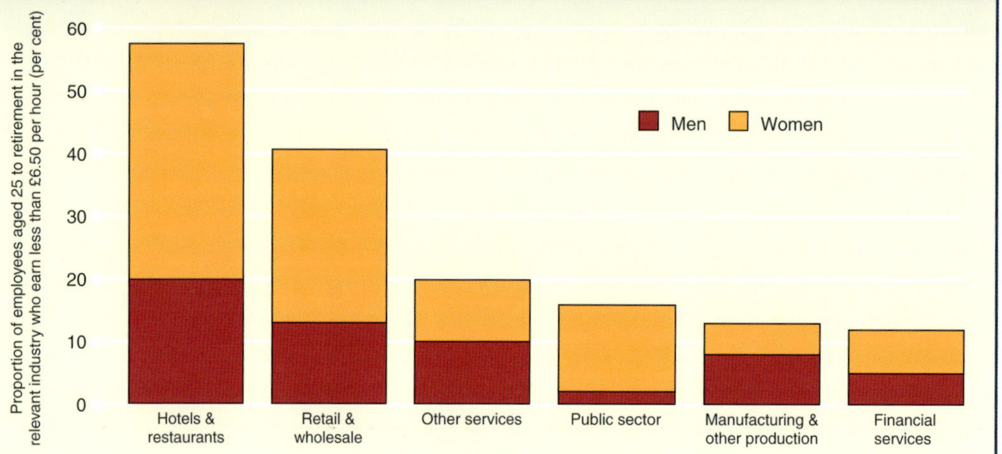

Source: Labour Force Survey, ONS; the data is for 2006; UK

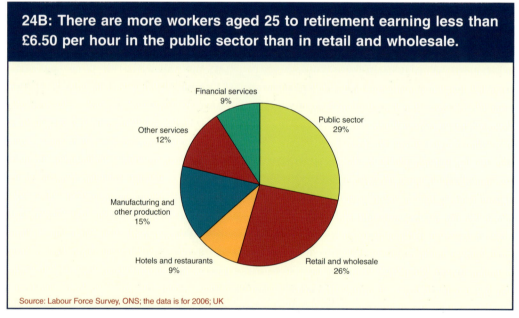

24B: There are more workers aged 25 to retirement earning less than £6.50 per hour in the public sector than in retail and wholesale.

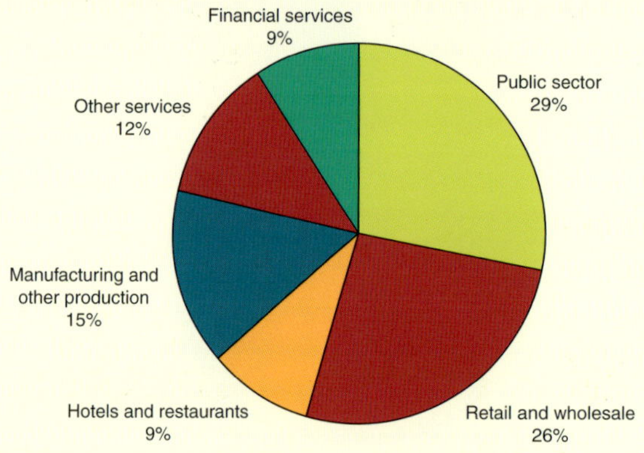

Source: Labour Force Survey, ONS; the data is for 2006; UK

The first graph shows how the proportion of workers aged 25 to retirement who were paid less than £6.50 per hour varies by industry sector, with the data shown separately for men and women.

The second graph shows the share of workers aged 25 to retirement paid less than £6.50 per hour by industrial sector.

Some of the sectors have been combined together for presentational purposes with the particular sectors shown being manufacturing and other production (industry code A-F); wholesale & retail (G); hotels & restaurants (H); public administration, education & health (L-N); other business activities (J-K); and other services (I & O-Q).

The data source for both graphs is the Labour Force Survey (equivalent data from the Annual Survey Hours and Earnings not being publicly available) and relates to the United Kingdom. The data is for 2006. People whose hourly pay rates cannot be calculated from the survey data have been excluded from the analysis.

Overall adequacy of the indicator: medium. The Labour Force Survey is a large, well-established, quarterly government survey, designed to be representative of the population as a whole, but there are some doubts about the reliability of its low pay data.

Pay inequalities

25A: Pay inequalities between men and women have reduced at the bottom but not at the top.

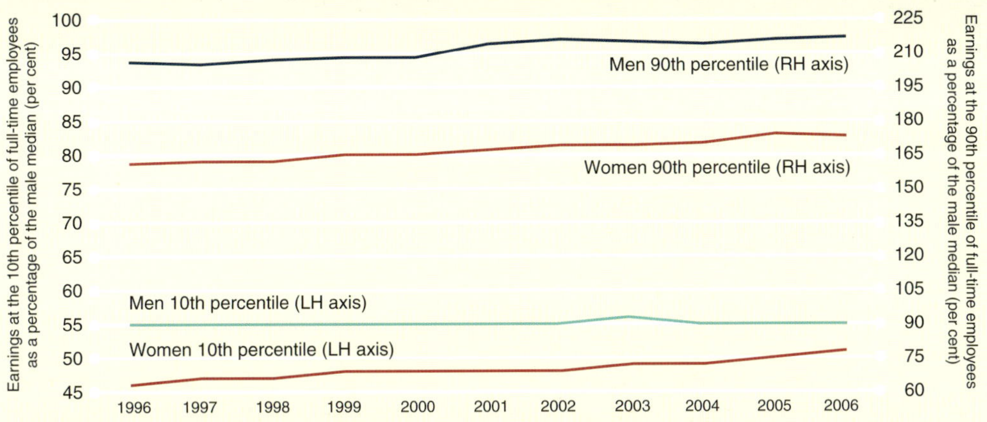

Source: Annual Survey of Hours and Earnings, ONS; UK

25B: Two-fifths of all part-time workers – both men and women – are paid less than £6.50 per hour.

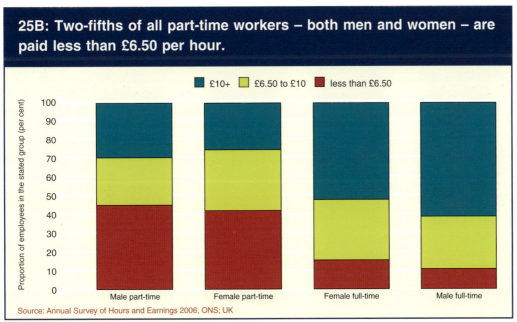

Source: Annual Survey of Hours and Earnings 2006, ONS; UK

The first graph focuses on pay differentials. It shows gross hourly pay for: full-time male employees at the 10th percentile (i.e. the pay of men one tenth of the way from the bottom of the male pay distribution); full-time female employees at the 10th percentile (i.e. the pay of women one tenth of the way from the bottom of the female pay distribution); full-time male employees at the 90th percentile (i.e. the pay of men one tenth of the way from the top of the male pay distribution); full-time female employees at the 90th percentile (i.e. the pay of women one tenth of the way from the top of the female pay distribution). In each case, the statistics are shown as a proportion of average (median) hourly pay of full-time male employees thus providing a measure of earnings inequalities. The left-hand axis shows proportions at the 10th percentile and the right hand axis shows the proportion at the 90th percentile.

The data source for the first graph is the New Earnings Survey (NES) for 1996 and the Annual Survey of Hours and Earnings (ASHE) from 1997 onwards. The two surveys use slightly different methods of calculation so the NES figures have had a small adjustment applied to cater for this. Some detailed changes were made to the ASHE survey base in 2004 and an adjustment has also been made for this.

The second graph shows, for the latest year, the distribution of employees across the pay spectrum with the data shown separately for part-time women, part-time men, full-time women and full-time men. The data source is ASHE and the data relates to the United Kingdom. The proportions have been calculated from the hourly rates at each decile using interpolation to estimate the consequent proportion earning in each of the pay groups.

Overall adequacy of the indicator: high. ASHE is a large annual survey of employers.

Disadvantage at work

The two indicators in this section point to a range of ways in which people can be disadvantaged in work other than through low pay. Both of them also show how one form of disadvantage (e.g. lack of qualifications) increases the likelihood of another (e.g. lack of training).

26 Insecure at work

(The proportion of men and women whose employment is insecure)

This indicator looks at the two aspects of insecure employment. The first graph shows the proportion of men and women making a new claim for the unemployment benefit Jobseeker's Allowance who were last claiming this benefit less than six months ago. The inference drawn is that these people have been employed in the interim, but for a period of less than six months. The supporting graph looks at how content people are to be in temporary employment, comparing it with how content people are to be in part-time employment.

Key points:

- Nearly half of the men and a third of the women making a new claim for Jobseeker's Allowance were last claiming that benefit less than six months ago. These proportions have changed little over the last decade. What this signifies is that a substantial proportion of those claiming unemployment benefit are alternating between spells of unemployment and spells of short-term employment.
- Only one-fifth of temporary employees reported that they did not want a permanent job. By contrast, the vast majority of part-time employees reported that they did not want a full-time job. This suggests that, whereas part-time employment is generally a positive choice, temporary employment is often not.

27 Lacking support at work

(The proportion of men and women lacking support at work)

The first graph shows the proportions of men and women, broken down by their hourly rate of pay, who belong to a trade union. The supporting graph shows the likelihood that employees aged 25 or over have received job-related training in the past three months, with the data broken down by their level of education.

Key points:

- Overall, around 30 per cent of both men and women belong to a trade union. The proportions are highest among those earning between £9 and £21 an hour (a third of men and a half of women) and only slightly lower (one-quarter of men and one-third of women) among those earning over £21 an hour. By contrast, among those earning less than £6.50 an hour, just one in eight of both men and women belong to a trade union. The pay range £6.50 to £9 an hour is the only one where the proportion of men in a trade union exceeds the proportion of women.

- While a quarter of employees aged 25 or over report having received some job-related training in the past three months, there are big differences according to the employee's level of education. So among those with higher education, almost two-fifths report having received some training; by contrast, among those with no qualifications, the proportion is just one in ten. This pattern, in which the higher the level of education the greater chance of training, appears to apply at every level of education.

Selected relevant research

Every year the government publishes data on trade union membership. In 2007[11], it showed that:

- Trends in union membership for men and women have been moving in the opposite direction in recent years. The proportion of women who are members of a trade union has risen from 28 per cent in 2001 to 30 per cent in 2006. By contrast, the proportion of men who are members of a trade union has fallen pretty steadily since the mid-1990s (the earliest point for which comparable data is available), from 35 per cent and now stands at 27 per cent.
- The proportion of employees belonging to a trade union is around three times higher in the public sector than the private sector (60 per cent compared to 20 per cent). It is this difference that explains women's higher membership rate – men in either sector are (slightly) more likely to belong to a union than women. However, women are more likely to work in the public sector, meaning that they work in areas that have higher union representation.
- There is also a significant overlap between temporary employment and lack of union recognition. Employees in full-time employment are twice as likely to be in a trade union as those on temporary contracts.

Other recent reports highlight the need for more in-work training.

- The Leitch report, *Prosperity for all in the global economy – world class skills*, commissioned by the Treasury in 2006, identified the shortage of skills and qualifications in the UK workforce as a barrier to economic growth and competitiveness. The report set a target that 90 per cent of the workforce should hold level 2 qualifications or higher by 2020.
- Analysis by the New Policy Institute NPI (MacInnes and Kenway, 2007) showed that, given that a large proportion of the workforce in 2020 are already in the workforce now, this places an emphasis on in-work training for those who do not currently hold qualifications.
- This, in turn, shifts the emphasis to employers offering in-work training. A report by the TUC (2007) shows that currently around 35 per cent of employers, covering 25 per cent of the workforce, offer no in-work training at all. This has been recognised by the Learning and Skills Council's *Train to gain* programme, which offers advice on training to employers. Employers are also encouraged to sign up to a 'skills pledge', a promise to train all their staff to at least level 2 qualifications.

Indicator 26

Insecure at work

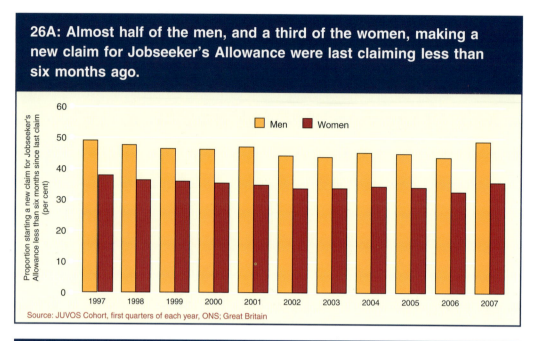

26A: Almost half of the men, and a third of the women, making a new claim for Jobseeker's Allowance were last claiming less than six months ago.

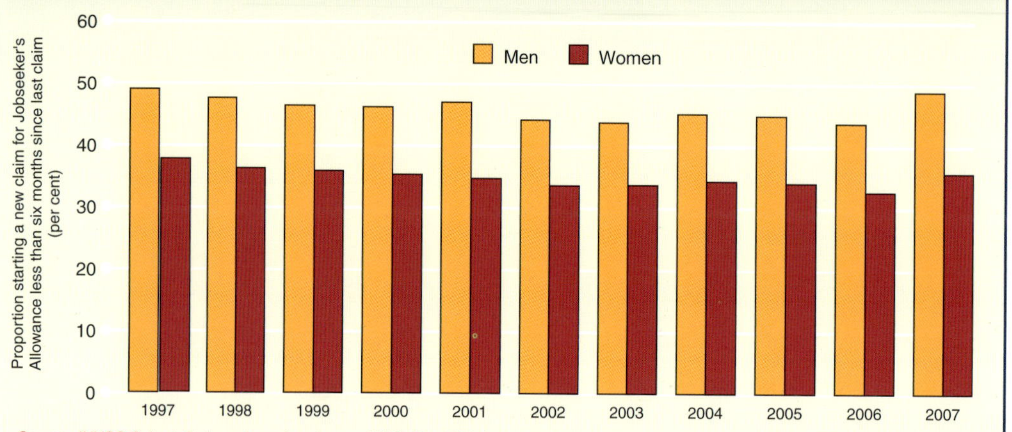

Source: JUVOS Cohort, first quarters of each year, ONS; Great Britain

26B: Most part-time employees do not want a full-time job – but only a fifth of temporary employees do not want a permanent job.

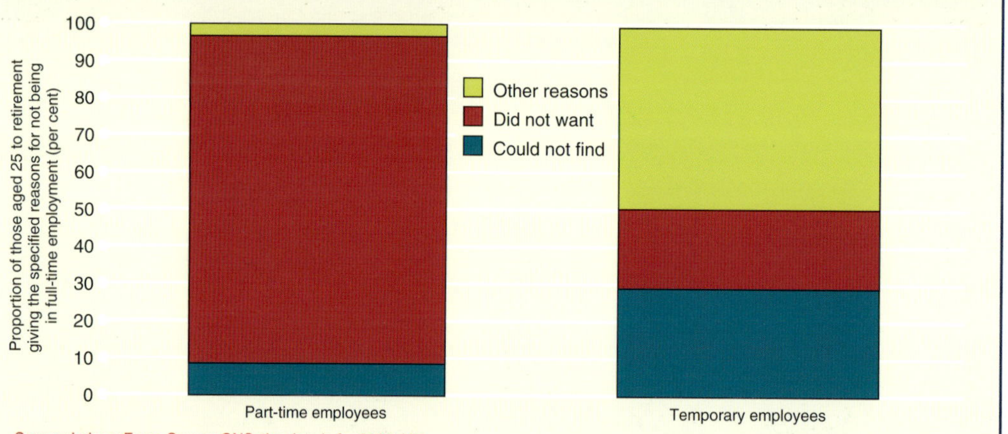

Source: Labour Force Survey, ONS; the data is for 2006; UK

The first graph tackles insecurity at work through the issue of people who find themselves taking a succession of jobs interspersed with periods of unemployment. It shows the probability that someone who makes a new claim for Jobseeker's Allowance was last claiming that benefit less than six months previously. This is effectively the same as the proportion of people finding work who then lose that work within six months. Figures are shown separately for men and women. The data relates to Great Britain and, for each year, is taken from the first quarter of the Joint Unemployment and Vacancies Operating System (JUVOS) cohort.

The second graph shows data for all employees aged 25 to retirement in part-time and temporary jobs (shown separately) by reason for the part-time or temporary employment. The data source is the Labour Force Survey and relates to the United Kingdom. The figures are the average for the four quarters of 2006.

Overall adequacy of the indicator: high. Note, however, that while the claimant count data is sound, the narrow definition of unemployment that it represents means that it understates the extent of short-term working interspersed with spells of joblessness.

Lacking support at work

27A: For both men and women, only one in eight workers earning less than £6.50 an hour belong to a trade union, far fewer than for those with higher hourly earnings.

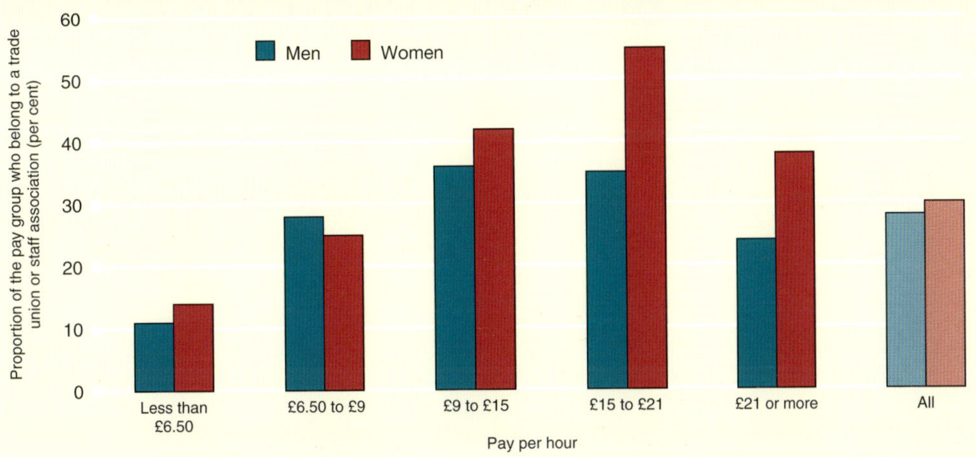

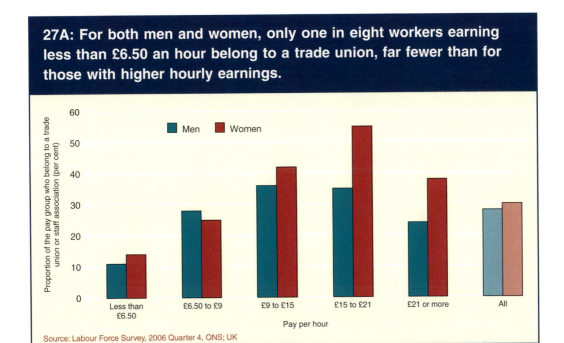

Source: Labour Force Survey, 2006 Quarter 4, ONS; UK

27B: The fewer qualifications a person has, the less likely they are to receive job-related training.

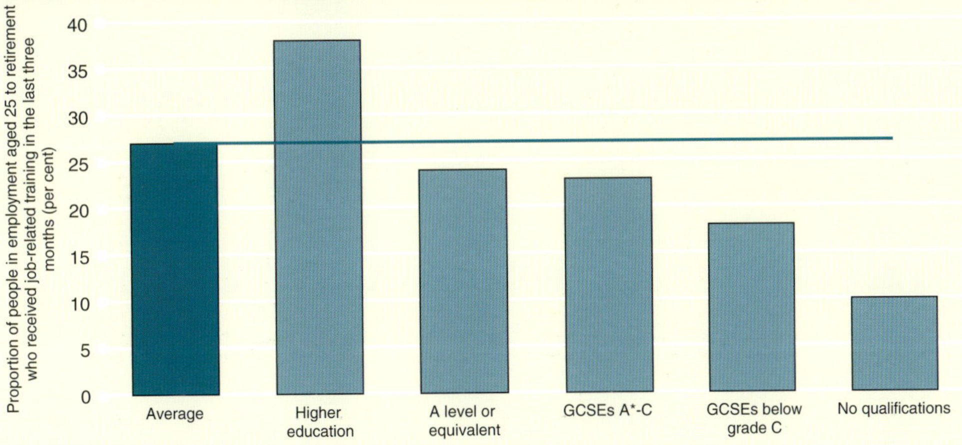

Source: Labour Force Survey, ONS; the data is for 2006; UK

The first graph shows the proportion of people currently employed who are members of a trade union or staff association, with the data shown separately for men and women and by level of pay.

The second graph shows the proportion of employees aged 25 to retirement age who have received some job-related training in the previous three months according to the level of the employee's highest qualification. Department for Children, Schools and Families (formerly DfES) equivalence scales have been used to translate vocational qualifications into their academic equivalents. The training includes that paid for by employers and by employees themselves.

The data source for both graphs is the Labour Force Survey (LFS) and relates to the United Kingdom. In the second graph, the figures for each year are the average for the four quarters of 2006 while the figures in the first graph are for the fourth quarter only (the data is only collected in the fourth quarter).

Overall adequacy of the indicator: high. The LFS is a large, well-established, quarterly government survey, designed to be representative of the population as a whole.

Chapter 4 **Education**

Lacking minimum levels of qualification

In keeping with the focus of this report on those who are doing least well (as opposed to what is happening on average), this section is concerned with those who lack what can reasonably be regarded as minimum levels of qualification. The importance of these qualifications to the likelihood of not having a job and being only poorly paid are explored later in the third section of this chapter. The material covers both children and working-age adults.

28 Educational attainment at age 11

(The proportion of 11-year-olds failing to reach minimum levels of qualification)

This indicator focuses on the 11-year-olds who have not reached Level 4 at Key Stage 2 (KS2) in English and maths. The first graph shows the proportion of 11-year-olds in this situation each year over the last decade, both for all maintained schools and for those schools where at least 35 per cent of pupils are eligible for free school meals. Since entitlement to free school meals is essentially restricted to families in receipt of out-of-work benefits, this should be thought of as a proxy for worklessness rather than low income. The supporting graph focuses on the same standard but uses pupil level data to show the differences between boys and girls, separately for those eligible and not eligible for free school meals.

Key points:

- Although the rate of improvement has slowed since the late 1990s, there continues to be year-on-year improvement in the proportion of 11-year-olds reaching Level 4 at KS2 in both English and maths. This improvement can be seen both for schools as a whole and for schools with high levels of pupils eligible for free school meals, albeit that the proportion failing to reach this minimum level is markedly higher for the latter group of schools (33 per cent for English, 35 per cent for maths) than for schools as a whole (20 per cent and 24 per cent respectively). The scale of progress is illustrated by the observation that results in schools with high levels of pupils eligible for free school meals are now actually better than the all-schools average was in 1997.
- At the level of the individual pupil, there are marked differences by gender between English and maths. In English, for a given free school meal status (that is, eligible for free school meals or not), boys do worse than girls by around ten percentage points. By contrast, in maths, for a given free school meal status there is no difference between boys and girls. In other words, there is a gender gap in English, but not in maths.
- The gender gap in English does not mean, however, that boys always do worse than girls. For example, 30 per cent of girls who are eligible for free school meals fail to reach Level 4 at KS2 compared with 20 per cent of boys who are not eligible for free school meals. In maths, both girls and boys who are eligible for free school meals are twice as likely to fail to reach Level 4 as girls and boys who are not eligible for free school meals (40 per cent compared with 20 per cent in each case).

29 Educational attainment at age 16

(The proportion of 16-year-olds failing to reach minimum levels of qualification)

This indicator focuses on 16-year-olds who either obtain no GCSEs or obtain fewer than five GCSEs at any grade. This, it should be noted, is different from the usual 'headline' measure for which the standard is five GCSEs at grade C or above.

The first graph shows the proportion of 16-year-olds for each year from 1996 onwards who fail to obtain (a) any GCSEs; (b) five GCSEs at any standard; and (c) five GCSEs at least grade C (i.e. the usual headline measure). The supporting graph focuses on those who do not obtain five GCSEs at any standard, using pupil level data to show the differences between boys and girls, separately for those eligible or not for free school meals and separately for those who are white British or from an ethnic minority.

Key points:

- In 2005/06, just 3.5 per cent of 16-year-olds in England and Wales obtained no GCSEs at all while a further 7.5 per cent obtained some, but fewer than five, GCSEs. The total of these two (11 per cent) has barely changed since the start of the decade. This lack of progress in the proportions obtaining at least five GCSEs is in stark contrast to the continued progress on the headline measure, where the proportion failing to obtain five GCSEs at grade C or above has come down steadily from 50 per cent in 1999/00 to 42 per cent in 2005/06.
- In 2005/06, 33 per cent of white British boys eligible for free school meals failed to obtain at least five GCSEs at any level, three times the average and a far higher proportion than for any other group of boys or girls. For example, among those eligible for free school meals, the 33 per cent of white British boys failing to obtain at least five GCSEs compares with 23 per cent of white British girls, 17 per cent of boys from ethnicity minorities, and 12 per cent of girls from ethnic minorities.
- As with the individual results at age 11, however, it is not as simple as boys always doing worse than girls; for example, the 23 per cent of white British girls eligible for free school meals who do not get five GCSEs is twice the equivalent proportion for white British boys not eligible for free school meals. Nor is it as simple as children from ethnic minorities always doing better than white British children; for example, among those not eligible for free school meals, the proportion who do not get five GCSEs is similar for both white British children and children from ethnic minorities.

30 Without a basic qualification at age 19

(The proportion of 19-year-olds lacking a basic qualification)

The next indicator shows the estimated proportion of 19-year-olds whose highest level of qualification, if any, is lower than an NVQ2 or the academic equivalent. The first graph shows how this proportion has changed year by year from 1997 onwards. The second graph shows how an age cohort's highest level of qualification – in this case, the cohort born in 1985 – alters between the ages of 16 and 21.

Key points:

- Over the past decade, the proportion of 19-year-olds without at least an NVQ2 has fluctuated between 24 per cent and 28 per cent.

- While there is no sign of any sustained progress on this measure, a study by the Department for Children, Schools and Families (DCSF) that uses administrative data finds a recent improving trend in the proportion without NVQ2 or equivalent, down from 34 per cent in 2004 to 29 per cent in 2006. DCSF explains this by arguing that there have been an increasing number of vocational qualifications which the survey data fails to capture. It is of note that, even though the trend is positive, the overall proportion without the necessary level of qualification is still higher in the DCSF results.
- The reason for picking NVQ2 as the key measure of minimum achievement at age 19 is that if people have not reached that level by age 19, they are unlikely to have gone on to do in the next few years. Taking those born in 1985 as an example: 34 per cent of them lacked at least an NVQ2 or equivalent at age 19, while 29 per cent of them still did so at age 21.

31 Working-age adults without qualifications

(The proportion of the working-age population with no formal qualifications)

This indicator looks at the working-age population from age 18 to retirement with no educational qualification at all. The first graph shows how this proportion has changed over the last decade. Besides the figure for the whole working-age population, it also shows the proportion of 18- to 29-year-olds with no qualification. The supporting graph shows how the proportion of both men and women with no qualification varies by age.

Key points:

- Over the last decade, the proportion of the working-age population with no qualifications has fallen by nearly a third, from 18 per cent in 1997 to 13 per cent in 2006. This is not because the proportion of young adults without a qualification has been falling but because older adults, where the proportion without a qualification is high, have been reaching pensionable age.
- Among those in their 20s and 30s, around 8 per cent of both men and women lack any qualification. By contrast, among those in their 40s, 11 per cent of men and 13 per cent of women lack any qualification, while above the age of 50 the proportions are higher still – 18 per cent for men and 25 per cent for women.
- While there are big differences between the older and younger parts of the working age population as far as basic qualifications are concerned, the similarity in the proportions among those in their 20s and 30s suggests that the shift to the new norm had actually taken place by the early 1990s, when those who are now in their mid 30s joined the working-age population, rather than more recently.

Selected relevant research

Some recent research has further explored the effect of ethnicity on school attainment:

- Using the same data source as the second graph in indicator 29, Kingdon and Cassen (2007a) looked further at the causes of low attainment at secondary school. They found that students from ethnic minority backgrounds often score less well than their white British classmates at age 11, largely due to the fact that children from ethnic minority backgrounds are less likely to speak English at home. This difference is reversed by age 16, as the discussion above illustrates.
- Further research by the same authors, *Tackling low educational achievement* (Kingdon and Cassen, 2007b), found that almost half of low achievers – for example those getting no GCSEs passes, or no passes in English or maths – were white British boys.
- Machin and McNally (2006) take a longer term view, looking at education as part of the overall anti-poverty strategy. Part of their study focused on the effectiveness of different interventions and concluded that targeting individual students who have dropped out can be costly and not always yield the returns expected. In particular, while such interventions might increase the probability of employment, they do not seem to affect wages.

Other research has looked at the longer term trends in levels of qualification in the UK workforce:

- The Leitch review of skills (2006), commissioned by the Treasury, recommended that 90 per cent of working-age adults should hold Level 2 NVQ2 or above by 2020. Research by the New Policy Institute (MacInnes and Kenway, 2007) showed that, on current trends, this target would not be reached. The research also found that a larger proportion of working women than working men achieved Level 2 once they joined the workforce.

Indicator 28

Educational attainment at age 11

28A: Progress continues to be made in the literacy and numeracy of 11-year-olds – including those in schools with high levels of deprivation.

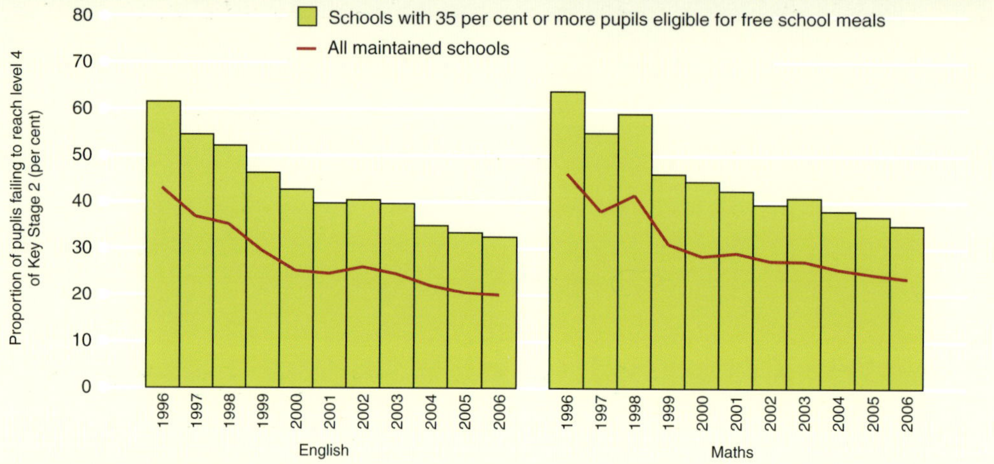

Source: DCSF Performance Tables; England

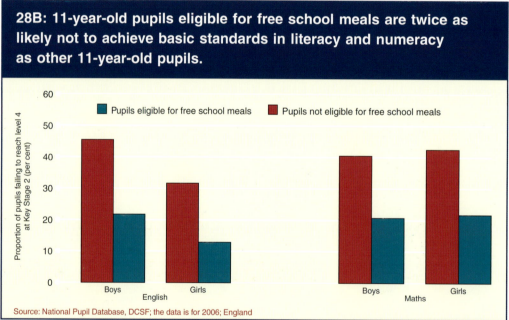

28B: 11-year-old pupils eligible for free school meals are twice as likely not to achieve basic standards in literacy and numeracy as other 11-year-old pupils.

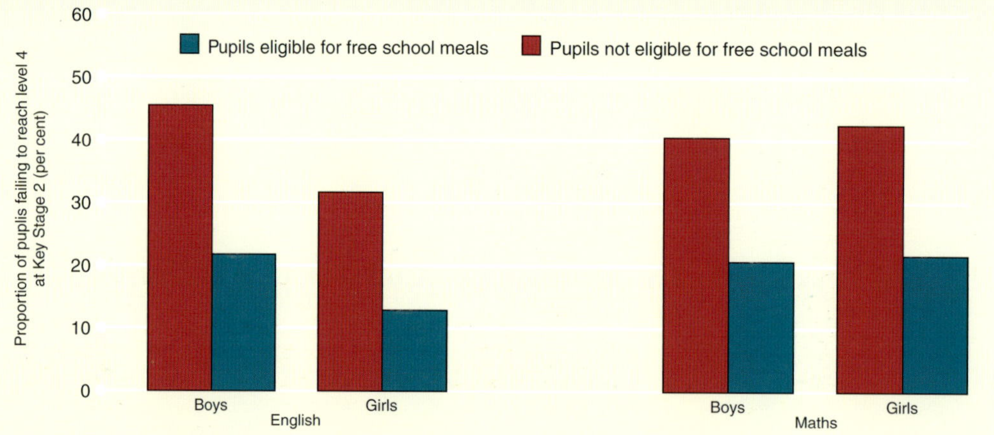

Source: National Pupil Database, DCSF; the data is for 2006; England

The first graph compares the proportion of children failing to reach Level 4 at Key Stage 2 (11-year-olds) in schools which have at least 35 per cent of pupils eligible for free school meals with that for all maintained mainstream schools. The graph shows maths and English separately and shows changes over time. The 35 per cent threshold is a level commonly used by the government itself when looking at examination results for schools with a high level of children with free school meals. The data source is Department for Children, Schools and Families (formerly DfES) performance tables. The data relates to England and covers all LEA maintained schools.

The second graph shows, for the latest year how the proportion of children failing to achieve Level 4 at Key Stage 2 varies by gender and whether or not the pupil is eligible for free school meals. The data source is the English National Pupil Database. The data relates to England and covers all maintained schools. The data is for 2006. Since entitlement to free school meals is restricted to families in receipt of out-of-work benefits, this should be thought of as a proxy for worklessness rather than low income.

Overall adequacy of the indicator: medium. While the data itself is sound enough, the choice of the particular level of exam success is a matter of judgement.

Educational attainment at age 16

29A: One in ten 16-year-olds still obtain fewer than five GCSEs, the same as in 1999/00. This lack of improvement contrasts with the continuing improvement for the higher threshold of five GCSEs at grade C or above.

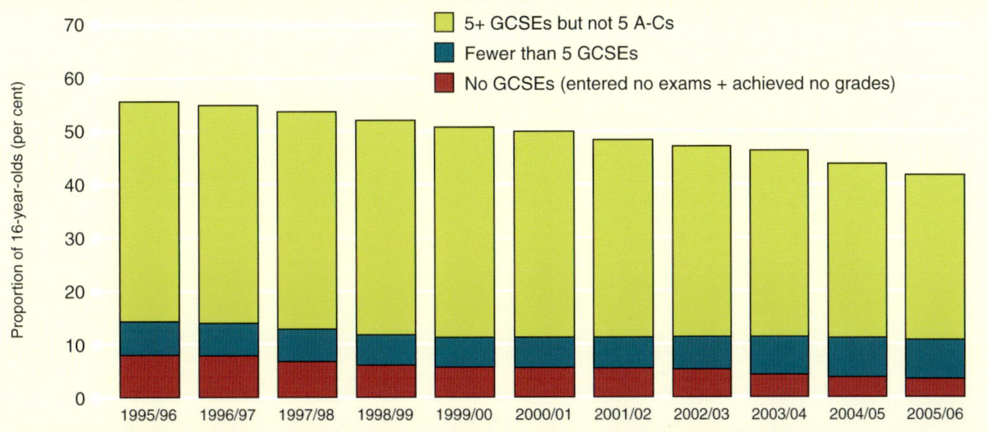

Source: Statistical Releases from DCSF (England) and the National Assembly for Wales (Wales); England and Wales

29B: A third of white British boys eligible for free school meals do not obtain five or more GCSEs, a much higher proportion than that for any other group.

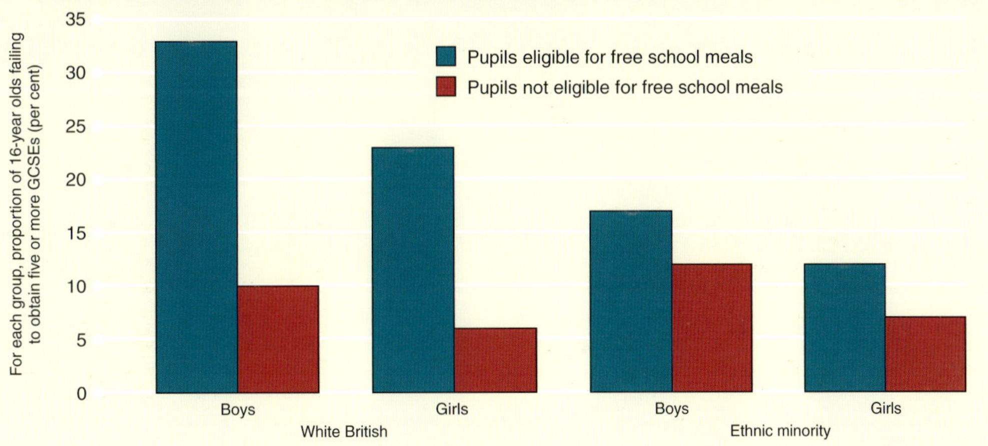

Source: National Pupil Database, DCSF; the data is for 2006; England

The first graph shows the proportion of students (defined as pupils aged 15 at 31 August in the calendar year prior to sitting the exams) failing to obtain five or more GCSEs (or equivalent) at grade C or above in England and Wales. The data is split between those who obtain no GCSE grades at all (either because they do not enter for exams or achieve no passes), those who do obtain some GCSEs but less than five, and those who obtain five or more GCSEs but less than five at grade C or above. The data sources are the Department for Children, Schools and Families (formerly DfES) and the Welsh Assembly. The data relates to England and Wales and covers all schools including city technology colleges and academies, community and foundation special schools, hospital schools, pupil referral units and non-maintained special schools. All the statistics relate to pupils passing either GCSEs or GNVQ etc equivalents. Note that the scope of what was counted as an 'equivalent' in England was widened in 2003/04, which is why the proportion considered to have no grades decreased in that year. This change does not, however, materially affect the higher thresholds of five GCSEs or GCSEs at grade C or above.

The second graph shows how the proportion of children failing to achieve five or more GCSEs (or GNVQ equivalents) varies by pupil characteristics; more specifically, gender, ethnic background and whether or not the pupil is eligible for free school meals. Since entitlement to free school meals is restricted to families in receipt of out-of-work benefits, this should be thought of as a proxy for worklessness rather than low income. The data source is the English National Pupil Database. The data relates to England and covers all maintained schools. The data is for 2006.

Overall adequacy of the indicator: medium. While the data itself is sound enough, the choice of the particular level of exam success is a matter of judgement.

Indicator 30

Without a basic qualification at age 19

30A: One in four 19-year-olds still fails to achieve a basic level of qualification and one in twelve has no qualifications at all.

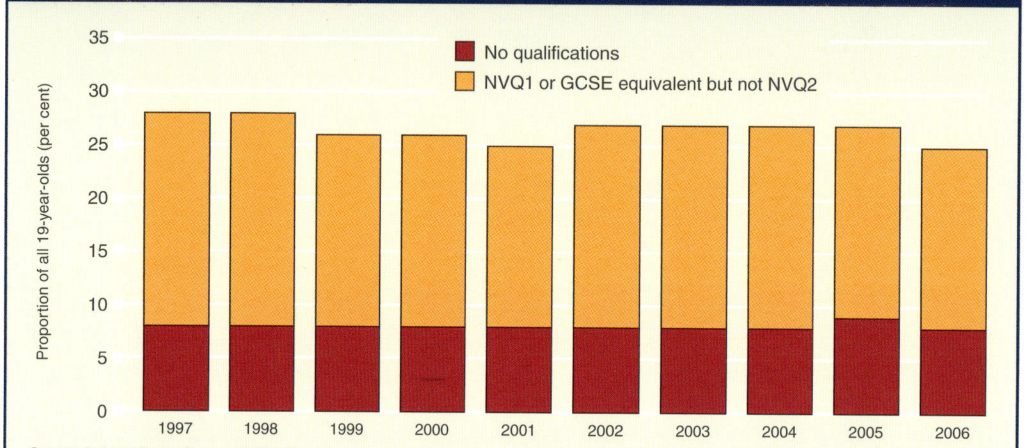

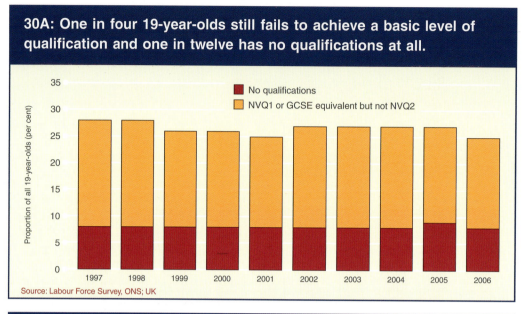

Source: Labour Force Survey, ONS; UK

30B: Most of those who first acquire a Level 2 qualification after the age of 17 have done so by the age of 19.

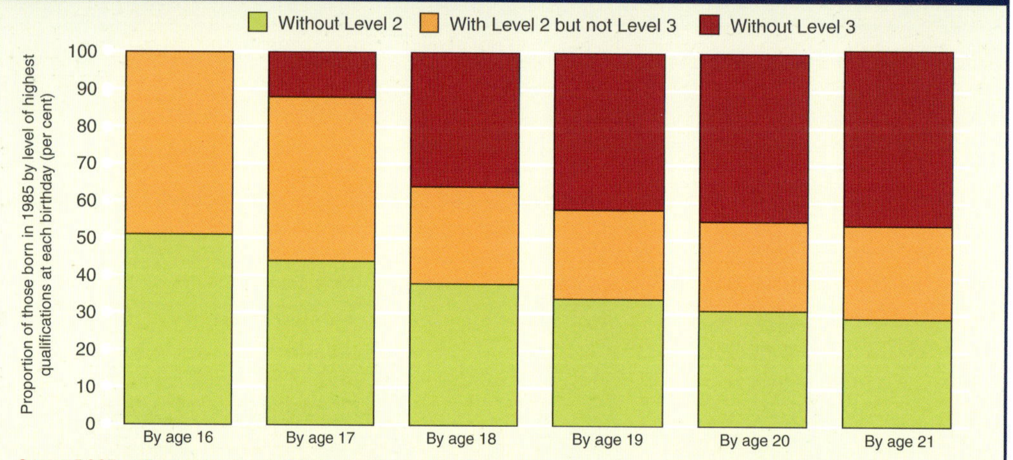

Source: DCSF publication based on matched administrative data; England

The first graph shows the proportion of 19-year-olds without a basic qualification, with the data shown separately for those without NVQ2 or equivalent and those without any qualifications. Department for Children, Schools and Families (DCSF) equivalence scales have been used to translate academic qualifications into their vocational equivalents. So, for example, 'NVQ2 or equivalent' includes those with five GCSEs at grade C or above, GNVQ Level 2, two AS levels or one A level. In line with these equivalence scales, 35 per cent of those with an 'other qualification' are considered to have NVQ2 or equivalent and a further 10 per cent are considered to have NVQ3 or equivalent. The data source is the Labour Force Survey (LFS) and relates to the United Kingdom. The figures for each year are the average for the four quarters of the relevant year (noting that prior to 2006, these four quarters ran from December to November).

DCSF has recently concluded that, at least in England, LFS appears to overstate academic achievement and, furthermore, that the range and diversity of vocational qualifications has grown in recent years and that it is difficult for LFS to accurately capture these. They therefore prefer to use newly introduced administrative sources to analyse levels of qualifications among young adults. Using this data, the second graph shows, for those pupils born in 1985, what proportion have achieved certain educational levels at each age from 16 (i.e. in 2001) to 21 (i.e. in 2006). The particular educational levels shown are below Level 2, Level 2 but not Level 3, and Level 3 or above, where Levels 2 and 3 are similar, but not quite identical, to NVQ2 and NVQ3 respectively.

Overall adequacy of the indicator: limited. As discussed above, it appears that the qualifications data in LFS at age 19 has some shortcomings but it is the only source for time trend data.

Working-age adults without qualifications

Indicator 31

31A: The proportion of the working-age population without any educational qualifications has fallen by a third over the last decade.

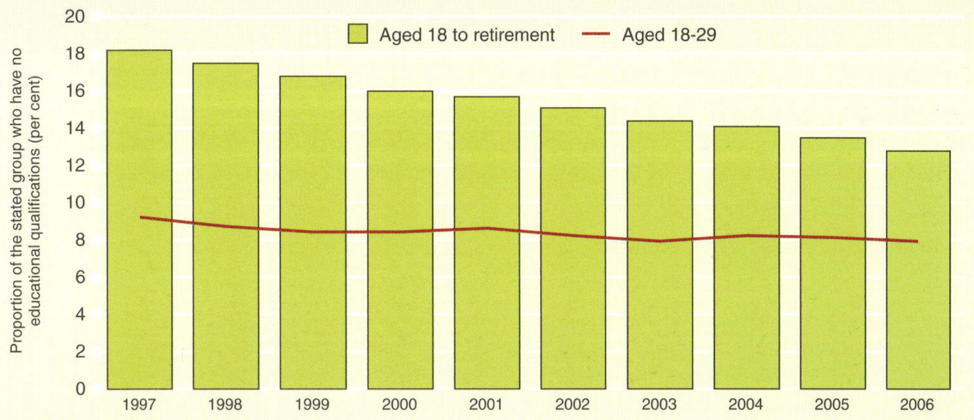

Source: Labour Force Survey, ONS; UK

31B: The proportion of people in their twenties without any educational qualifications is much smaller than the proportion for people aged 40 and over but similar to the proportion for people in their thirties.

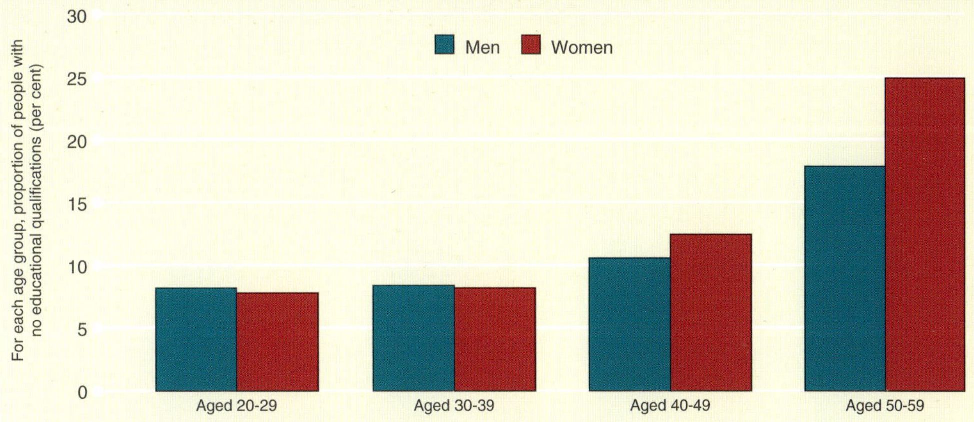

Source: Labour Force Survey, ONS; the data is for 2006; UK

The first graph shows the proportion of adults aged 18 to retirement without any educational qualifications. For comparison purposes, the equivalent proportion for those aged 18 to 29 is also shown.

The second graph shows, for the latest year, the proportion of adults without educational qualifications by gender and for selected age groups.

The data source for both graphs is the Labour Force Survey (LFS) and relates to the United Kingdom. The figures for each year are the average for the four quarters of the relevant year (noting that prior to 2006, these four quarters ran from December to November).

Overall adequacy of the indicator: high. The LFS is a well-established, quarterly survey designed to be representative of the population as whole.

Children at a disadvantage

Poor educational outcomes are not the only form of childhood disadvantage associated with poverty. Ill-health, one aspect of which is discussed in chapter 5 (child deaths) is another. This section of the report looks at some other aspects of extreme childhood disadvantage, namely children excluded from school, children in care, children with a criminal record and the number of under-age pregnancies.

The context for this is provided by a recent UNICEF study on childhood well-being in rich countries which placed the UK at the bottom of the 21 countries examined.[12] That study's use of subjective measures means that its scope is very different from this report. But the boost that it has given to awareness of non-material aspects of deprivation is welcome. For while some matters covered here have certainly been the subject of government concern, they have not always had the prominence that the severity of their consequences deserves.

32 School exclusions

(The number of children permanently excluded from school)

This indicator shows the numbers of boys and girls who have been permanently excluded from school in Great Britain in each of the last ten years. The supporting graph shows the proportion of children permanently excluded from school in England in the latest year, broken down by ethnic group.

Key points:

- Some 10,000 children in England, Wales and Scotland were permanently excluded from school in 2005/06, the latest year for which there is data. Of these, around 8,000 were boys and 2,000 were girls.
- The number of exclusions has remained close to the 10,000 mark in each of the last seven years. In the mid-1990s, however, the figure was around 13,000 a year. The fall, from 13,000 to 10,000, took place during a two-year period, from 1997/98 to 1999/00.
- On average, around 12 children per 10,000 were excluded from English schools in 2005/06. This average figure is also the one for white children. The proportion is markedly lower for Bangladeshi and Pakistani children (and lower still for children in the Indian group). For black children, by contrast, the rates are higher: slightly so for black African children (16 per 10,000) but substantially so for black Caribbean children (40 per 10,000).
- The exclusion rate in Scotland, of around 4 per 10,000 children (in 2004/05) is far lower than the rate for either England (12 per 10,000) or Wales (10 per 10,000).

33 Looked-after children

(The number of looked-after children)

This indicator concerns children in local authority care in England. The first graph shows the number of children in care year by year since 1996 (that is, the number in care at a point in time – 31 March – rather the total number who were in care at some point in the year in question). The supporting graph compares the outcomes for children in care compared with all children on two key measures, namely: the proportion with no GCSEs whatsoever at age 16 (more precisely, in Year 11); and the proportion not in employment, education or training at age 19. The extremely adverse outcome shown in this graph for children in care is what provides the justification for focusing on this group of children in this report.

Key points:

- Around 60,000 children were in care in England in 2006, just over half of them boys. The number of children in care has been at this level since 2002. In 1996, by contrast, the number stood at 50,000, some 10,000 fewer.
- A number of key educational outcomes for children in care (looked-after children) are an order of magnitude worse than for children as a whole. More than a third of looked-after children in Year 11 obtained no GCSEs whatsoever in 2005/06, compared with just 2 per cent for all Year 11 pupils.[13] Children with no GCSEs comprise both those not entered for any exams, and those who were but who achieved no grades.
- A further fifth of looked-after children in Year 11 obtained fewer than five GCSEs at any grade. Taken together with those who obtained none, this means that almost 60 per cent of looked-after children in Year 11 failed to obtain a minimum level of qualification, six times the rate for children as a whole.
- One in every three of 19-year-olds who were previously looked after were not in employment, education or training that year. This compares with one in every seven for 19-year-olds as a whole.

34 Under-age pregnancies

(The number of girls conceiving a child before the age of 16)

This indicator addresses an issue which has long been a subject of government concern, namely the number of under-age pregnancies, measured here by the number of girls in Great Britain who conceive under the age of 16. The first graph shows the number of such girls each year between 1995 and 2005. The total is divided according to whether conception leads to a birth or to an abortion. The second graph, also for Great Britain, shows the proportion of live births where the mother is aged 15 to 19, divided by social class. It should be noted that this is a very different measure from the first indicator. Whatever concerns there may be about 18- or 19-year-olds giving birth, such mothers are adults and the sexual intercourse that gave rise to the conception will have been legal. In these two, vital respects, their situation is very different from that of girls conceiving before the age of 16.

Key points:

- In 2005, there were about 8,500 pregnancies among girls who conceived before the age of 16. This number is similar to a decade previously.
- Around two-fifths of such pregnancies result in birth and the other three-fifths in abortion. The proportion resulting in birth is somewhat lower than a decade ago, when it was half.
- In 2005, 9 per cent of births among those classified as having a 'routine or manual background' were to mothers aged 19 or under. By contrast, among those classified as having a 'professional or managerial background', the proportion was little more than 1 per cent.

35 With a criminal record

(The number of children with a criminal record)

The final indicator in this section addresses the subject of the numbers of children with a criminal record. The first graph shows the number of such children aged 10 to 17 either found guilty, or cautioned for, an indictable offence in each of the years 1995 to 2005. The supporting graph, for the latest year, categorises these offences according to the type of crime involved, and whether committed by boys or girls.

Key points:

- In 2005, around 120,000 children aged 10 to 17 were either found guilty, or cautioned for, an indictable offence. This represents a noticeable rise, of around 20,000, compared with just two years earlier. Prior to that, the number had been falling, from 130,000 in 1995, and around 120,000 in the late 1990s.
- Within these totals, the number of children found guilty has varied little over the decade, fluctuating between 40,000 and 50,000 a year and with no real trend. By contrast, the number of children cautioned has changed substantially, from a high of 90,000 in 1995, to a low of 55,000 in 2002 before rising to 75,000 in 2005.
- A breakdown of the 2005 total by age shows a nearly equal division between those aged 17, 16, 15, 14 and 10 to 13, that is a fifth in each case. Another way of putting this is to say that more than half of the 120,000 offences were committed by children aged 15 or under.
- Nearly half of the offences committed in 2005 involved theft with a further fifth involving violence against the person. Drug offences and burglary accounted for a further tenth each.
- Three quarters of the offences in 2005 were committed by boys and one quarter by girls. Among girls, theft is by far the most likely crime to be committed, accounting for two-thirds of all crimes committed by girls. By contrast, although still the largest single category, theft accounts for just a third of the crimes committed by boys.

Selected relevant research

Some recent research has looked at the different experiences of care for young people from different ethnic groups:

- A report by Barn, Andrew and Mantovani (2005) found that white young people fared the worst in terms of placement instability, leaving care early, low educational attainment, homelessness, and criminal behaviour, including drug misuse.
- White, black Caribbean, and children of mixed parentage tended to spend longer in care, while Asian and black African children often entered care in adolescence. The length of time in care appeared to have as great a bearing on the child's outcomes as their ethnicity.

There has also been some research carried out into the links between poverty and teenage motherhood:

- Research by Bradshaw (2006) and Bradshaw and Mayhew (2005) found that teenage mothers were more than three times as likely to be poor as mothers in their 30s. Babies born to teenage mothers were 40 per cent more likely to be born underweight and the teenage mothers themselves were 50 per cent more likely to be depressed.
- However, Bradshaw concludes that reducing the number of teenage mothers would not make a significant difference to the numbers of children in poverty because the actual number of births to teenage mothers is, while high compared to other countries, actually quite small.

School exclusions

Indicator 32

32A: The number of permanent exclusions has remained broadly unchanged over the last six years.

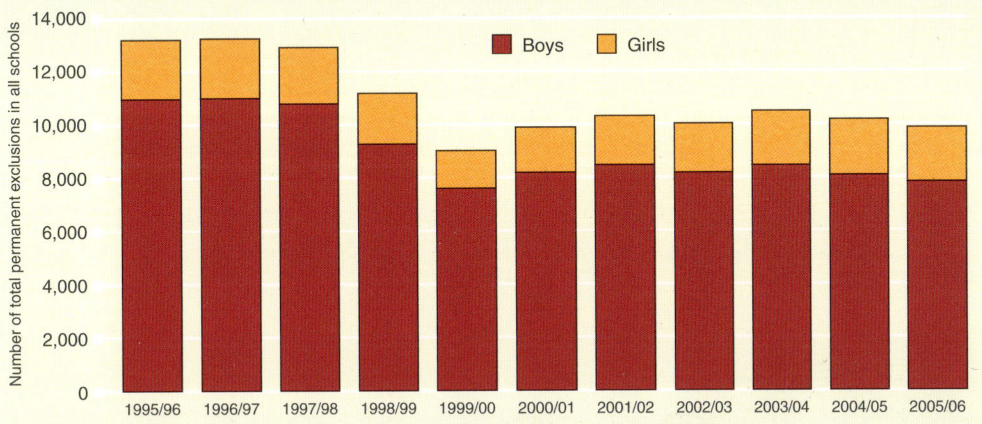

Source: DCSF Statistical Bulletin, National Assembly for Wales and the Scottish Executive; Great Britain

32B: Black Caribbean pupils are three times as likely to be excluded from school as white pupils.

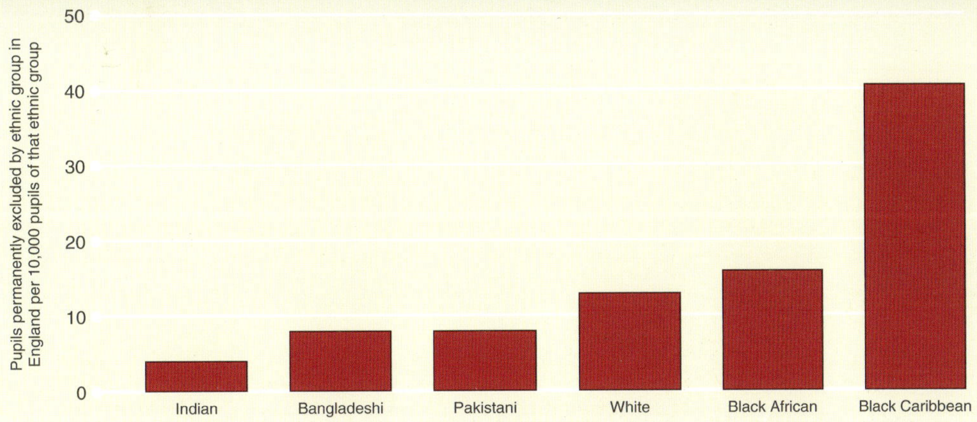

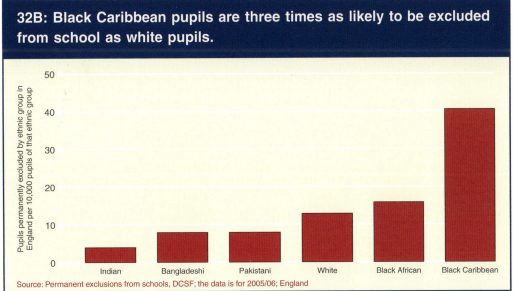

Source: Permanent exclusions from schools, DCSF; the data is for 2005/06; England

The first graph shows the number of pupils permanently excluded from primary, secondary and special schools, with the data shown separately for boys and girls. The data relates to Great Britain. A gender breakdown is not available for Scotland, so these numbers have been estimated by assuming that the gender split is the same as in England and Wales.

The second graph shows, for the latest year, how the rate of permanent exclusions varies for children from different ethnic backgrounds. The data relates to England only.

Overall adequacy of the indicator: medium. Exclusions are susceptible to administrative procedures; for example, the officially recorded numbers may well under-represent the true number of exclusions if parents are persuaded to withdraw their child rather than leave it to the school to exclude them.

Looked-after children

33A: There are 60,000 looked-after children in England, 10,000 more than a decade ago.

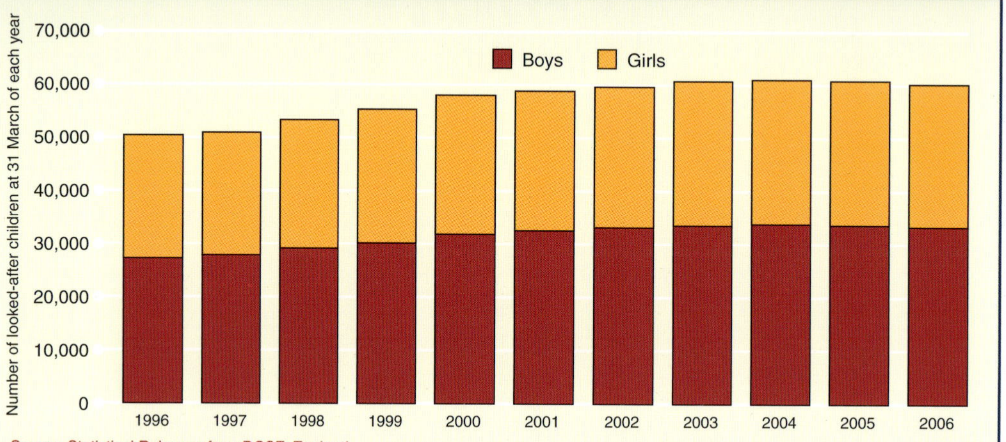

Source: Statistical Releases from DCSF; England

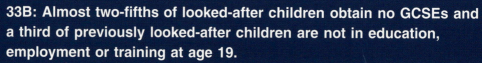

33B: Almost two-fifths of looked-after children obtain no GCSEs and a third of previously looked-after children are not in education, employment or training at age 19.

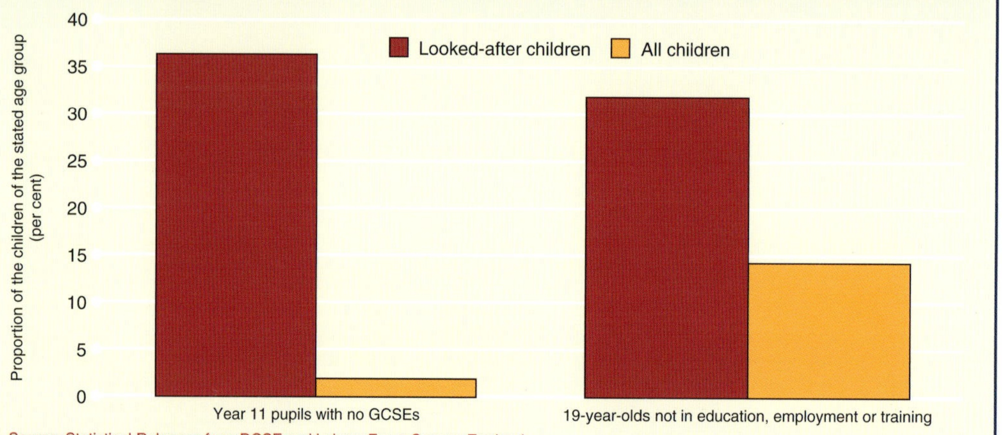

Source: Statistical Releases from DCSF and Labour Force Survey; England

The first graph shows the number of looked-after children at 31 March each year, with the data shown separately for boys and for girls.

The second graph shows the proportion of looked-after children in year 11 who failed in 2005/06 to obtain any GCSEs (or equivalent) plus the proportion of those 19-year-olds who were being looked after at age 16 (i.e. three years previously) who were not in education, employment or training in 2006. For comparison purposes, the equivalent proportions for all children are also shown.

The data source for both graphs is the Department for Children, Schools and Families (formerly DfES) and the data relates to England. The figures exclude children looked after under an agreed series of short-term placements. In the second graph, those with whom the Department had lost touch are excluded from the analysis. Note that the 'all' for 19-year-olds who were not in education, employment or training in 2006 is from the Labour Force Survey.

Overall adequacy of the indicator: high. The data is well-established administrative counts.

Under-age pregnancies

34A: The overall number of under-age conceptions is similar to a decade ago, although a lower proportion now lead to actual births.

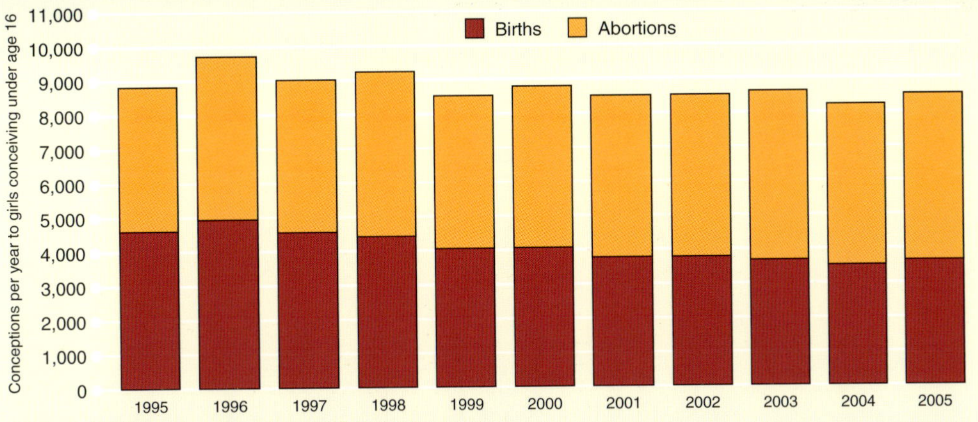

Source: Health Statistics Quarterly, ONS and ISD Scotland; Great Britain

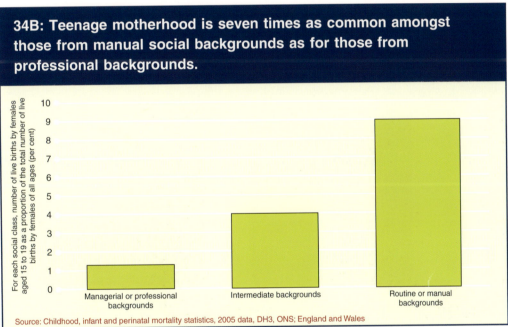

34B: Teenage motherhood is seven times as common amongst those from manual social backgrounds as for those from professional backgrounds.

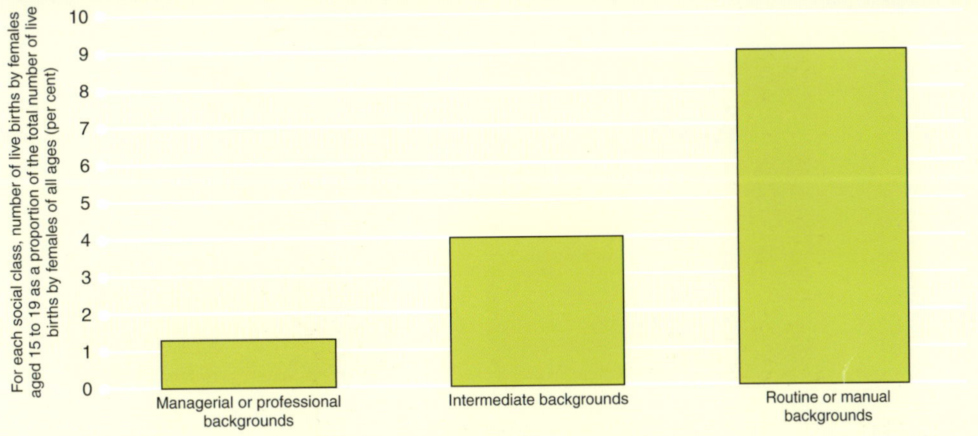

Source: Childhood, infant and perinatal mortality statistics, 2005 data, DH3, ONS; England and Wales

The first graph shows the number of conceptions per year to girls conceiving under the age of 16, with the data shown separately for delivered babies and for abortions. The data relates to Great Britain. English and Welsh conceptions leading to births are counted during the actual year of conception, while Scottish conceptions are counted after the birth of the child, which is commonly in the calendar year following conception. ONS population projections have been used for the number of 15-year-old girls.

The second graph shows, for the latest year, the number of live births by females aged 15 to 19 in each social class as a proportion of the total live births by females of that social class. The data source is the DH3 mortality statistics from ONS and the data is for England and Wales. The analysis is based on the recorded social class of the father of the baby and, as such, it does not include the 25 per cent of births to females aged 15 to 19 which were sole registrations.

Overall adequacy of the indicator: medium. The collection of the conception and births statistics is an established process.

With a criminal record

35A: The number of children found guilty for indictable offences has remained steady, while the number cautioned fell up to 2002 but has been rising since then.

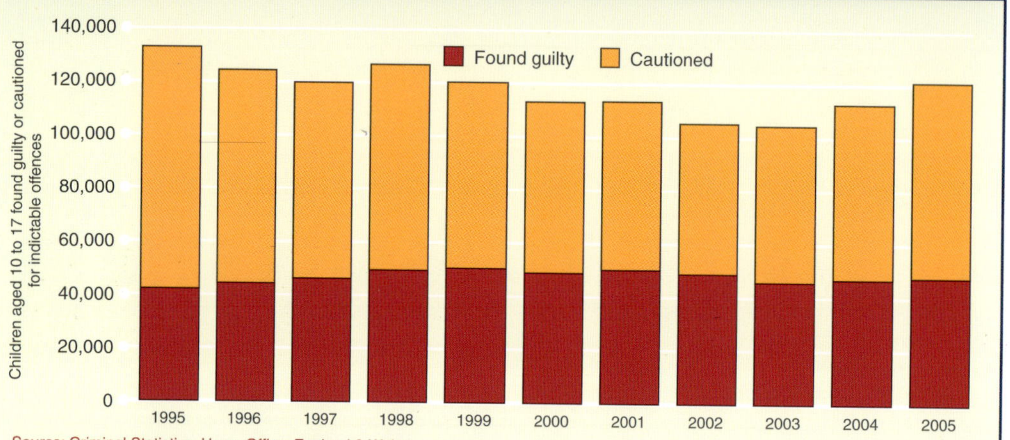

Source: Criminal Statistics, Home Office; England & Wales

35B: Three times as many boys are found guilty or cautioned of indictable offences as girls but the difference is much less for theft.

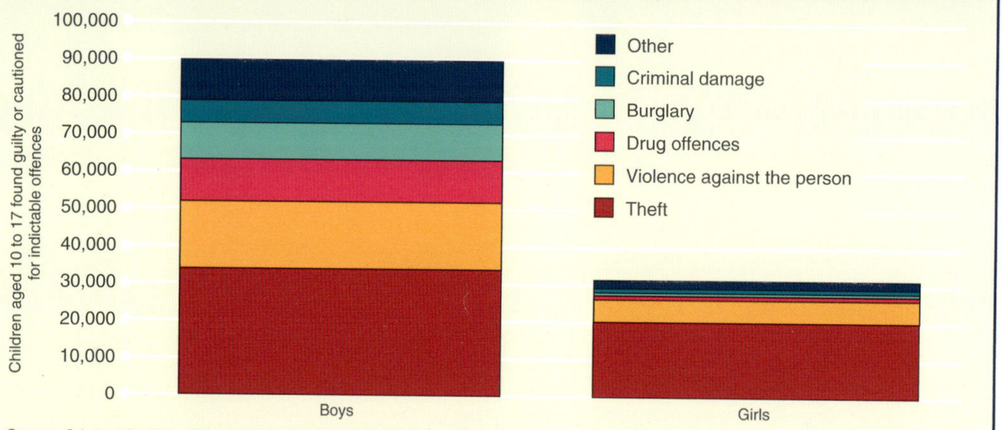

Source: Criminal Statistics, Home Office; the data is for 2005; England and Wales

The first graph shows the number of children between the ages of 10 and 17 who were either formally cautioned for, or convicted of, an indictable offence, with the data shown separately for boys and for girls.

The second graph shows, for the latest year, the number of indictable offences by gender and type of offence.

The data source for both graphs is Home Office Criminal Statistics and the data relates to England and Wales. Note that the cautions are formal cautions only.

Overall adequacy of the indicator: medium. The figures are police-recorded crime only and should not be taken as accurate estimates of the total extent of crime carried out by children.

Impact of qualifications on work

This section contains two indicators that show the link between the level of educational qualifications and the likelihood that someone is either lacking but wanting paid work or is in work but is low paid (defined as being paid less than £6.50 an hour). Each indicator classifies people according to their highest level of education, namely: a degree or equivalent; A levels or equivalent; GCSEs at grades A to C; GCSEs but below grade C; or no qualifications.

36 Impact of qualifications on work: young adults

(The proportion of 25- to 29-year-olds wanting work, or low-paid, by qualification level)

The first indicator looks at those in their late 20s, in effect the youngest age cohort who have almost all completed their education. The first graph shows the proportions lacking but wanting paid work according to the highest level of qualification, divided in each case between those who are unemployed and those who are economically inactive but wanting work. The second graph shows the proportion who are low paid.

Key points:

- The lower a young adult's qualifications, the more likely they are to be lacking but wanting paid work. Among those with degrees or the equivalent, just 5 per cent are in this situation. By contrast, among those with no qualifications, more than 20 per cent lack, but want, paid work. Even low GCSEs appear to confer a marked advantage compared with having no qualifications. A levels or their equivalent also appear to confer a marked advantage compared with just good GCSEs.
- On the face of it, the risk of low pay seem to follow a similar pattern: the lower a young adult's qualifications the higher their risk of being low paid if in work. Thus, among those in work with degrees or equivalent, around 10 per cent are low paid while among those with no qualifications the proportion exceeds 50 per cent. All levels of qualifications appear to make a noticeable difference compared with the level below.
- But while the pattern appears the same, the scale is very different. Thus, despite the higher risks of lacking work associated with lower qualifications, it remains the case that the great majority will be in work in their late 20s, even for those with no qualifications. By contrast, a majority of those with no qualifications in work will be low paid.

37 Impact of qualifications on work: disabled adults

(The proportion of 25- to 50-year-olds wanting work, or low paid, by qualification level and disability status)

The second indicator presents the same analysis but for the 25 to 50 age group, comparing the risks for those with a work-limiting disability to the risks for those without. As before, the first graph shows the proportions lacking but wanting paid work according to the highest level of qualification while the second graph shows the proportion who are low paid.

Key points:

- At all levels of qualification, the proportion of people with a work-limiting disability who lack, but want, paid work is much greater than for those without a disability. Indeed, at almost 15 per cent, the proportion of people with a work-limiting disability with degrees or equivalent who lack, but want, paid work is as high as the proportion of people without a work limiting disability with no qualifications who lack, but want, paid work. And, for people with a work-limiting disability with some qualifications but not degrees, the proportion who lack, but want, paid work is, at 20-35 per cent, much higher.
- At all levels of qualification, the proportion of people with a work-limiting disability who are low paid is somewhat greater than for those without a disability. But the differences are much less than the differences for lacking but wanting paid work discussed above.

Selected relevant research

Disability and low qualifications overlap to a substantial extent and some recent research has looked at this in more detail.

- A report by the Social Market Foundation (Evans, 2007) showed that around one third of all those without any formal qualifications are disabled. Three-fifths of disabled people are qualified up to Level 2 compared to three-quarters of non-disabled people.
- According to this study, of those disabled people without any qualifications, one-third have mobility impairments, one-third have long-term conditions, one-sixth have mental health problems and one in sixteen have learning difficulties.

Other research has tried to quantify more precisely the effects of different levels of qualification on employment and pay.

- Grinyer (2005) found that literacy had a pronounced effect on employment, particularly for women. Women who had Level 1 literacy – equivalent to D-G at GCSE – were 7 per cent more likely to be employed that those with lower literacy skills. Women with Level 1 skills earned, on average, 26 per cent more than those with lower skills.

Impact of qualifications on work: young adults

36A: The lower a young adult's qualifications, the more likely they are to be lacking but wanting paid work. Even so, most young adults with no qualifications are in work.

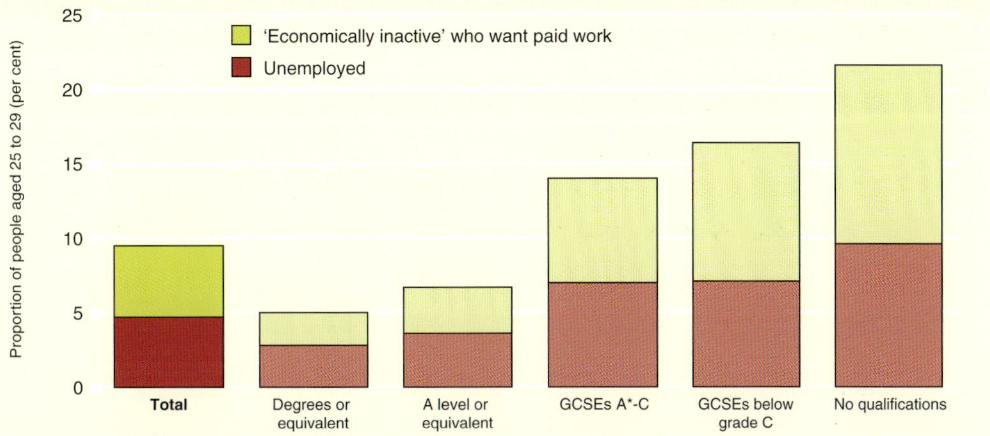

Source: Labour Force Survey, ONS; the data is for 2006; UK

36B: The lower a young adult's qualifications, the more likely they are to be low paid. A majority of young adults with no qualifications are low paid.

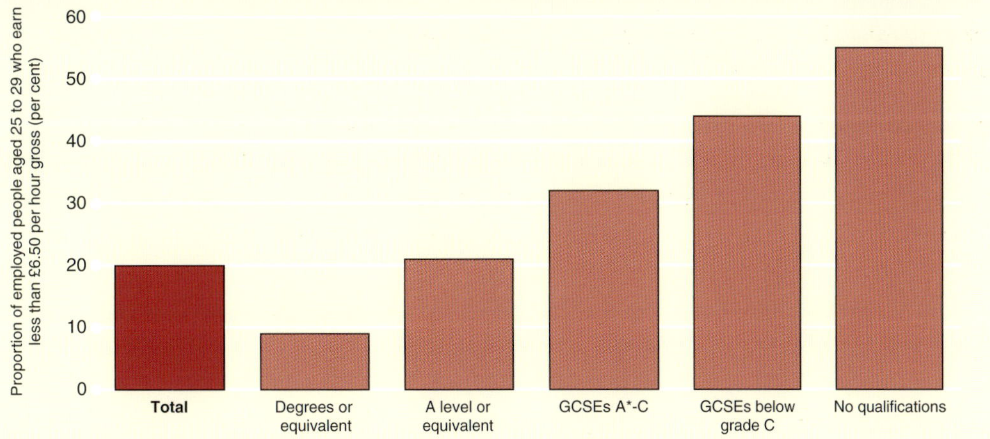

Source: Labour Force Survey, ONS; the data is for 2006; UK

The first graph shows the proportion of 25- to 29-year-olds who lack, but want, paid work, with the data broken down by level of highest qualification. The data is shown separately for those who are unemployed and those counted as 'economically inactive' who nevertheless want paid work. 'Unemployment' is the ILO definition and includes all those with no paid work in the survey week who were available to start work in the next fortnight and who either looked for work in the last month or were waiting to start a job already obtained. The economically inactive who want paid work includes people not available to start work for some time and those not actively seeking work.

The second graph shows the proportion of 25- to 29-year-olds in employment who were paid less than £6.50 per hour, with the data broken down by level of highest qualification.

In both graphs, the lower age limit of 25 has been chosen on the grounds that a) the vast majority of people will have completed their formal education by that age and b) they will no longer be in casual employment (as, for example, students often are).

The data source for both graphs is the Labour Force Survey (LFS) and relates to the United Kingdom. To improve statistical reliability, the data is the average for the four quarters of 2006.

Overall adequacy of the indicator: medium. The LFS is a well-established, quarterly survey designed to be representative of the population as a whole. However, the low pay data in the second graph is considered by ONS to be less reliable than the non-income data in the first graph.

Indicator 37

Impact of qualifications on work: disabled adults

37A: At all levels of qualification, the proportion of people with a work-limiting disability who lack, but want, paid work is much greater than for those without a disability.

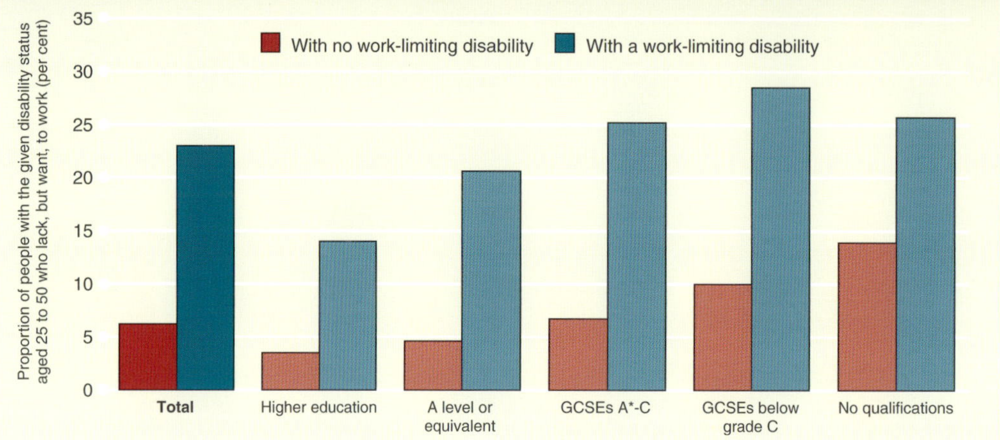

Source: Labour Force Survey, ONS; the data is for 2006; UK

37B: At all levels of qualification, the proportion of people with a work-limiting disability who are low paid is somewhat greater than for those without a disability.

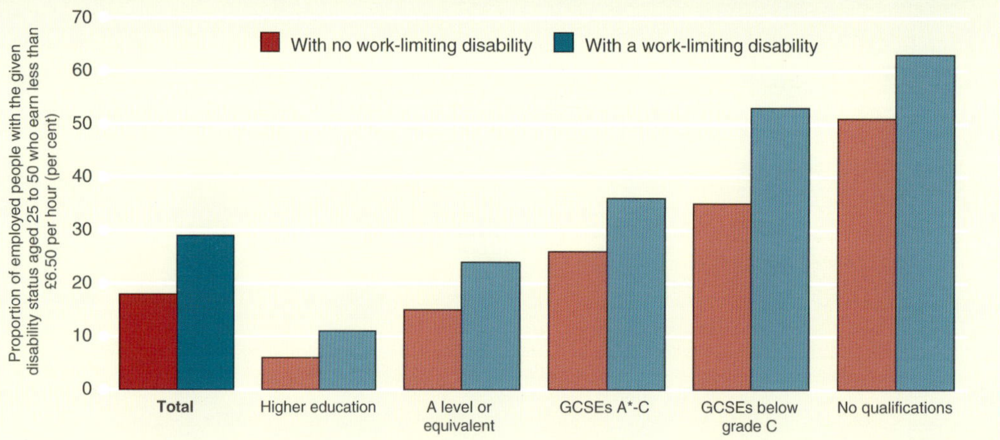

Source: Labour Force Survey, ONS; the data is for 2006; UK

The first graph shows how the proportion of disabled adults aged 25 to 50 who lack, but want, paid work varies by level of disability and level of highest qualification. 'Work-limiting disability' comprises those people who stated that they have had health problems for more than a year and that these problems affect either the kind or amount of work that they can do. 'Unemployment' is the ILO definition and includes all those with no paid work in the survey week who were available to start work in the next fortnight and who either looked for work in the last month or were waiting to start a job already obtained. The economically inactive who want paid work includes people not available to start work for some time and those not actively seeking work.

The second graph shows how the proportion of employees aged 25 to 50 who were paid less than £6.50 per hour varies by level of disability and level of highest qualification.

The data source for both graphs is the Labour Force Survey (LFS) and relates to the United Kingdom. To improve statistical reliability, the data is the average for the four quarters of 2006.

Overall adequacy of the indicator: medium. The LFS is a well-established, quarterly survey designed to be representative of the population as a whole. However, the low pay data in the second graph is considered by ONS to be less reliable than the non-income data in the first graph.

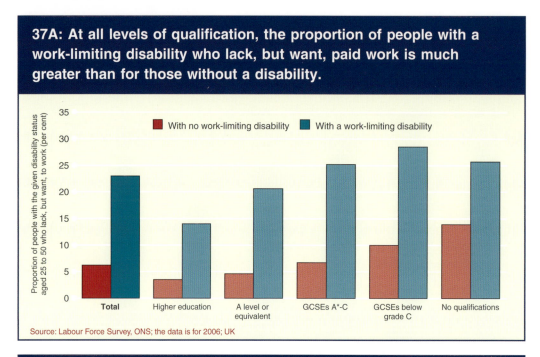

Chapter 5 **Ill-health**

Disability

The importance of the connection between disability and poverty is clearly demonstrated elsewhere within this report: disabled working-age adults are twice as likely as non-disabled adults to be in poverty; disability substantially reduces the likelihood that someone is in work; and, if they do not have dependent children, working-age adults in receipt of benefits have steadily fallen further behind as they have not shared in the growth in incomes over the last decade. Against this background, a better understanding of the situation and characteristics of people who are disabled is obviously important.

38 Long-term working-age recipients of out-of-work benefits

(The number of long-term, working-age recipients of out-of-work benefits)

This indicator shows the number of people of working-age receiving out-of-work benefits for two years or more, according to whether they are disabled, a lone parent, unemployed or a carer. The figures, for Great Britain, are shown for each year between 1997 and 2007. The supporting graph shows a breakdown of the medical conditions that long-term recipients of disability out-of-work benefits (either Incapacity Benefit or Severe Disablement Allowance) have.

Key points:

- In 2007, 3 million working-age people were receiving out-of-work benefits which they had been receiving for two years or more. Three-quarters of these (some 2.2 million) were sick or disabled.
- Over the last decade, the total number of long-term recipients of out-of-work benefits has not changed very much. Within that total, however, the number who are sick or disabled has risen (from 1.9 million a decade ago to 2.2 million), with that rise having taken place in the years up to 2003.
- Over the same decade, the number of long-term unemployed recipients has fallen from 0.3 to 0.1 million. To all intents and purposes, there has been virtually no unemployed people long-term reliant on benefits for several years.
- The number of long-term lone parent recipients of benefits has also come down, from 0.7 to 0.5 million. The number of long-term carer recipients has risen slightly to around 0.3 million.
- Among those receiving disability benefits for two years or more, 40 per cent have mental or behavioural disorders. This is by far the largest single category. Musculoskeletal disorders, the second largest category, account for a further 20 per cent.
- The numbers receiving disability benefits for two years or more can also be broken down by age. This shows that around a third are aged 55 to retirement, a further third are aged 45 to 54, and the final third are aged under 45. Long-term disability is therefore by no means confined to, or even concentrated especially among, older working-age adults.

39 Long-standing illness/disability

(The proportion of older working-age adults with a limiting long-standing illness or disability)

This indicator shows the proportion of people aged 45 to 64 who report that they are suffering from a limiting long-standing illness or disability. The first graph shows these proportions, for men and women separately, for each year (for which data is available) since 1995/96. The supporting graph, for the latest year (2005), shows how these proportions vary according to the level of household income. These figures are for Great Britain.

Key points:

- In 2005, some 25 per cent of both men and women aged 45 to 64 reported that they were suffering from a limiting long-standing illness or disability. These proportions are similar to those in 1995/96.
- The proportion of men and women with such a condition varies markedly according to the level of household income. Among men, 45 per cent of those in the poorest fifth reported such a condition, compared with 25 per cent for men on average incomes and barely more than 10 per cent for men in the richest fifth. More than 40 per cent of men in the second poorest fifth also reported such a condition. The figures for women show a similar gradient, although rather less pronounced, from 40 per cent among those in the poorest fifth, to around 15 per cent for those in the richest fifth.

40 Mental health

(The proportion of working-age adults judged at high risk of developing a mental illness)

This indicator is concerned with mental health and uses health survey data for England which includes an assessment of whether a person is at high risk of developing a mental illness. The first graph shows this proportion, separately for men and women, for each year that is available from 1995 to 2005. The second combines data from the three most recent years in order to show how these proportions, again for men and women separately, vary according to the level of household income. In both cases, the results are for people age 25 to retirement.

Key points:

- In 2005, some 10 per cent of men and some 15 per cent of women were assessed as being at high risk of developing a mental illness. Although the figures for men and women have fluctuated from year to year during the past decade, it does appear that the proportions a decade ago were about 5 per cent higher for both men and women, that is, around 15 per cent and 20 per cent respectively.
- Over the three most recent years, twice as many people in the poorest fifth of the population have been deemed at high risk of mental illness as people on average incomes.
- Depending on their income, there are some marked differences in the pattern of 'at-risk' rates between men and women. So among men and women in the poorest fifth, the proportions at high risk are judged to be the same: 25 per cent in each case. There is a similar equality, albeit at around 15 per cent, for men and women in the second poorest fifth. With average and above average incomes, by contrast, a higher proportion of women than men are judged to be at high risk: between 8 per cent and 10 per cent of men depending on their income, but between 12 per cent and 16 per cent of women.

Selected relevant research

Some recent research has looked at different health outcomes for different groups. For example:

- A report by the Social Exclusion Unit (2004) showed that mothers of young children suffer the highest levels of depression, along with lone parents and those who are economically inactive. Over a quarter of lone parents have common mental health problems.

- A report by the Disability Rights Commission (2006) looked at the physical health inequalities suffered by people with mental health problems. Among their findings were that people with learning disabilities were more likely to suffer from obesity and respiratory disease and that those with mental health problems were more likely to suffer from a range of illnesses, including obesity, heart disease, high blood pressure, respiratory disease, diabetes and stroke. The report makes the point that, while social deprivation may explain some of these additional risks of ill-health, it does not explain it all. For example, they found that part of the explanation lies in access to primary care, with people with mental health problems being less likely to receive standard treatments and tests from their GP, meaning diseases were sometimes able to progress before being treated.

Long-term working-age recipients of out-of-work benefits

Indicator 38

38A: Three-quarters of working-age people receiving a key out-of-work benefit for two years or more are sick or disabled.

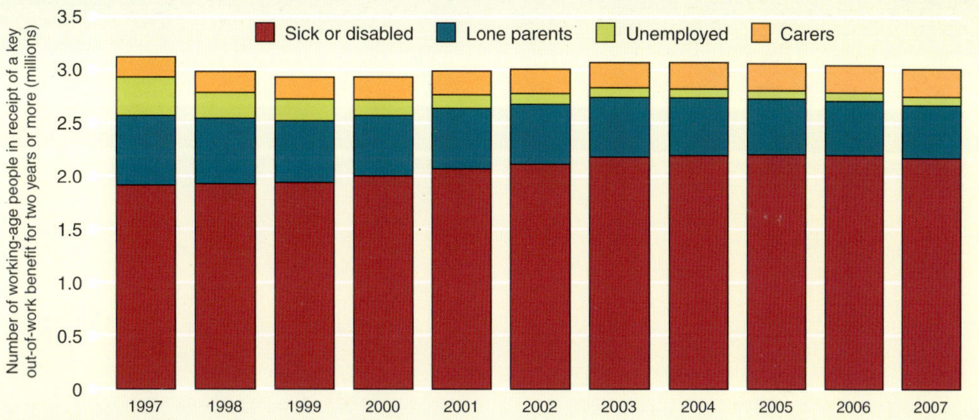

Source: Work and Pensions Longitudinal Study, DWP; Great Britain

38B: Two-fifths of all long-term claimants of Incapacity Benefit or Severe Disablement Allowance have mental or behaviour disorders.

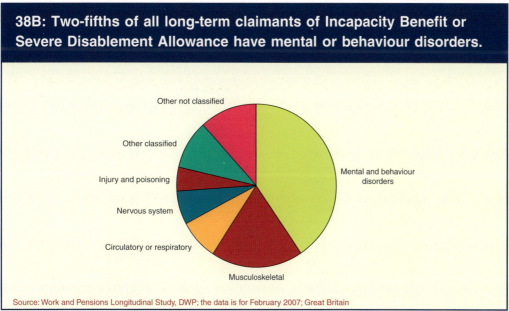

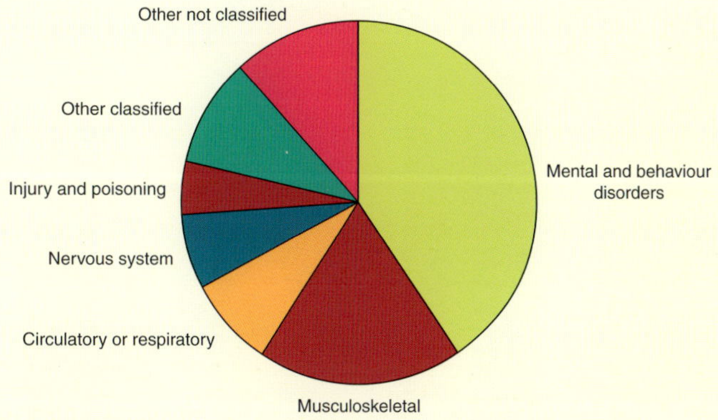

Source: Work and Pensions Longitudinal Study, DWP; the data is for February 2007; Great Britain

The first graph shows all those of working age who were in receipt of a 'key out-of-work benefit' for two years or more. 'Key out-of-work benefits' is a DWP term which covers the following benefits: Jobseeker's Allowance, Income Support, Incapacity Benefit, Severe Disablement Allowance and Carer's Allowance. Note that this list is slightly different from 'key benefits', which also include Disability Living Allowance. For each year, the total is broken down by type of claimant, namely: unemployed, sick or disabled, lone parents and carers. Note that a small number of 'others' have been omitted from the graph.

As can be seen from the first graph, the majority of long-term claimants of key out-of-work benefits are sick or disabled. In this context, the second graph shows, for the latest year, a breakdown by reason for those who have either been in receipt of Incapacity Benefit for two years or more or are in receipt of Severe Disablement Allowance.

The data source for both graphs is the DWP Work and Pensions Longitudinal Study. The data relates to Great Britain and is for the month of February of each year. The data has been analysed to avoid double-counting of those receiving multiple benefits by matching data from individual samples.

Overall adequacy of the indicator: high. The data is thought to be very reliable and is based on information collected by the DWP for the administration of benefits.

Indicator 39

Long-standing illness/disability

39A: A quarter of adults aged 45-64 report a long-standing illness or disability which limits their activity.

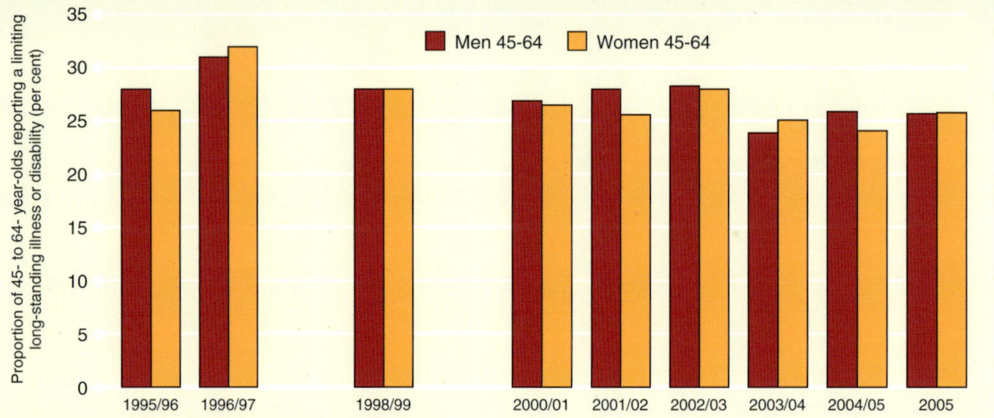

Source: General Household Survey, ONS; Great Britain

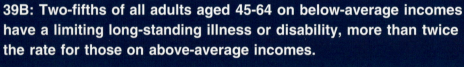

39B: Two-fifths of all adults aged 45-64 on below-average incomes have a limiting long-standing illness or disability, more than twice the rate for those on above-average incomes.

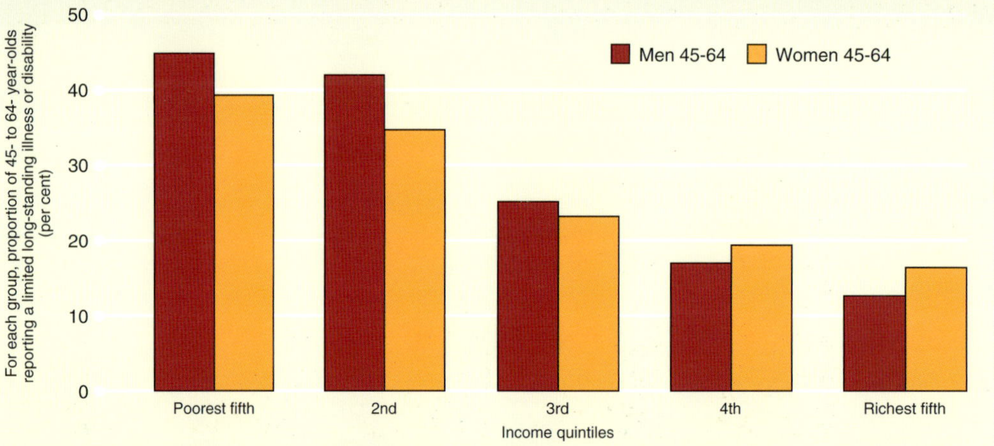

Source: General Household Survey, ONS; the data is the average for the three years to 2005; Great Britain

The first graph shows the proportion of adults aged 45 to 64 who report having a long-term illness or a disability that limits the activities they are able to carry out. The data is shown separately for men and women.

The second graph shows how the proportions vary by household income. Again, the data is shown separately for men and women. To improve its statistical reliability, the data is the average for the latest three years. The division into income quintiles is based on net, equivalised income.

The data source for both graphs is the General Household Survey (GHS) and relates to Great Britain. The question asked was: 'Do you have any long-standing illness, disability or infirmity? Long-standing is anything that has troubled you over a period of time or that is likely to affect you over a period of time. Does this illness or disability limit your activities in any way?' Note that GHS moved from financial years to calendar years in 2005. Also, note that the data for 1997/98 and 1999/00 is missing because the GHS was not carried out in those years. Finally, note that the data for 1996/97 onwards is weighted but is unweighted for 1995/96.

Overall adequacy of the indicator: medium. While the GHS is a well-established government survey designed to be representative of the population as a whole, the inevitable variation in what respondents understand and interpret as 'long-standing' and 'limiting activity' diminishes the value of the indicator.

Mental health

40A: The proportion of adults aged 25 to retirement who are deemed to be at a high risk of developing a mental illness is somewhat lower than a decade ago. Women are more at risk than men.

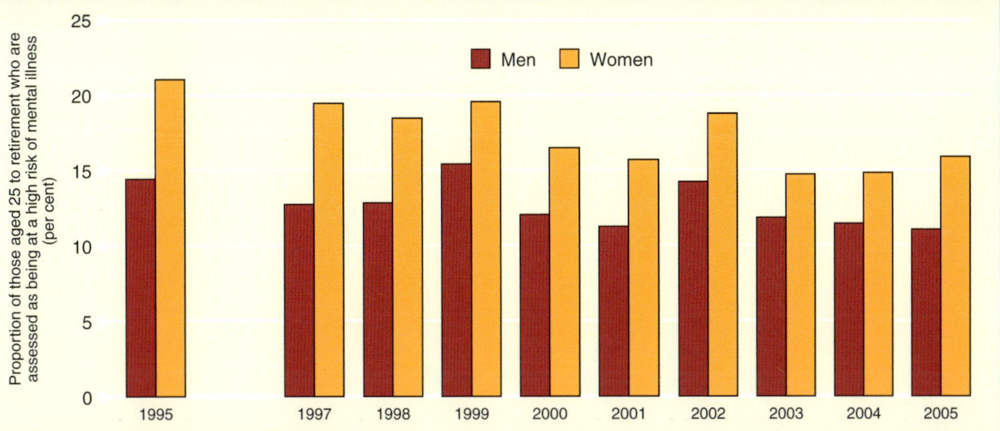

Source: Health Survey for England, DH; England

40B: Adults in the poorest fifth are around twice as likely to be at risk of developing a mental illness as those on average incomes. The differences are greater for men than for women.

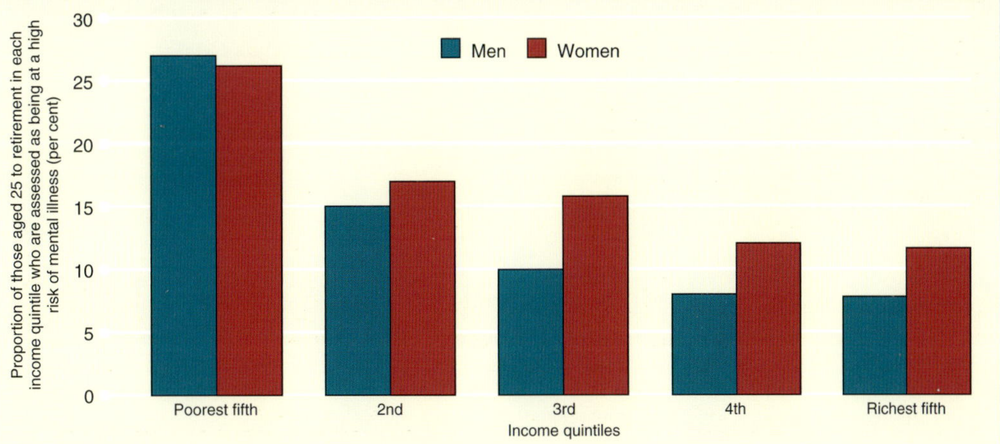

Source: Health Survey for England, DH; the data is the average for 2003 to 2005; England

The first graph shows the proportion of adults aged 25 to retirement who are classified as being at high risk of developing a mental illness, with the data shown separately for men and women. A high risk of mental illness is determined by asking informants a number of questions about general levels of happiness, depression, anxiety and sleep disturbance over the previous four weeks, which are designed to detect possible psychiatric morbidity. A score is constructed from the responses, and the figures published show those with a score of four or more. This is referred to as a 'high GHQ12 score'.

The second graph shows how the proportions vary by household income, with the data shown separately for men and women. The division into income quintiles is based on gross, equivalised income.

The data source for both graphs is the Health Survey for England (HSE) and relates to England only. To improve statistical reliability, the data in the second graph has been averaged over the latest three years. Note that the data from 2003 onwards is weighted whereas the earlier data is unweighted.

Overall adequacy of the indicator: medium. While the HSE is a large survey which is designed to be representative of the population in England as a whole, the data only allows a partial analysis of mental health.

Mortality

In principle, statistics on death belong in a report like this only insofar as they reflect differences in death rates that are connected to levels of income, or class, or a proxy for them. There are, however, two problems with this position. The first is that such a breakdown is not available for some of our chosen measures on a timely basis. Given the importance of the subject, and the fact that the data exists within government but is not made available, this is a surprising gap. The second is that the classification of social class used by government statisticians was changed a few years ago. As a result, for some statistics, it is not possible to compare how the class inequality has evolved over the last decade since the two classifications are not comparable.

41 Child deaths

(The rate of infant death and the number of accidental deaths among children)

The first indicator shows measures of two death rates among children. The first is the rate of infant death, measured as the proportion of children born each year who die before their first birthday. Babies who are stillborn are excluded from this measure. The first graph, for England and Wales, shows this rate, for each year between 1995 and 2005, separately for those in social classes 1 to 4 and those in classes 5 to 8. The second graph shows the number of accidental deaths among those aged under 16, in this case, for Great Britain.

Key points:

- In 2005, the rate of infant deaths among children in social classes 1 to 4 was just under 4 per 1,000 live births. By contrast, the rate among those in social classes 5 to 8 was around 5.5 per 1,000.
- Ten years earlier both rates were higher, by 1-1.5 per 1,000 live births, that is, about 5 deaths per 1,000 for those in classes 1 to 4 and around 7 for those in classes 5 to 8. The fall over the intervening ten years has been very steady, with no sign that progress for either group is slowing down.
- In 2005, there were just under 300 accidental deaths among children aged up to 16. Compared with ten years earlier, when more than 500 died, this is a 50 per cent fall.
- Up-to-date data on the difference in accidental death rates by social class is not available. However, over the period 1995 to 2001 for which data on the old basis is available, the accidental death rate among children in manual social classes (IIIM to V) fell from 5 to 3.5 per 100,000 while that for non-manual social classes (I to IIINM) fell from 3.5 to 2.5 per 100,000. As with infant deaths, therefore, there is a marked difference by social class, and while the numbers are coming down for all, the difference remains the same.

42 Premature deaths

(The rate of premature deaths by gender)

The second indicator refers to the rate of premature deaths. We prefer such a measure to the more commonly used 'life expectancy' since its meaning is plain (and involves none of the assumptions that are essential in order to construct the latter). The first graph shows the overall rate of premature deaths, expressed as the number of deaths among those aged under 65 as a proportion of the total population in that age group. These rates are shown for men and women separately and for each year from 1996 to 2006. The supporting graph shows the proportion of people aged 35 to 65 dying from either lung cancer or heart disease. The figures are shown separately for men and women, and separately too for those in manual and non-manual backgrounds. But due to the problems with classification referred to above, these data refer to 1997 to 1999 only, more recent data being unavailable.

Key points:

- In 2006, some 240 men under the age of 65 died per 100,000 of that population. The comparable figure for women was around 150.
- Ten years earlier, the premature death rates for men and women stood at nearly 300, and 180, per 100,000 respectively. This means that rates for both men and women have fallen by a sixth in a decade. Over that period, the falls have been steady and there is no sign of progress slowing on either.
- Recent data on the differences in premature rates of death by class does not seem to be available. However, certain major causes of death have long afflicted some classes more than others. For example, over the period 1997 to 1999, rates of both heart disease and lung cancer among those aged 35 to 64 were much higher for those from manual social backgrounds than for those from non manual ones, by 50 per cent for heart disease and by 150 per cent for lung cancer.

Selected relevant research

The government has set Public Service Agreement targets to reduce health inequalities between the most and least deprived areas in England, measured by infant mortality and life expectancy at birth. According to the most recent figures:

- 66 per cent of the most deprived areas had higher than average infant mortality rates, compared to 27 per cent of all other areas (Wanless *et al.*, 2007).
- Similarly, life expectancy has improved for men and women across the population. However, average life expectancy for males in the group of most deprived areas, known as the spearhead group, is still two years lower than for males elsewhere. This gap has not closed in the last decade.

Indicator 41

Child deaths

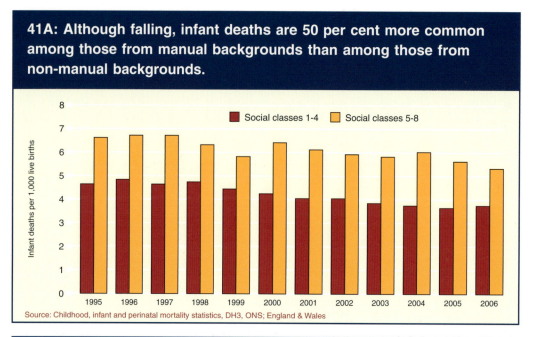

41A: Although falling, infant deaths are 50 per cent more common among those from manual backgrounds than among those from non-manual backgrounds.

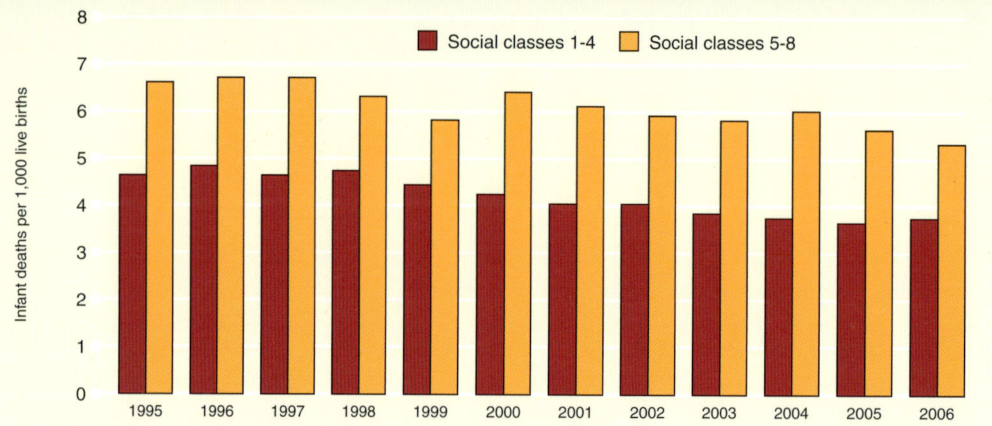

Source: Childhood, infant and perinatal mortality statistics, DH3, ONS; England & Wales

41B: Accidental deaths among the under-16s have almost halved over the last decade.

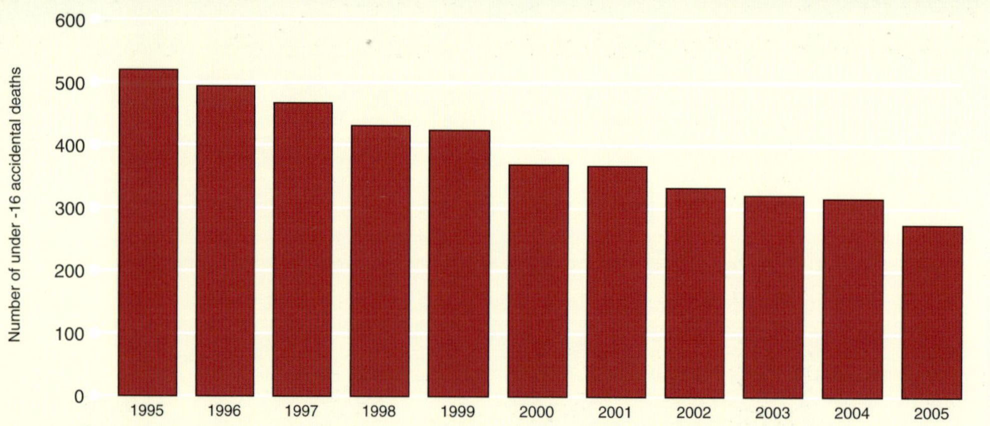

Source: Data for England and Wales supplied by ONS; data for Scotland supplied by General Registrar Office; Great Britain

The first graph shows the annual number of infant deaths per 1,000 live births, with the data shown separately according to the social class of the father. Infant deaths are deaths which occur at ages under one year. The social class classifications are those recently introduced which range from 1 (higher managerial and professional) to 8 (never worked and long-term unemployed). The data source is ONS DH3 childhood, infant and perinatal mortality statistics. The data relates to England and Wales and is based on a 10 per cent sample of live births. The data is based on year of occurrence. Cases where the social class of the father is unknown (including all births where the registration is solely in the name of the mother) have been excluded from the analysis.

The second graph shows the annual number of deaths due to external causes among those under 16. The data relates to Great Britain. 'Accidental deaths' encompasses all forms of accidental death, including traffic accidents, poisoning, falls and drowning as well as suicides and homicides (ICD-10 codes V01-X59). The data is based on year of occurrence rather than year of registration.

Overall adequacy of the indicator: high. The sample sizes in the first graph are substantial and relatively few (5 per cent) have not been coded to a social class.

Premature deaths

42A: The rate of premature death has fallen by a sixth over the last decade. It is, however, still one-and-a-half times as high among men as among women.

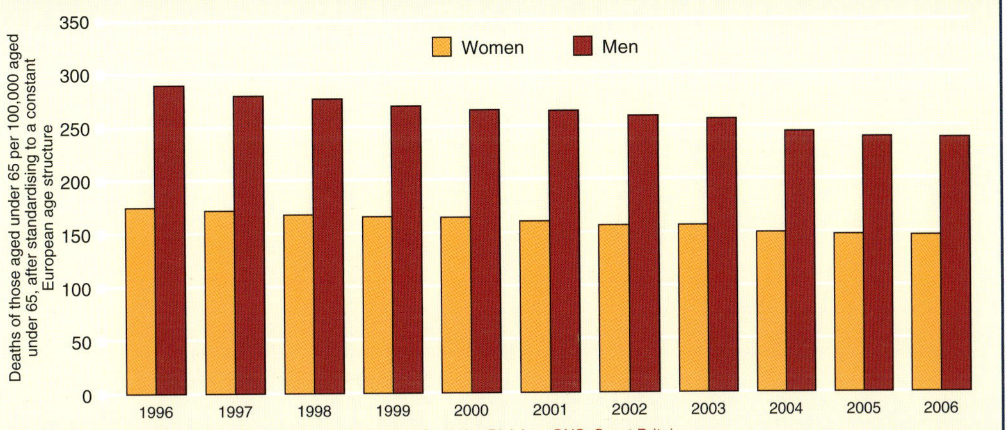

Source: General Register Office for Scotland and Mortality Statistics Division, ONS; Great Britain

42B: Death rates from heart disease and lung cancer – the two biggest causes of premature death – for people aged 35 to 64 are around twice as high among those from manual backgrounds as from non-manual backgrounds.

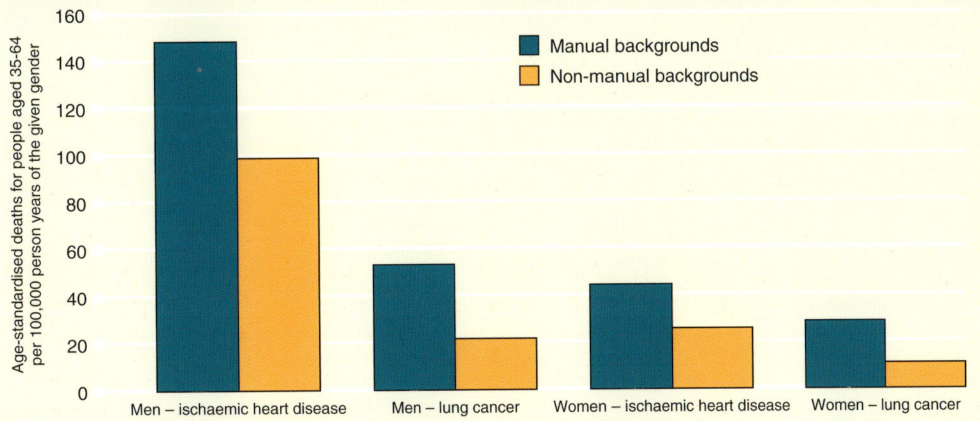

Source: Health Statistics Quarterly 20, ONS; the data is the average for 1997 to 1999; England & Wales

The first graph shows the number of deaths of people aged under 65 per 100,000 population aged under 65, with the data shown separately for males and females. The data source is the General Register Office (Scotland) and Mortality Statistics Division, ONS (England and Wales). The data relates to Great Britain and all data has been standardised to a constant European age structure.

The second graph compares death rates among those aged 35 to 64 by social class and gender for the two biggest causes of premature death, namely ischaemic heart disease and lung cancer. The data source is Health Statistics Quarterly 20 (Winter 2003) published by ONS. The data is the average for the years 1997 to 1999 and covers England and Wales. The data is the latest publicly available and the age group is the only one for which published data is available. Each death is coded using the Ninth Revision of the International Classification of Diseases and Related Health Problems (ICD-9). The data for ischaemic heart disease is ICD-9 codes 410 to 414 and that for lung cancers is ICD-9 code 162.

Overall adequacy of the indicator: high. The underlying data are deaths organised according to the local authority area of residence of the deceased by the ONS in England and Wales and by the Registrar General for Scotland.

Chapter 6 **Housing and exclusion**

Lacking adequate housing

The four indicators in this section relate to different aspects of the links between poverty and housing. These links run both ways. High housing costs, especially when mortgage costs and rents are rising, can tip some households over the edge into poverty. But at least as important are the various ways that poverty impacts upon housing, in extremis leading to homelessness but more widely limiting access and restricting choice, undermining sustainability and obliging people to put up with poor housing conditions.

43 Unmet housing need

(The number of households with an unmet housing need)

The first graph provides a measure of the number of households in need of new, subsidised housing, broken down according to their existing housing tenure and the reason why they need new housing. The supporting graph focuses on overcrowding, showing the number of adults in accommodation that is officially classified as overcrowded broken down according to whether they are the owner/tenant (or their spouse) or not, and whether they are living with dependent children.

Key points:

- According to estimates prepared by the housing charity Shelter, there are around one million households in England currently needing new, subsidised housing.
- Just under half of this one million households currently have no self-contained accommodation, including those who are homeless, living in temporary accommodation or sharing with others. A further one third of a million are currently living in social housing but either in overcrowded accommodation or with children in flats above the ground floor.
- Official estimates show that there are 1.4 million adults living in overcrowded conditions in England. Of these, around 500,000 are neither the owner/tenant nor their spouse and are in effect therefore living in someone else's home (usually their parents'). Of this 500,000, 300,000 are aged under 25 and 200,000 aged 25 or over.

The key points above are concerned with the backlog of unmet need. In addition, because of demographic change, the number of households requiring subsidised housing is increasing by around 48,000 per year in England.[14] But the amount of new housing built or acquired to meet this need has been well below this level in each of the last nine years.[15]

44 Newly homeless

(The number of households newly recognised as homeless)

This indicator refers to the number of households in England newly recognised by their local authority as unintentionally homeless. It is important to note that this is not a measure of the number of households at any one time who are homeless since it does not include those recognised as homeless in previous years but still homeless. Furthermore, not everyone who is homeless applies to their local authority to be classified as such, particularly those who would not qualify for accommodation even if so classified.

The first graph shows the number of households officially recognised as newly homeless in each year over the last decade. Households with and without dependent children are shown separately. For those judged to be 'in priority need', the supporting graph provides a breakdown of the immediate reasons why they became homeless.

Key points:

- The number of households newly recognised as homeless in England has fallen sharply in recent years, down from 200,000 in 2004 to just over 100,000 in 2006. This latter level is also now substantially below the level in the late 1990s, when it was running at around 150,000 a year.
- In 2006, the majority (three-fifths) of the newly homeless households did not contain dependent children. This proportion has remained fairly steady throughout the previous decade despite the large variation in the total number recognised as homeless.
- For those judged to be 'in priority need', the most common reason given as the immediate cause of homelessness is loss of accommodation with family or friends (two-fifths), with a further fifth each being due to relationship breakdown or loss of tenancy. Mortgage and rent arrears account for just one in twenty.

45 In temporary accommodation

(The number of homeless households in temporary accommodation)

The number of homeless households placed in temporary accommodation can be seen as a measure of the capacity of local authorities to meet the needs of those homeless households whom they have a duty to accommodate. The first graph shows the number of homeless households in temporary accommodation at the end of the March each year since 1997. The supporting graph looks at those who left temporary accommodation in 2006, breaking them down according to how long they spent there, from less than six months to two years or more.

Key points:

- 100,000 homeless households were in temporary accommodation in Great Britain in March 2007. This is about 10,000 fewer than in 2005 (the peak year) but still double the number of a decade ago.
- In 2006, just over half of those leaving temporary accommodation had been there for six months or less. Around one quarter, however, had been there for one year or more while one in seven had been there for two years or more. It is a moot point whether stays of such a long duration can properly be described as 'temporary', or indeed whether 'temporary accommodation' is appropriate for such long stays.

46 In mortgage arrears

(The number of mortgage holders in serious arrears or facing repossession)

This indicator looks at owner occupiers with a mortgage who are either in difficulty with that mortgage or whose economic circumstances make it more likely that they could get into difficulty.

The first graph shows the number of UK mortgage holders, year by year since 1990, who are either more than twelve months in arrears with their mortgage payments or who have been served with a court order for repossession. The supporting graph looks at the economic circumstances of households with mortgages where the head of the household is not in full-time employment.

Key points:

- In 2006, around 14,000 mortgage holders were in arrears by twelve months or more. Although slightly higher than two years earlier, this number is still lower than it was even at the start of this decade – and just a tenth what it was in the early 1990s.
- In 2006, around 47,000 court orders were served for repossession, some three times the number in 2003. The number of orders is now back to what it was in the early 1990s.
- In 2005/06, one in seven heads of household with a mortgage was not in full-time employment. Though little different from the late 1990s, this is nearly three times as high as at the start of the 1980s, when all but 5 per cent of heads of households with a mortgage were in full-time employment.

Selected relevant research

Affordability, notably the perceived lack of affordable housing, is often seen as one of the key problems relating to housing in this country. New Policy Institute work in this area (Palmer *et al*, 2006) shows that:

- In large part because of falling interest rates, annual mortgage costs for first-time buyers have risen much less than house prices over the last five years. Nevertheless, they have still risen sharply and, compared to earnings, had by 2005 reached levels previously only recorded in 1990.
- Housing costs comprise one quarter of net household income for households in the poorest fifth of the population, compared to 15 per cent on average and 10 per cent for the richest fifth.
- For those in the poorest fifth who are owner-occupiers with a mortgage, housing costs represent around a third of their net household income.

Unmet housing need

43A: There are estimated to be around a million households currently needing new subsidised housing.

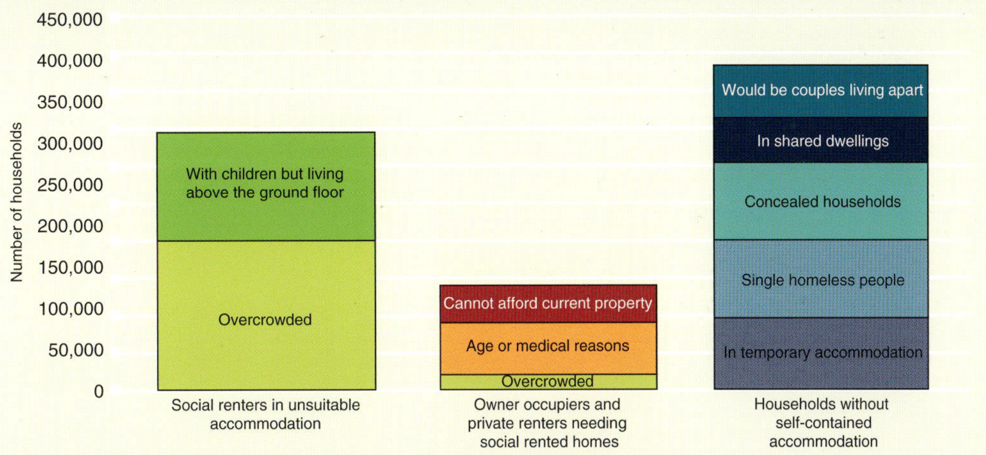

Source: A Shelter report entitled *Building for the future: 2005 update*; England; updated July 2007

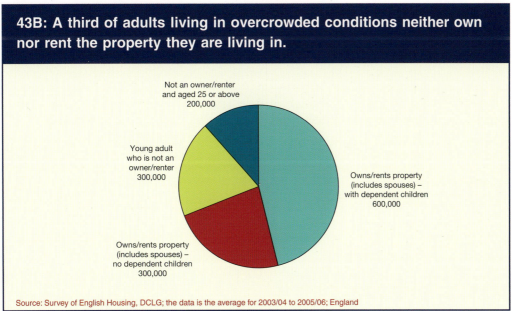

43B: A third of adults living in overcrowded conditions neither own nor rent the property they are living in.

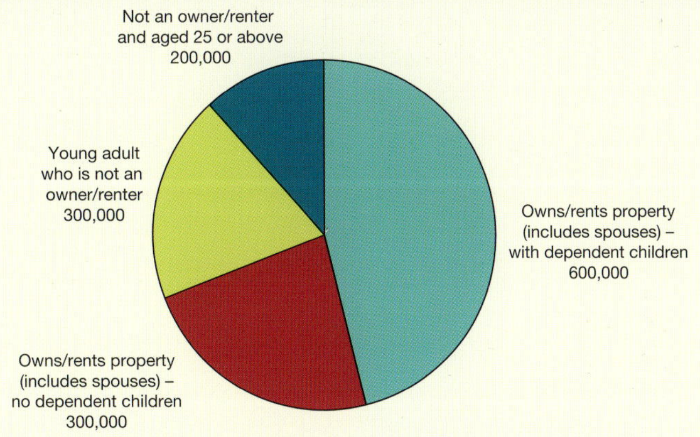

Source: Survey of English Housing, DCLG; the data is the average for 2003/04 to 2005/06; England

The first graph shows Shelter's latest estimates of the number of households who require new 'sub-market housing', with the data broken down into the categories used in the 2004 Barker report, *Review of housing supply*, sponsored by HM Treasury. 'Sub-market housing' is a phrase used by Barker to describe housing which, for cost reasons, has to be provided by the social sector, either via social rented accommodation or low-cost home ownership. The data is from table 4 of Shelter's 2005 report entitled *Building for the future: 2005 update*.

The second graph provides a breakdown of adults who are living in overcrowded conditions by age, presence or otherwise of children and owner/renter status. Overcrowding is defined in the 'bedroom standard', a measure of occupation density calculated in relation to the number of bedrooms and the number of household members and their relationship to each other. The various owner/renter statuses are owner of the property, renter of the property, spouse of the owner or renter, and neither owner/renter nor spouse. This division has been chosen as those who are not owners/renters or spouses do not have an obvious 'licence to occupy' the property and thus could potentially be considered to be homeless. The age separation between those aged 16-24 and 25+ has been chosen because, while those aged 24 and below are often still in the transition from dependent to independent living, the vast majority of those aged 25 and over have reached a more settled living arrangement. The data source is the Survey of English Housing and relates to England.

Overall adequacy of the indicator: medium. The Shelter estimate involves a range of assumptions being made about who requires new housing.

Indicator 44

Newly homeless

44A: The number of newly homeless households has fallen sharply since 2004 but is still around 100,000 households a year.

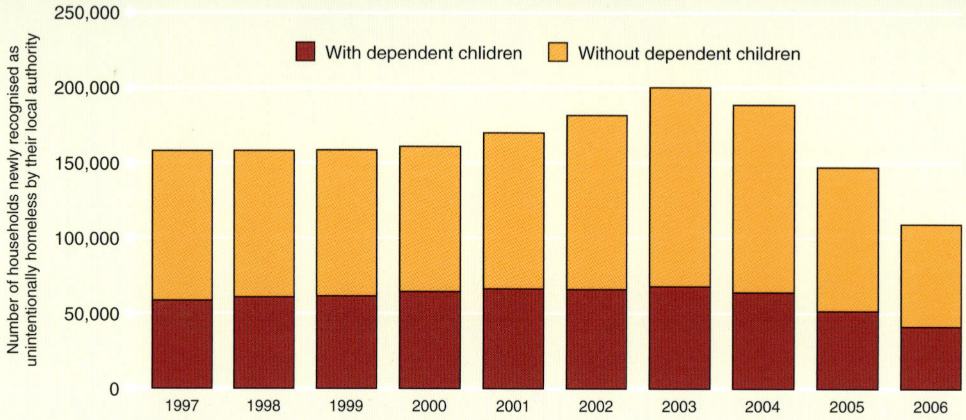

Source: Statutory Homelessness England, Statistical Releases, DCLG

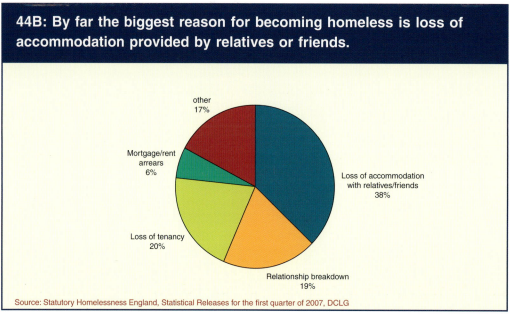

44B: By far the biggest reason for becoming homeless is loss of accommodation provided by relatives or friends.

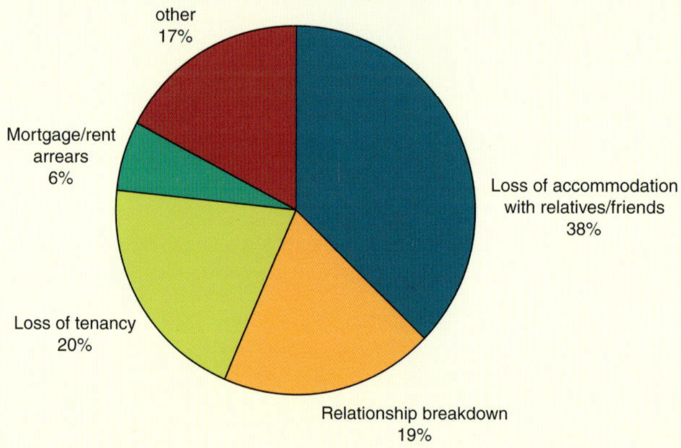

Source: Statutory Homelessness England, Statistical Releases for the first quarter of 2007, DCLG

The first graph shows the number of households in England who were newly recognised as homeless by their local authority in each of the stated years, with the data split between those with and without dependent children. It includes both those 'in priority need' and those 'not in priority need' but excludes those deemed to be intentionally homeless (a relatively small number) as division by family type is not available for this group. In line with Department of Communities and Local Government (DCLG) guidance, the numbers with children are assumed to be the same as the numbers who are in priority need because they have children. Scotland, Wales and Northern Ireland are not included in this graph because the legislative environment is different.

The second graph provides, for the first quarter of 2007, a breakdown of the households that were newly recognised by local authorities in England as being both homeless and 'in priority need' (no equivalent statistics are kept for those 'not in priority need') according to the reason why the household became homeless.

The data source for both graphs is the DCLG Statutory Homelessness England, Statistical Releases.

Overall adequacy of the indicator: medium. While there is no reason to believe there is any problem with the underlying data, the extent to which it leaves 'homelessness' dependent on administrative judgement is not satisfactory. In particular, the figures may not include many single people who are effectively homeless, as local authorities have no general duty to house such people and therefore many may not apply.

In temporary accommodation

45A: The number of homeless households placed in temporary accommodation has doubled over the last decade.

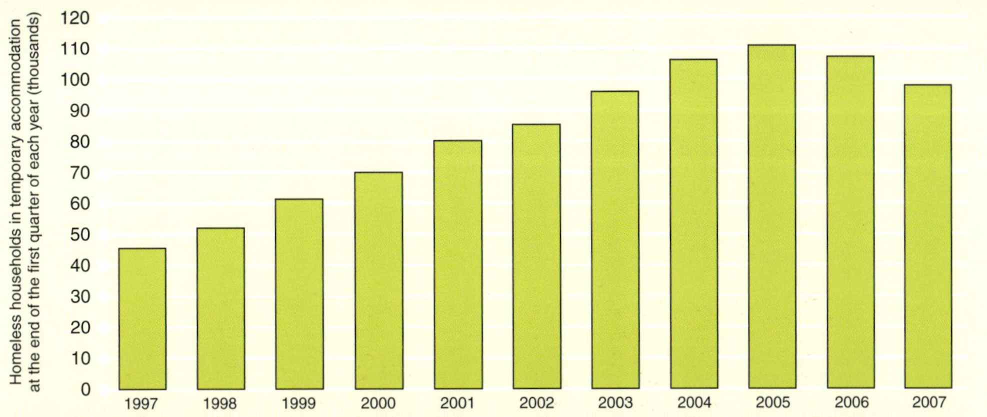

Source: Homelessness Bulletins, DCLG; Statistical Bulletin Housing Series, Scottish Executive; Welsh Office Housing Statistics; Great Britain

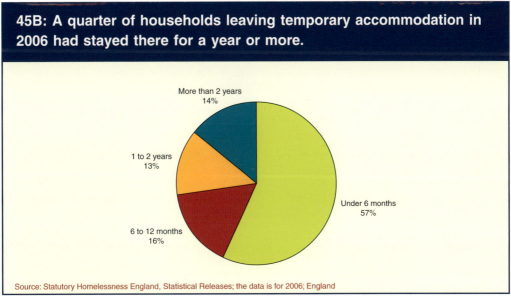

45B: A quarter of households leaving temporary accommodation in 2006 had stayed there for a year or more.

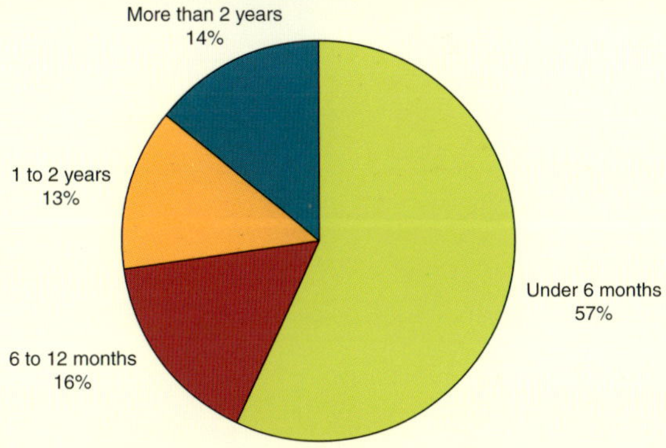

Source: Statutory Homelessness England, Statistical Releases; the data is for 2006; England

The first graph shows the number of homeless households who were in temporary (as opposed to permanent) accommodation arranged by their local authority, measured at the end of the first quarter of each year. The data is for Great Britain. 'Temporary accommodation' includes bed and breakfast, hostel accommodation, private renting and other. Households who are 'homeless at home' are excluded from the analysis as this data is not available for Scotland. The data source is the Department of Communities and Local Government (DCLG) Statutory Homelessness England, Statistical Releases, Scottish Executive Housing Statistics and Welsh Office Housing Statistics.

The second graph provides a breakdown of those households leaving temporary accommodation in 2006 by the length of time they had spent there. Note that equivalent data for earlier years is not directly comparable as it relates to households leaving temporary accommodation under the provisions of the 1996 Housing Act rather than all households leaving temporary accommodation. The data source is DCLG Statutory Homelessness England, Statistical Releases and the data relates to England only.

Overall adequacy of the indicator: high. The data is a complete count.

Indicator 46

In mortgage arrears

46A: While the number of mortgage holders in serious arrears remains very low, court orders for repossession are rising sharply and are now back to the levels of the early 1990s.

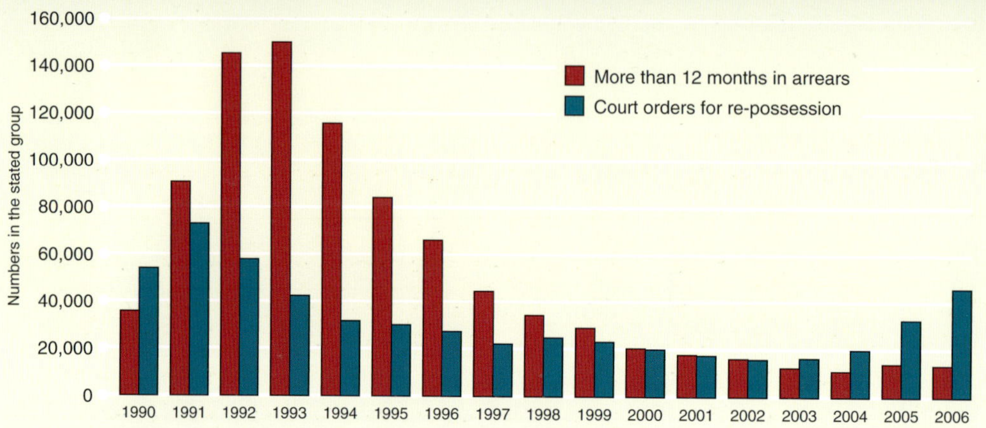

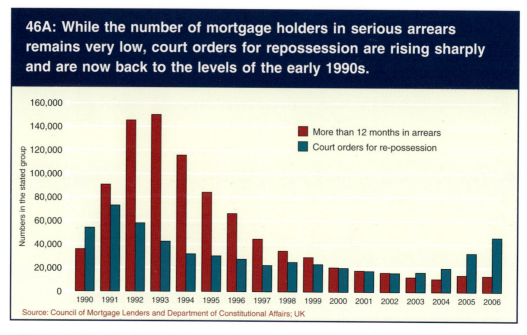

Source: Council of Mortgage Lenders and Department of Constitutional Affairs; UK

46B: One in seven working-age heads of households with a mortgage is in an economically vulnerable position – in part-time work, unemployed or economically inactive.

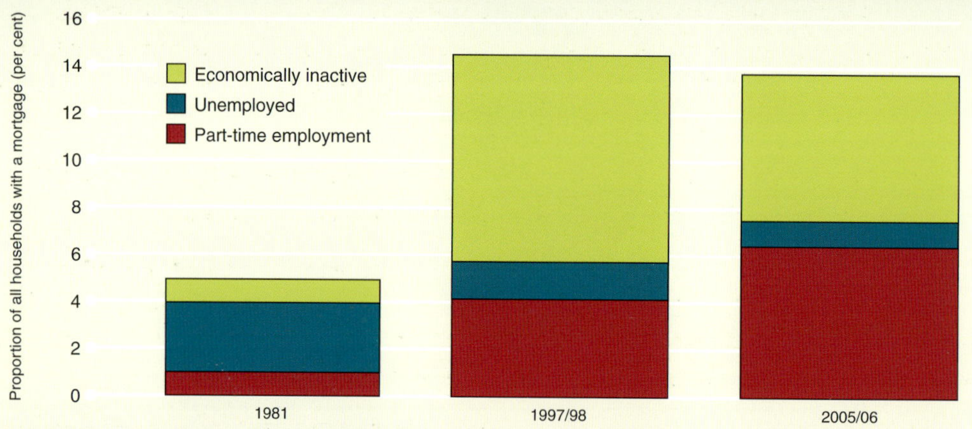

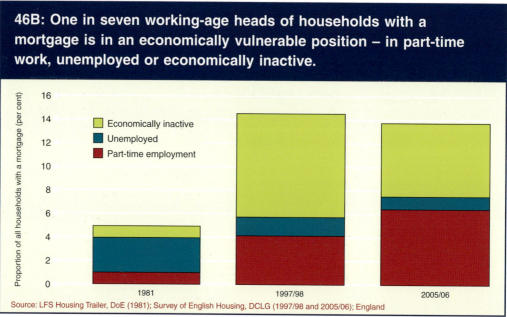

Source: LFS Housing Trailer, DoE (1981); Survey of English Housing, DCLG (1997/98 and 2005/06); England

The first graph shows both the number of residential mortgage holders who were a year or more in arrears with their mortgage repayments at the end of each of the years shown and the number of court orders made for mortgage repossession during each year. Note the number of orders excludes suspended orders, as these do not directly relate to repossessions. The data source for mortgage arrears is the Council of Mortgage Lenders (CML) and relates to the United Kingdom. The figures are based on a sample which typically averages 85 per cent of the total mortgage market in any given year. The data source for court orders is the UK Housing Review table 53, which in turn obtained its data from the Department for Constitutional Affairs (DCA), and the data relates to England and Wales.

The second graph shows the proportion of households with mortgages where the head of the household has the economic status shown. The data is from the Survey of English Housing and relates to England only.

Overall adequacy of the indicator: high. The data for both arrears and court orders is produced regularly and is considered to be reliable.

Access and exclusion

Whether it is the direct result of the policies and practices of institutions, or simply the result of a lack of resources, lacking access to those services that it is normal for most people to have is an important part of the experience of poverty and social exclusion. This theme presents four indicators on this subject, two relating to mobility and two relating to essential financial services. Differences between men and women are an aspect of the first pair, though not the second.

47 Access to services with and without a car

(The proportion of households finding access to essential local services difficult by with/without a car)

This indicator focuses on the ease with which people can access various key local services, pairing that with information on the groups within the population most likely to lack a car. The first graph shows the proportion of households who report that they find it difficult to access shops, supermarkets, post offices, doctors and hospitals, with results shown separately for households with and without cars. The supporting graph shows the proportion of men and women who either live in a household without a car, or live in one where there is a car but where they themselves do not have a full driving licence.

Key points:

- For all essential local services, households without a car are more likely to report difficulties accessing the service than households with a car. More specifically, around 5 per cent of those with cars report difficulties accessing corner shops, supermarkets, post offices and doctors compared with around 20 per cent for those without a car. Access to hospitals is much more difficult for both groups, with 20 per cent of those with a car and 40 per cent of those without a car reporting difficulties.
- In 2006, 20 per cent of women and 15 per cent of men lived in households that did not have a car. Thirty years ago, both these proportions were about twice as high.
- While the gap between men and women in terms of household car ownership is only 5 per cent, the gap in terms of who can drive the car is much larger, with 25 per cent of men but 40 per cent of women either lacking a car in their household or not having a driving licence. These proportions have both halved over the last 30 years.
- Looking at car ownership by family type, couples are much more likely than singles to have a car. So whereas only 10 per cent of working-age couples and 20 per cent of pensioner couples lack a car, 40 per cent of working-age singles (both with and without dependent children) and 65 per cent of single pensioners lack a car.[16]

48 Anxiety

(The proportion of men and women aged 60+ who feel very unsafe outside at night)

This indicator touches on an important aspect of exclusion, namely, the extent to which people feel unsafe when outside their home. The two graphs are closely related. The first shows the proportions of both men and women aged 60 and over who report feeling very unsafe walking alone at night, the figures being for each year of the last decade. The second shows the differences by both gender and income.

Key points:

- In 2005/06, 25 per cent of women aged 60 and over reported feeling very unsafe walking alone at night. This is about four times the figure for men.
- Although there is a degree of uncertainty about the precise year-by-year numbers, the proportions of both men and women aged 60 and over feeling very unsafe walking at night have been lower in both of the last two years than they had been in earlier years (for example 35 per cent of women and 10 per cent of men reported feeling very unsafe at night in 2001/02).
- The proportion feeling very unsafe at night varies noticeably according to their level of income. So, for example, more than 30 per cent of women aged 60 and over with a household income of less than £10,000 a year report feeling very unsafe walking alone at night compared with 20 per cent of other women. The comparable figures for men are 10 per cent and 5 per cent respectively. It is noteworthy that gender is more important than income here (that is, the proportion of men in low income households feeling unsafe at night is smaller than the proportion of women in non-low income households).

49 Without a bank account

(The proportion of households without a bank account)

This indicator is the first of two which addresses a subject of renewed government interest, namely financial exclusion. Its subject is households which lack a bank account and the recent government interest in the subject is reflected by their agreement with the banks in 2004 for targets to reduce the numbers lacking a bank account.[17]

The first graph shows the proportion of households who lack any kind of bank or building society account. The figures here are shown for each year over the past decade, separately for those in the poorest fifth of the population and those with average incomes. Of those who do have an account, some just have basic bank accounts while others just have Post Office Card Accounts (POCA). These accounts, only introduced in 2003, have proved popular (with nearly five million such accounts in existence in April 2006). But as they do not have all the features of a bank account, people who only have a POCA are not regarded by the Treasury as being fully 'financially included'. The second graph shows, for 2005/06 (the first year for which separate data is available), the proportions with no account, a POCA only, and a basic bank account only, with the data shown separately for each level of household income.

Key points:

- In recent years, the proportion of households without a bank account has come down sharply, to just 6 per cent for households in the poorest fifth in 2005/06 and 3 per cent for households with average incomes.
- The fall has been especially sharp for households in the poorest fifth, where the proportion without such an account a decade ago was between 20 per cent and 25 per cent. Much of this fall has been in the last few years, a halving in fact, from 16 per cent in 2003/04.

- The fall in the proportion of low income households without a bank account has largely coincided with the introduction of two new types of account, namely basic bank accounts and especially POCA. If the latter are not counted as a proper account because of their limited functionality, the proportion of low income households without an account in 2005/06 rises from 6 per cent to 11 per cent.
- Half of all households with a POCA only are in the poorest fifth of households, with most of the remainder in the second poorest fifth. Although some 2 per cent of households with above-average incomes have no account whatsoever, almost none have a POCA only.
- The statistics above are for households rather than individuals. Looking at individuals, around 5 per cent of adults did not have a bank account, with the proportion being similar for both men and women.[18]

50 Without home contents insurance

(The proportion of households without home contents insurance)

The last indicator deals with the subject of home contents insurance. As long ago as 1999, home contents insurance was identified alongside bank accounts as a key aspect of financial exclusion by the government's Policy Action Team 14 report *Access to financial services*.[19] In the wake of the 2007 floods and the damage they caused, home contents insurance – or rather the lack of it – has ceased to be just a matter of academic or policy interest.

The first graph shows the proportion of households without home contents insurance, with the results shown separately for each fifth of the income distribution. These proportions are shown both for 2005/06 and for ten years earlier, 1995/96. The second graph shows the connection between having such insurance or not, and the likelihood of being burgled. More precisely, for each year since 1999, the graph shows the proportions of households suffering a burglary in the previous year according to whether or not they have home contents insurance.

Key points:

- 50 per cent of households in the poorest fifth of the population lacked home contents insurance in 2005/06, more than twice the level for households with average incomes and five times the level for households in the top fifth of the income distribution.
- The fact that 10 per cent of the richest lack home contents insurance shows that not everyone regards home contents insurance as essential (by comparison, the proportion in the top fifth without bank accounts is negligible). However, the gap between the poorest fifth and the average is both large and has changed little since at least the mid-1990s.
- This lack of progress in reducing the gap on home contents insurance contrasts unfavourably with the progress that has been made with bank accounts, particularly since the first government-inspired study into this question, namely the 1999 *Access to financial services* report, called for the gaps between income groups in insurance as well as banking and insurance to be eliminated by 2005.
- In 2005/06, 7 per cent of households without home contents insurance suffered a burglary, compared with just 2 per cent for those with such insurance. While the underlying crime statistics show that the likelihood of burglary has fallen for both households with and without home contents insurance, this unfavourable 4:1 ratio has remained broadly constant.

Selected relevant research

Single parents and single pensioners are the most likely to be without access to a car. Given that both groups are mainly female, the importance of public transport to women is clear.

- A study for the Department for Transport (Hamilton, Hoyle and Jenkins, 2002) found that women are the majority of public transport users but that routes and services are not designed with them in mind. In particular, women are more likely to be travelling with young children and travelling along routes other than those going into the centres of towns. Common route design, while good for commuters, meets women's needs much less well.
- Green (2007) looked at the experiences of people in poverty in Scotland. Some of the findings centred around access to public services, and the importance of public transport in this. In particular, disabled people often found it hard to rely on public transport as disabled provision on buses was so limited.

Financial exclusion, and how it varies across different groups, has been a common theme of some recent research:

- Nandy (2005) carried out research for Centrepoint into debt among young homeless people, finding that lack of access to affordable credit and resulting reliance on more expensive forms of credit was one of the main reasons they got into debt. This can in turn lead to a poor credit rating, meaning a young homeless person cannot move into their own home and is stuck in the hostel system.
- A report by Help the Aged (2007) found that older people were often excluded from financial services such as mortgages, internet banking and premium bank accounts.
- People living in rural areas have more restricted access to financial services. The State of the Countryside report (Commission for Rural Communities, 2007) reported that around one in eight banks and building societies are in rural areas, though these areas contain one fifth of the population. Under one tenth of all cashpoints are in rural areas; furthermore, fewer of these are free to use – around 45 per cent compared with 60 per cent in urban areas.

Access to services with and without a car

47A: The proportion of households who find it difficult to access essential local services is much higher for those without a car than for those with a car.

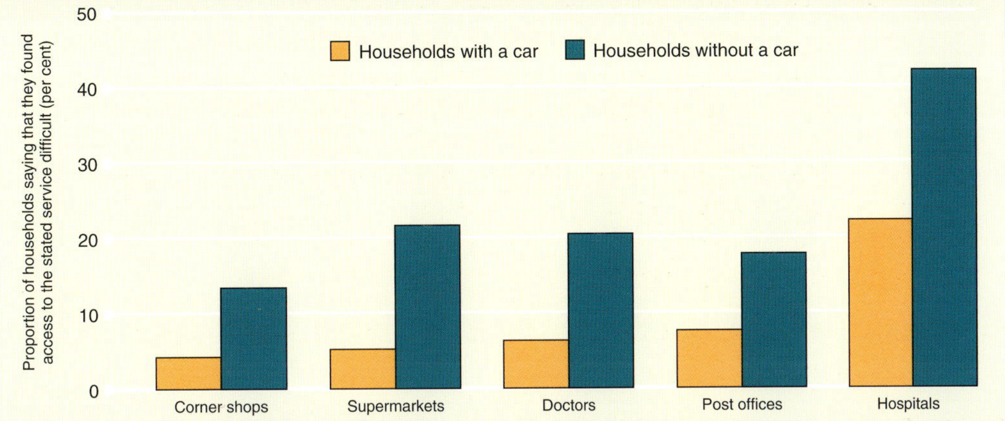

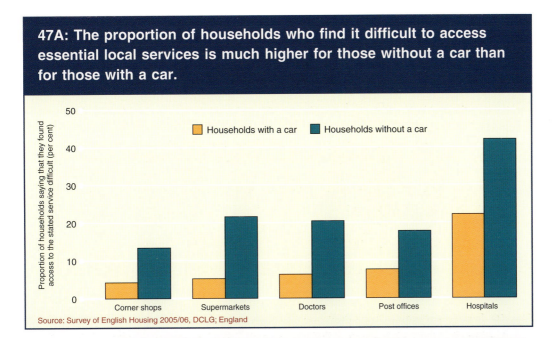

Source: Survey of English Housing 2005/06, DCLG; England

47B: Although the proportion is coming down, two-fifths of women still do not drive. This compares with a quarter of men.

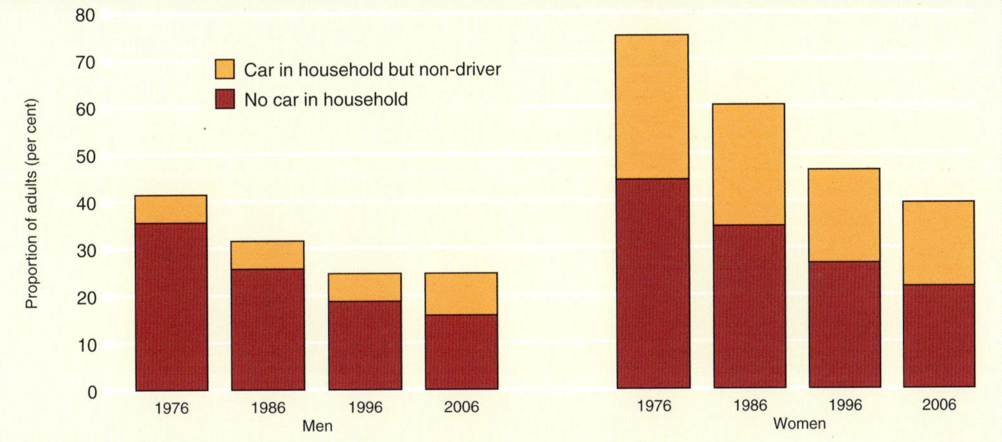

Source: 2006 National Travel Survey, DfT; Great Britain

The first graph shows the proportion of households who say that they find it difficult to access a selection of essential local services, with the data shown separately for households with and without a car. The data source is the Survey of English Housing and the data is for England only.

The second graph shows, by gender, the proportion of adults who do not have access to a car, with the data divided between households without a car and adults who do have a car in their household but do not themselves have a full driving licence. The data source is the National Travel Survey and the data relates to Great Britain.

Overall adequacy of the indicator: limited. The National Travel Survey and Survey of English Housing are both well-established annual government surveys, designed to be nationally representative, but it is not at all clear that the data fully captures the problems of transport in relation to poverty and social exclusion, particularly given the absence of any good data on the adequacy of public transport as an alternative to car ownership.

Indicator 48

Anxiety

48A: Among those aged 60 or over, women are around four times as likely as men to feel very unsafe out at night.

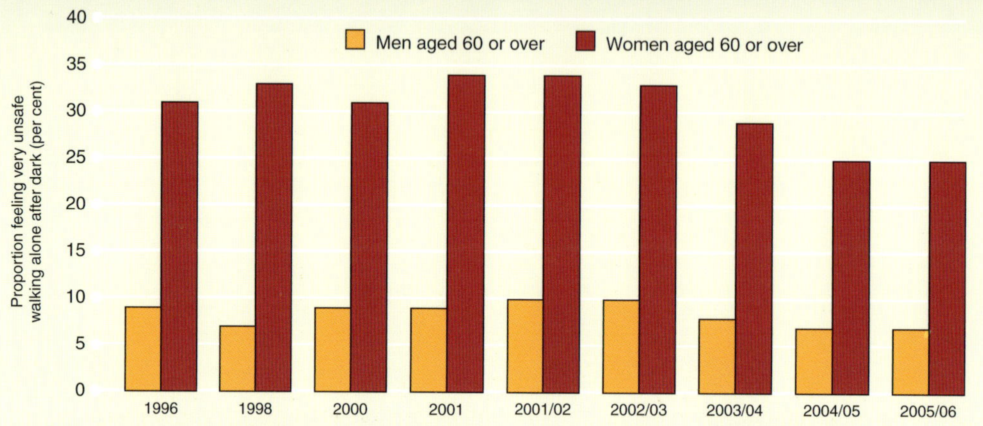

Source: British Crime Survey, Home Office; England and Wales

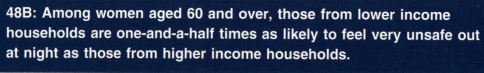

48B: Among women aged 60 and over, those from lower income households are one-and-a-half times as likely to feel very unsafe out at night as those from higher income households.

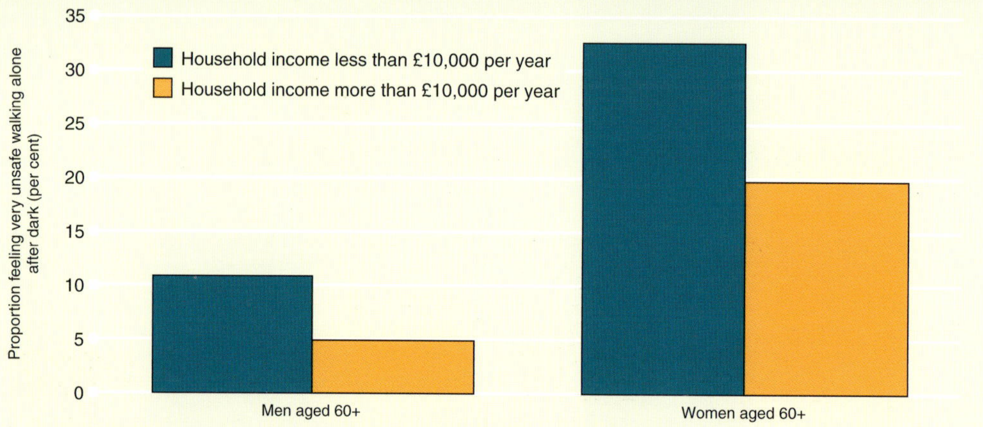

Source: British Crime Survey, Home Office; the data is the average for 2003/04 to 2005/06; England and Wales

The first graph shows the proportion of people aged 60 or over who say that they feel very unsafe walking alone in their area after dark, with the data shown separately for men and women.

The second graph shows, for the latest year, a breakdown of the statistics according to whether the people lived in households with an annual income of more or less than £10,000.

The data source for both graphs is the British Crime Survey (BCS) and the data relates to England and Wales. Note that there is no BCS survey data for either 1997 or 1999.

Overall adequacy of the indicator: medium. The BCS is a well-established annual government survey and the fact that the proportions feeling very unsafe have changed little over successive surveys suggests a degree of robustness to this result. However, it is unclear to what extent these feelings reflect anxiety more generally or simply with respect to walking at night.

Without a bank account

49A: The proportion of low income households with no bank or building society account has fallen sharply in recent years.

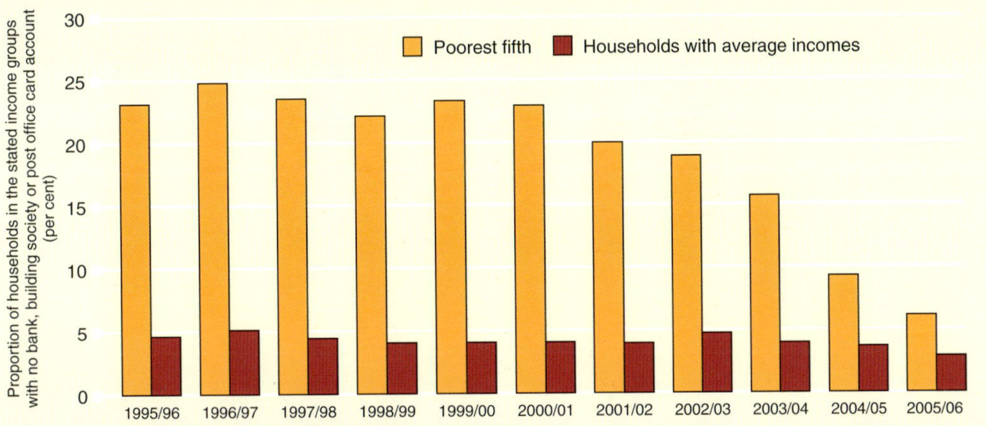

Source: Family Resources Survey, DWP; Great Britain

49B: While only one in 20 of the poorest fifth of households now have no account, this rises to one in 10 if Post Office Card Accounts are not considered to be accounts.

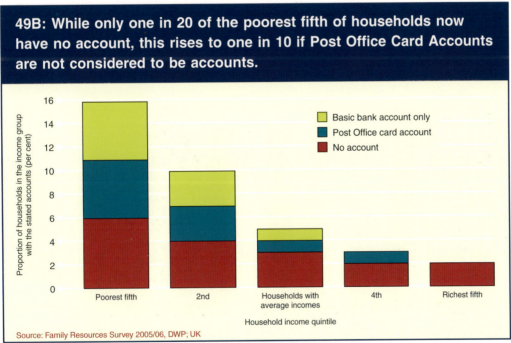

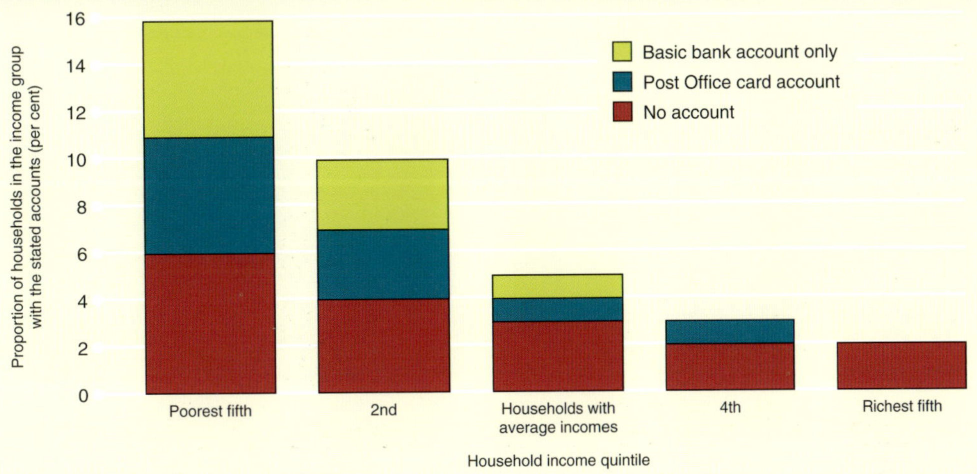

Source: Family Resources Survey 2005/06, DWP; UK

The first graph shows the proportion of households without a bank, building society or any other kind of account. The data is split to show households in the poorest fifth of the income distribution and for households on average incomes (middle fifth of the income distribution) separately. Income is household disposable income, equivalised to take account of household composition and is measured after deducting housing costs. The data source is the Family Resources Survey (FRS) and the data relates to Great Britain. As well as bank and building society accounts, the figures also count any savings or investment accounts as well as post office card accounts but do not include stocks and shares, premium bonds, gilts, Save As You Earn arrangements or Credit Unions.

The recent fall shown in the first graph has largely coincided with the introduction of two new types of account, namely basic bank accounts and post office card accounts. Some people argue that these new types of account, particularly the post office card account, should not be considered to be true accounts as they have only limited functionality. In this context, the second graph shows, for the latest year and for differing levels of household income, the proportion of households with only a basic bank account or a post office card account. Note that such an analysis was not possible for years prior to 2005/06. Also note that the small number of households with both a basic bank account and a post office card account but no other accounts are included in the 'basic bank account only' category.

Overall adequacy of the indicator: medium. FRS is probably the most representative of the surveys that gather information on the extent to which people have bank and other types of account but the inclusion in recent years of people with post office card accounts only is arguably distorting the trends over time.

Indicator 50

Without home contents insurance

50A: Half of the poorest households do not have home contents insurance, the same as a decade ago.

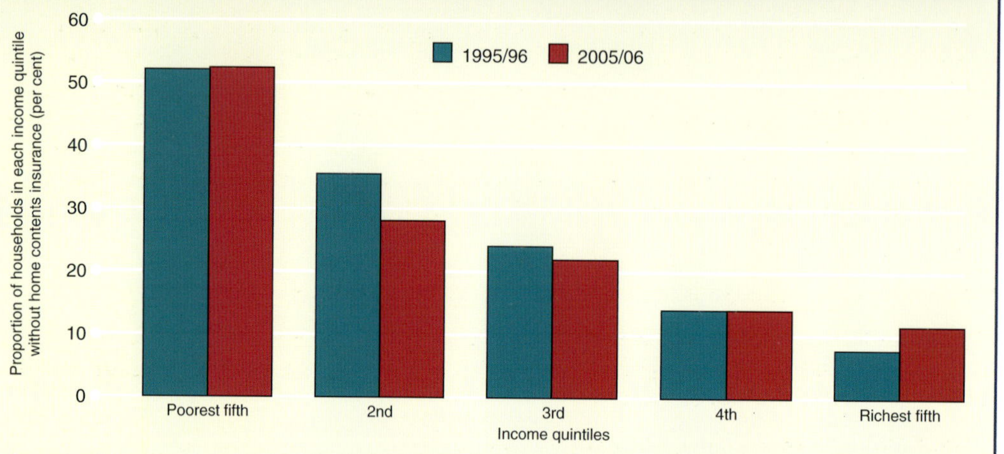

Source: The Family Expenditure Survey (1995/96) and The Expenditure and Food Survey (2005/06), ONS; UK

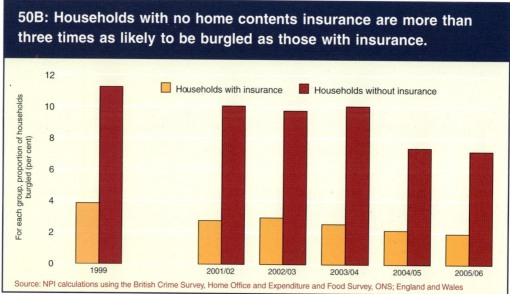

50B: Households with no home contents insurance are more than three times as likely to be burgled as those with insurance.

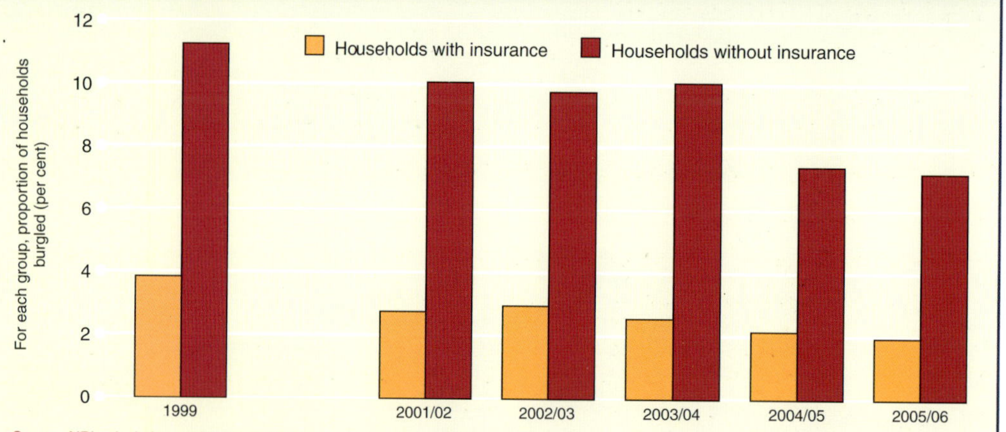

Source: NPI calculations using the British Crime Survey, Home Office and Expenditure and Food Survey, ONS; England and Wales

The first graph shows, for the latest year, how the proportion of households without home contents insurance varies according to the household's income. The division into income quintiles is based on gross, equivalised income. The data source is the Expenditure and Food Survey (EFS) and relates to the United Kingdom. For comparison purposes, the equivalent data from the Family Expenditure Survey for a decade earlier is also presented, although survey limitations mean that the division into income quintiles here is based on unequivalised and unweighted income.

The second graph shows the proportion of households with, and without, home contents insurance that were victims of a burglary one or more times in each of the years shown. The rates have been estimated using data on burglaries from the British Crime Survey (BCS) and data on household insurance from EFS. The estimates are for England and Wales. Note that data for years earlier than 1999 has not been included in the graph as it was collected on a different basis (via a direct question in the BCS) and is therefore not directly comparable.

Overall adequacy of the indicator: medium. The BCS and EFS are well-established government surveys, which are designed to be nationally representative.

Notes

[1] Data on income poverty in Northern Ireland has only been available for the last four years and was not included in the income poverty analysis in earlier reports, which strictly speaking were therefore for Great Britain. By contrast, all the income poverty analysis in this report is for the whole of the UK.

[2] The technically correct term for 'family', as defined here, is 'benefit unit'.

[3] This process is known as 'equivalisation'. In line with a recent government decision to adopt OECD methods for the adjustment, all household income figures in this report have been equivalised using the OECD equivalisation factors rather than the McClements factors which were used in previous reports. For income before deducting housing costs, these factors are 0.67 for the first adult, 0.33 for each subsequent adult and for each child aged 14 years or over, and 0.2 for each child aged under 14. For income after deducting housing costs, the factors are 0.58 for the first adult, 0.42 for each subsequent adult and for each child aged 14 years or over, and 0.2 for each child aged under 14.

[4] The Family Resource Survey.

[5] Although there is an indicator on this subject at www.poverty.org.uk/05/index.shtml.

[6] See www.poverty.org.uk/03d/index.shtml, noting that the statistics in this indicator are for income before, rather than after, deducting housing costs as this is the only income data available from the relevant data source (the British Household Panel Survey).

[7] Downloadable at www.poverty.org.uk/reports/ethnicity.pdf.

[8] Table 8.11 from *Households below average income: a statistical analysis 1979-1994/95*, Department of Social Security, 1997.

[9] See www.poverty.org.uk/28b/index.shtml.

[10] Third graph of www.poverty.org.uk/28/index.shtml.

[11] *Trade Union membership* 2006, DTI, 2007.

[12] UNICEF (2007) *Poverty in perspective: child well-being in rich countries.*

[13] Note that this 2% is not the same as the 3.5% discussed in indicator 29 because the former statistic relates to Year 11 pupils whereas the latter relates to pupils aged 15 at the start of the academic year.

[14] From *Review of housing supply*, Barker K.(2004) for HM Treasury.

[15] First graph of www.poverty.org.uk/49b/index.shtml.

[16] Fourth graph of www.poverty.org.uk/46/index.shtml.

[17] HM Treasury (2004) *Promoting financial inclusion.*

[18] Family Resources Survey 2005/06, using the same definition of bank account as in the graphs and excluding those who either refused to answer the question or where the answer was 'don't know'.

[19] HM Treasury 1999.

References

Barker (2004), *Review of housing supply*, HM Treasury, available at http://www.hm-treasury.gov.uk/consultations_and_legislation/barker/consult_barker_index.cfm

Barn R., Andrew L. and Mantovani N. (2005) *Life after care: the experiences of young people from different ethnic groups*, available at http://www.jrf.org.uk/bookshop/eBooks/1859351921.pdf

Bivand P. (2005) *Rising workless households threaten child poverty aim*, available at http://www.cesi.org.uk/statsdocs/0508/WB167-p17-18.pdf

Bradshaw J. and Mayhew E. (2005) *Mothers, babies and the risks of poverty*, available at http://www.cpag.org.uk/info/Povertyarticles/Poverty121/mothers-babies-poverty.pdf

Bradshaw J. (2006) *Teenage births*, available at http://www.jrf.org.uk/bookshop/eBooks/9781859355046.pdf

Bradshaw J., Finch N., Kemp P., Mayhew E. and Williams J. (2003) *Gender and poverty in the UK*

Bradshaw J., Finch N., Mayhew E., Ritakallio V.M. and Skinner C. (2006) *Child poverty in large families*, available at http://www.jrf.org.uk/bookshop/eBooks/9781861348777.pdf

Commission for Rural Communities (2007) *State of the countryside 2007*, available at http://www.ruralcommunities.gov.uk//projects/stateofthecountryside2007/overview

Disability Rights Commission (2006) *Equal treatment, closing the gap*, available at http://www.drc.org.uk/library/health_investigation.aspx

Edwards S. (2003) *In too deep, CAB clients' experience of debt*, available at http://www.citizensadvice.org.uk/in-too-deep.pdf

Evans S. (2007) *Disability, skills and work: raising our ambitions*, available at http://www.smf.co.uk/assets/files/publications/Disability,%20skills%20and%20work.pdf

Field F. and White P. (2007) *Welfare isn't working*, available at http://www.reform.co.uk/filestore/pdf/070511%20Welfare%20isn't%20Working%20-%20NDYP.pdf

Goode J., Callender C. and Lister R. (1998) *Purse or wallet? Gender inequalities and income distribution within families on benefits*, summary available at http://www.jrf.org.uk/knowledge/findings/socialpolicy/spr468.asp

Gordon D., Adelman L., Ashworth K., Bradshaw J., Levitas R., Middleton S., Pantazis C., Patsios D., Payne S., Townsend P. and Williams J. (2000) *Poverty and social exclusion in Britain*. York: Joseph Rowntree Foundation

Green M. (2007) *Voices of people experiencing poverty in Scotland: everyone matters?* http://www.jrf.org.uk/bookshop/eBooks/2020-experiencing-poverty-scotland.pdf

Grimshaw D. and Rubery G. (2007) *Undervaluing women's work*

Grinyer J. (2005) *Literacy, numeracy and the labour market: further analysis of the Skills for Life survey*. London: Department for Education and Skills

Hamilton K., Hoyle R. and Jenkins L. (2002) *The public transport gender audit*, available at http://www.uel.ac.uk/womenandtransport/gender.html

Help the Aged Policy, *Financial services, Help the Aged policy statement 2007*, available at http://policy.helptheaged.org.uk/NR/rdonlyres/ezuvtnkzzxhucmemwr57zz3kd4vrc3dxpa4hnurw22pccy6hmtktlecnwzp6l4v2v4n65uwzag6j7mjald2q4i22ldb/financialpolicystatement040607.pdf

Hirsch D. (2006) *What will it take to end child poverty? Firing on all cylinders*, available at http://www.jrf.org.uk/bookshop/details.asp?pubID=804

Holmans, Monk, Luanaigh and Whitehead (2005), *Building for the future: 2005 update*, Shelter, available from
http://england.shelter.org.uk/policy/policy-825.cfm/ct/1/sb/22/pg/1/plitem/190

Johnson G. and Semmence J. (2006) *Individual incomes of men and women, 1996/97-2004/05*, available at http://www.womenandequalityunit.gov.uk/indiv_incomes/report2006.pdf

Joshi H. and Paci P. (1998) *Unequal pay for women and men: evidence from British birth cohort studies*. Cambridge, MA: MIT Press

Kenway P. and Winkler V. (2006) *Dreaming of £250 a week: a scoping study into in work poverty in Wales*, available at
http://www.npi.org.uk/reports/in-work%20poverty%20in%20wales.pdf

Kingdon G. and Cassen R. (2007a) *Understanding low achievement in English schools*, available at http://sticerd.lse.ac.uk/dps/case/cp/CASEpaper118.pdf

Kingdon G. and Cassen R. (2007b) *Tackling low educational achievement*, available at http://www.jrf.org.uk/knowledge/findings/socialpolicy/2095.asp

Leitch Lord A. (2006) *Prosperity for all in the global economy: world class skills*, available at http://www.hm-treasury.gov.uk/media/6/4/leitch_finalreport051206.pdf

Machin S. and McNally S. (2006) *Education and child poverty: a literature review*, available at http://www.jrf.org.uk/bookshop/details.asp?pubID=797

MacInnes T. and Kenway P. (2007) *UK skills: step change or leap into the unknown?*, available at http://www.npi.org.uk/leitch%20070312.htm

Manning A. and Swaffield J. (2005) *The gender gap in early career wage growth*. CEP Discussion Paper No. 700. London: Centre for Economic Performance, London School of Economics. Available at: http://cep.lse.ac.uk/pubs/dp.asp?prog=CEPDP

Manning A. and Petrongolo B. (2005) *The part-time pay penalty*. Women and Equality Unit, Department for Trade and Industry, available at
http://www.womenandequalityunit.gov.uk/research/part_time_paypenalty.pdf

McKay S. (2007) *Saving lives: women's lifetime savings patterns*. London: Fawcett Society. Summary available at http://fawcett.wholething.co.uk/documents/Saving%20Lives.pdf

Middleton S., Ashworth K., Braithwaite I. (1997) *Small fortunes: spending on children, childhood poverty and parental sacrifice*. York: Joseph Rowntree Foundation.

Millar J. and Gardiner K. (2004) *Low pay, household resources and poverty*. Joseph Rowntree Foundation summary available at http://www.jrf.org.uk/knowledge/findings/socialpolicy/n64.asp

Nandy L. (2005) *Too much too young: problem debt among homeless young people*, available at http://www.centrepoint.org.uk/documents/Centrepoint_TooMuchTooYoung-report.pdf

Office of National Statistics (2007) *Work and worklessness among households*, available at http://www.statistics.gov.uk/pdfdir/work0807.pdf

Olsen W. and Walby S. (2004) *Modelling gender pay gaps*, available at http://www.eoc.org.uk/PDF/modelling_gender_pay_gaps_wp_17.pdf

Palmer G., Kenway P. and Wilcox S. (2006) *Housing and neighbourhoods monitor*, available at http://www.jrf.org.uk/bookshop/details.asp?pubID=825

Pantazis C. and Ruspini E. (2006) Gender, poverty and social exclusion. In: Pantazis C., Gordon D. and Levitas R. (eds) *Poverty and social exclusion in Britain. The Millennium Survey.* Bristol: Policy Press

Preston G. and Robinson M. (2006) *Out of reach: benefits for disabled children.* London: Child Poverty Action Group.

Purcell K. and Elias P. (2004) *Higher education and gendered career development – researching graduate careers seven years on*, available at: http://www2.warwick.ac.uk/fac/soc/ier/research/completed/7yrs2/rp4.pdf

Rennison J., Maguire S., Middleton S. and Ashworth K. (2005) *Young people not in education, employment or training: evidence from the Education Maintenance Allowance Database*, available at http://www.dfes.gov.uk/research/data/uploadfiles/RR628.pdf

Rigg J. (2005) *Labour market disadvantage among disabled people: a longitudinal perspective*, available at http://sticerd.lse.ac.uk/dps/case/cp/CASEpaper103.pdf

Salway S., Platt L., Chowbey P., Harriss K. and Bayliss E. (2007) *Long-term ill health, poverty and ethnicity*, available at http://www.jrf.org.uk/knowledge/findings/socialpolicy/2060.asp

Shaw J. (2007) *Eradicating child poverty*, available at http://www.ifs.org.uk/publications.php?publication_id=3869

Smith N., Middleton S., Ashton-Brooks K., Cox L. and Dobson B. with Reith L. (2004) *Disabled people's cost of living*, available at http://www.jrf.org.uk/bookshop/eBooks/1859352375.pdf

Social Exclusion Unit (2004) *Mental health and social exclusion*, available at http://archive.cabinetoffice.gov.uk/seu/page5717.html?id=257

TUC (2007) *Time to tackle the training divide*, available at http://www.tuc.org.uk/extras/trainingdivide.pdf

Walby S. and Olsen W. (2002) *The impact of women's position in the labour market on pay and the implications for UK productivity*, available at http://www.womenandequalityunit.gov.uk/publications/weu_pay_and_productivity.pdf

Wanless D., Appleby J., Harrison A. and Patel D. (2007) *Our future health secured?* Available at http://www.kingsfund.org.uk/publications/kings_fund_publications/our_future.html

Further reading

Bellamy K. and Cameron S. (2006) *Gender inequality in the 21st Century: modernising the legislation*, available at http://www.fawcett.wholething.co.uk/documents/low_res_final2.pdf

Blackaby D.H., Clark K., Leslie D.G., Murphy P.D. (1997) *The distribution of male and female earnings 1973-91: Evidence for Britain*, Oxford Economic Papers, New Series, Vol. 49, No. 2 (Apr. 1997), pp. 256-272

Blackaby D.H., Moore N.J., Murphy P.D., O'Leary N. (2001) *The gender pay gap in Wales*, Equal Opportunities Commission

Campbell D., Carruth A., Dickerson A. and Green F. (2007) *Job insecurity and wages*, Economic Journal, March

Department for Trade and Industry (2007) *Trade union membership 2006*, available at http://www.berr.gov.uk/files/file39006.pdf

Dorling D., Rigby J., Wheeler B., Ballas D., Thomas B., Fahmy E., Gordon D. and Lupton R. (2007) *Poverty, wealth and place in Britain 1968 to 2005*, available at http://www.jrf.org.uk/knowledge/findings/housing/2077.asp

Equal Opportunities Commission (2007) *The gender agenda*

Evans M. and Scarborough J. (2006) *Can current policy end child poverty in Britain by 2020?* Available at http://www.jrf.org.uk/knowledge/findings/socialpolicy/0376.asp

Fagan C., Urwin P. and Melling K. (2006) *Gender inequalities in the risks of poverty and social exclusion for disadvantaged groups in thirty European countries*, available at: http://ec.europa.eu/employment_social/emplweb/publications/publication_en.cfm?id=86

Forth J. and Millward N. (2000) *The determinants of pay levels and fringe benefit provision in Britain. NIESR Discussion Paper No. 171*. London: National Institute of Economic and Social Research.

Furlong A. and Cartmel F. (2005) *Early labour-market experiences of graduates from disadvantaged families*, available at http://www.jrf.org.uk/knowledge/findings/socialpolicy/0505.asp

Gould N. (2006) *Mental health and child poverty*, available at http://www.jrf.org.uk/bookshop/eBooks/9781859354919.pdf

Gregg P., Harkness S. and MacMillan L. (2006) *Welfare to work policies and child poverty: a review of issues relating to the labour market and economy*, available at http://www.jrf.org.uk/bookshop/eBooks/9781859355107.pdf

Joshi H. and Hinde P.R.A. (1993) *Employment after child-bearing in post war Britain: cohort study on evidence of contrasts within and across generations*, European Sociological Review 9 (3): 203-227

Katungi D., Neal E. and Barbour A. (2006) *People in low-paid informal work: 'need not greed'*, available at http://www.jrf.org.uk/bookshop/details.asp?pubID=793

Kenway P. (2007) *A snapshot of financial inclusion policy and practice in the UK 2007*, available at http://www.friendsprovident.co.uk/doclib/snapshot_report.pdf

Macran S., Joshi H. and Dex S. (1996) *Employment after childbearing: A survival analysis.* Work, Employment and Society, 10 (2): 273-296

Magadi S. and Middleton M. (2007) *Severe child poverty in the UK*, available at http://www.savethechildren.org.uk/en/docs/sevchildpovuk.pdf

Office of National Statistics (2007) *Gender pay gap: median pay gap narrows*, available at http://www.statistics.gov.uk/cci/nugget.asp?id=167

Organisation for Economic Co-operation and Development (OECD) (1998) *The concentration of women's employment and relative occupational pay*, in OECD (ed.) The Future of Female-Dominated Occupations. Paris: OECD

Tackling the pay gap between women and men (2007) *Communication from the Commission to the Council, the European Parliament, the European Economic and Social Committee and the Committee of the Regions*, available at http://ec.europa.eu/employment_social/news/2007/jul/genderpaygap_en.pdf

The Low Pay Commission (2000) *The minimum wage: the story so far, second report of the Low Pay Commission*, available at http://www.lowpay.gov.uk/lowpay/report2/complete.pdf

Vogler J. and Pahl C. (1994) *Money, power and inequality within marriage*. Sociological Review 42 (2): 263-288.

Women's Budget Group *Women's and children's poverty, making the links*, available at http://www.wbg.org.uk/documents/WBGWomensandchildrenspoverty.pdf